Architectural Design

Design Through Making

Guest-edited by Bob Sheil

 WILEY-ACADEMY

Architectural Design

Vol 75 No 4 July/August 2005

ISBN-10 0470090936

ISBN-13 9780470090930

Profile No 176

Editorial Offices
International House
Ealing Broadway Centre
London W5 5DB
T: +44 (0)20 8326 3800
F: +44 (0)20 8326 3801
E: architecturaldesign@wiley.co.uk

Editor
Helen Castle

Design and Editorial Management
Mariangela Palazzi-Williams

Art Direction/Design
Christian Küsters (CHK Design)

Design Assistant
Hannah Dumphy (CHK Design)

**Project Coordinator
and Picture Editor**
Caroline Ellerby

Advertisement Sales
Faith Pidduck/Wayne Frost
01243 770254
fpidduck@wiley.co.uk

Editorial Board
Will Alsop, Denise Bratton, Adriaan
Beukers, André Chaszar, Peter Cook,
Teddy Cruz, Max Fordham, Massimiliano
Fuksas, Edwin Heathcote, Anthony Hunt,
Charles Jencks, Jan Kaplicky, Robert
Maxwell, Jayne Merkel, Monica Pidgeon,
Antoine Predock, Michael Rotondi, Leon
van Schaik, Ken Yeang

Contributing Editors
André Chaszar
Craig Kellogg
Jeremy Melvin
Jayne Merkel

Subscription Offices UK
John Wiley & Sons Ltd.
Journals Administration Department
1 Oldlands Way, Bognor Regis
West Sussex, PO22 9SA
T: +44 (0)1243 843272
F: +44 (0)1243 843232
E: cs-journals@wiley.co.uk

Printed in Italy by Conti Tipicolor.
All prices are subject to change
without notice.
[ISSN: 0003-8504]

AD is published bimonthly and is available
to purchase on both a subscription basis
and as individual volumes at the following
prices.

Single Issues
Single issues UK: £22.50
Singles issues outside UK: US$45.00
Details of postage and packing charges
available on request.

Annual Subscription Rates 2005
Institutional Rate
Print only or Online only: UK£175/US$290
Combined Print and Online: UK£193/US$320
Personal Rate
Print only: UK£99/US$155
Student Rate
Print only: UK£70/US$110

Prices are for six issues and include
postage and handling charges. Periodicals
postage paid at Jamaica, NY 11431. Air
freight and mailing in the USA by
Publications Expediting Services Inc, 200
Meacham Avenue, Elmont, NY 11003

Individual rate subscriptions must be paid
by personal cheque or credit card.
Individual rate subscriptions may not be
resold or used as library copies.

Postmaster
Send address changes to *AD* Publications
Expediting Services, 200 Meacham Avenue,
Elmont, NY 11003

Design Through Making
Guest-edited by Bob Sheil

What the exact nature of the relationship between design and making might be is a perennial question for architecture. Ever since architects first hung up their hats as 'master builders' and asserted themselves as a profession, with a dedicated training, it has been necessary to consider the price of acquiring their own exclusive body of knowledge. How can it be possible to make up the ground they once had as supervisors of works who gained their position having passed through the ranks as an apprentice and then mason, procuring a hands-on knowledge of materials and construction on the way? Can learning ever make up for the shortfall of immediate experience? The distance between the architect and fabrication on site has, it seems, only intensified in the last couple of decades with the emergence of middle men – project managers – and design and build, and then been further exasperated by the emergence of the global market in professional services that has enabled the subcontracting out of production drawings.

The role of the architect may have been in danger of being pared right down to the concept sketch, whether the conventional Modernist signature napkin drawing jotted down in a moment of inspiration, or a slickly presented computer-generated blob. However, in the last few years this situation has been potentially inverted. The onset of CAD/CAM interfaces that allow designers to design directly for manufacture has placed production potentially back in the hands of the architect. This is a position that was advocated by the New York practice Sharples Holden Pasquarelli (SHoP) in their 2002 issue of △ Versioning: Evolutionary Techniques in Architecture, when they asserted a notion of 'the vertical' that put the architect back at the top of the pile. For many younger architects, control over the production process is an important means of recovering creative control.

Even though everything may have seemed to have colluded against architects' involvement in overseeing the fabrication of their buildings in the late 20th century, a vibrant preoccupation with making has never waned within architecture. It has been enthusiastically and faithfully pursued by many designers, who make it their business to investigate materials and construction, whether in the pursuit of the intricately crafted or for the sheer adrenalin of discovering innovative structures and systems. Guest-editor Bob Sheil – a member of sixteen*(makers) and a tutor at the Bartlett – is by his own admission a passionate advocate of design through making. And this issue of △ is therefore a testament to both the passion with which fabrication is pursued, using both craft and new technologies, and the very divergent questions that a pursuit of making throws up. △

Ian David, Intensive Care, Queen Elizabeth Hospital, London, 2004
One of a series of installations at the former Queen Elizabeth Hospital, now a dilapidated and abandoned assembly of unoccupied rooms. The work presents a dense cluster of unique fragile plaster-castings where each piece is either suspended or supported from precarious stainless-steel rods. The work recognises the present sense of delicate decay as the hospital slides into a weak and hazardous condition. The castings randomly smash to the floor as slight changes in temperature or air circulation disturb their environment.

 Introduction **Bob Sheil**

DESIGN THROUGH MAKING: AN INTRODUCTION

Should a sound understanding and experience of making underpin design skills? In an age of design data, what does the architect still have to gain from the physical and tacit? **Bob Sheil**, guest-editor of *Design Through Making*, outlines the ideas behind the issue and how they have prompted intriguing and impassioned responses from a diverse array of contributors.

FIRST IMPRESSIONS

Most architects do not make buildings – they make information for buildings. They turn ideas into drawings, models, texts and data, where many results inform the production of buildings and others do not. Among the host of critical and diverse traits required in architectural production, the making of buildings demands an expertise that is familiar with the tactile and the physical. It is a body of knowledge and experience that goes beyond the production of information; it is an area that is sporadically documented and, despite the often extraordinary outcome, it involves a level of skill that many designers cannot claim to fully possess or practise. *Design Through Making* takes a look at this expertise and the shifting territory of where it resides. Its collection of essays from theorists, designers, makers, educators and researchers casts a new light upon skills associated with

making and design. It investigates how making is associated with definitions and methodologies of architectural practice. But most of all, its central proposition concerns the fundamental manner in which this relationship is changing.

About a year ago, I invited a diverse team of contributors to be involved in the subject of this issue. Central to my purpose in preparing a broad discourse on a subject for which I maintain a passion was my ambition to measure it against differing points of view and context. It seemed to me it would serve less purpose to engage the reader on one frequency than offer the subject as a question in

Detail of Ian David's Intensive Care installation at the Queen Elizabeth Hospital, London, 2004.

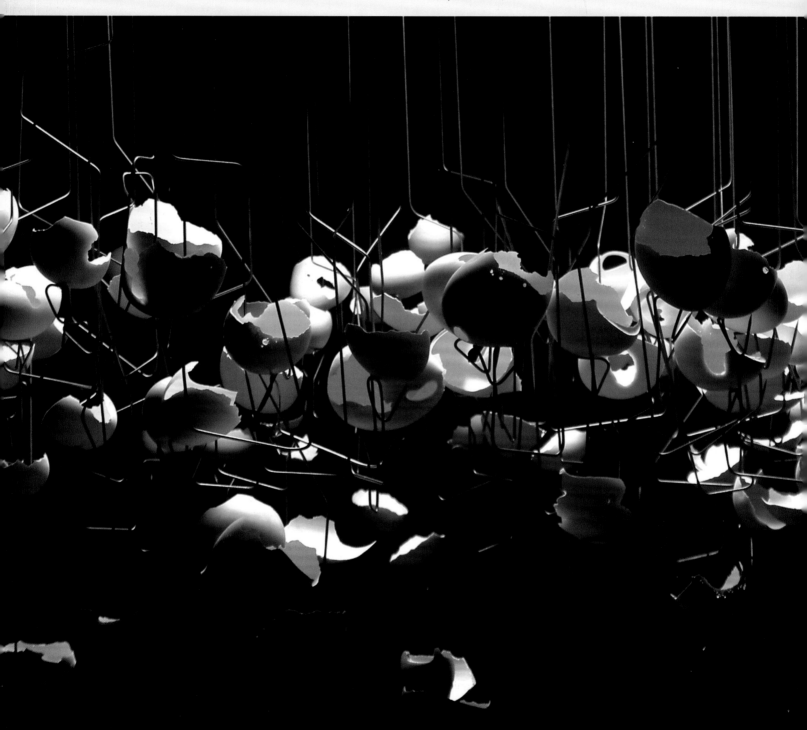

which many positions are valid. I could not help but guess what I might receive in return later on, and was gratified when this turned out not only to be surprising, but also personally illuminating. Subsequently, what views I took for granted have now been enriched by sharper insight and broader scope.[1] Even so, I am quite sure the question can go much further, and look forward to pursuing the ideas and issues raised within, again and again, in collaboration with my inspiring colleagues and students in architectural practice and education.

I must at first pause and refer to one of my final editorial tasks, and probably your first impression of this issue – the book cover and on it the image of Orgone Reef. I first encountered an earlier generation of this artefact at an exhibition in central London against the formidable backdrop of trade-show paraphernalia. Its presence was instantly spellbinding. It glistened, twitched, and dispersed its feathery entrails as my senses were well and truly switched on. The sight before my eyes was truly special. I soon understood how it was made and the obsessive reasons why. I was pleased that the conglomeration of enthusiasts its designer and maker Philip Beesley gathered together fulfilled their innovative research as something exquisite. Nevertheless, despite the care taken to reproduce the work as an exquisite image, what you see is not the real thing. And therein lies the greatest hurdle for anyone wishing to convey a message on the physical and tactile nature of design through printed matter.

TECHNIQUE

The prospect of realising ideas into built form is a transition during which some qualities are gained and others lost. As immaterial and intangible ideas develop, the question of how things are made generates a period of opportunity. If equipped with a critical understanding of the rich potential of this phase, the designer will approach this transition with confidence, prepared for the indeterminate nature of working with resistance,[2] and adapt to change accordingly. Architectural design does not end as the tools of fabrication are put into action. On the contrary, making is a discipline that can instigate rather than merely solve ideas – in other words a design process.

Some architects, such as the members of Rural Studio, do make buildings, and they make them without a dependency on conventional design information. Theirs is a process where, for instance, the finding of affordable and reappropriated materials is instigated as the requirements of the project emerge in conversation with the user. It is a process where outcomes are expected to evolve throughout the act of making the building rather than performing the process as a contingent event of a preceding design strategy. A first-hand account by John Forney explores this territory later.

EXPERTISE

In piecing together this issue, I wish to present a new connection between design practice and its physical and tactile outcome. In doing so, I believe it will be recognised

Tom McGlynn, *Under Observation*, Queen Elizabeth Hospital, London, 2004
Between theatres 1 and 2 is housed an aperture of cross-observation. Eliminating sound and preventing touch, all surfaces that once emanated function and utilisation gather dust and germs. Surrounding the aperture is a new system of twinned light fittings and polished plate-glass. The new system is tailormade, but is useless: it exists merely to draw attention to abandonment and absence. Fading in and fading out, occupants on either side activate the system, which causes their image to appear, merge and then disappear on the glass plane between them.

that we have entered an era where expertise in making is becoming repositioned at the centre of architectural practice. For architects, the new era is most clearly defined by the revolutionary change in making information. It is led by a convergence in the properties of digital drawing and the automated techniques of manufacturing into the hybrid and adaptive technology of CAD/CAM (computer-aided design/computer-aided manufacturing).[3] Armed with an array of new tools that draw and make, the CAD/CAM operative is neither a designer nor a maker, but both.

The operative is presented with new synthetic tasks where the consequences of information generate an immediate and mirrored response. It has taken time, however the gap between information and making has been bridged, and is irreversible. As the technology of digital fabrication gathers momentum in architecture, this journal is an acknowledgement of its effect as a new catalyst within a broad reappraisal of making and design practice. Old skills have reappeared alongside new as complex automation technology offers exciting potential to readdress everything from mass industrial to handmaking techniques. Digital fabrication has indeed sparked a revolution in many technological respects, but it has also implied that the expertise of designers and practitioners must also be revolutionised. Reforming a fundamental component of architectural discipline is clearly more than a matter of technique; it is also one of culture and context. It is therefore a principal aim of this issue to position this change in a broad context of theory, culture, history and craft. The selection of texts included is therefore varied in its purpose, origin and outlook.

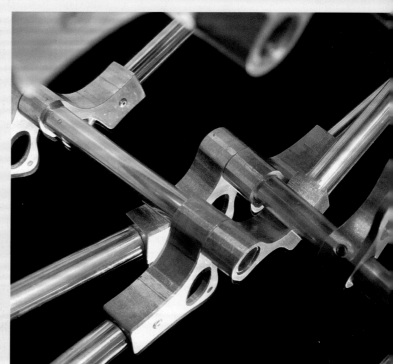

Top and above
Alastair McDonald, Eavesdropping, Queen Elizabeth Hospital, London, 2004
Contained within the reveal of a basement sash window, the work incorporates a fitted and curiously modulated surface concealed behind a hinged privacy screen. The project investigates the relationship between immediately adjacent public and confidential spaces and their reappropriation for devious and intimate purposes – something akin to twitching net curtains.

DRAWING

Not surprisingly, the most difficult aspects to convey in this medium are acts of making. Like the allusive nature of the nonillustrated recipe book, in which the outcome is somewhat of a surprise, acts of making are not documented to the same extent as instructions to make. My contributors hail from diverse backgrounds: not all are people who make, but all address the relationship between the craft of design and making in terms particular to their expertise. The series opens with Jonathan Hill's 'Building the Drawing', a characteristically lucid account of

Above
Martin Xavier Perez Broby, Digital craft 1, Queen Elizabeth Hospital, London, 2004
Universal components for anatomical enclosure, an assembly to form a reconfigurable series of suspended wings and frames.

Martin Xavier Perez Broby, Digital craft 2, armature component, London, 2005
Recent investigation into merging traditional and digital fabrication
techniques for 1:1 furniture components in cast pewter and laminated wood.

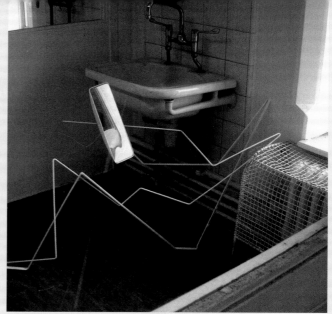

Christos Lefakis, The 10th Occupant, Queen Elizabeth Hospital, London, 2004
The isolation ward on the mezzanine level is characterised by a series of nine adjacent rooms, each separated from one another and a corridor by a half-glazed partition and door. Through a series of new inhabitants, each emitting a unique pulsating and incremental frequency, the work investigates conditions of occupancy, surveillance, attendance and absence. Visitors are immediately absconded into a duty of care for all bleating patients.

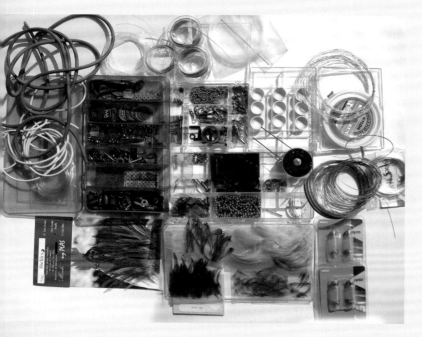

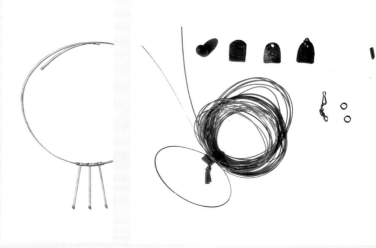

Architect, maker and calligrapher Louis Lafargue transforms ad-hoc objects such as bullet casings, fishing tackle and electrical components into curious and exquisite jewellery for people and places.

histories in the practice of architecture based upon drawing as the primary product of the architect. Hill highlights the multiple applications that drawings serve, the drawing as analogue, drawing the immaterial, and drawing through making.
It is the place we must begin, the place where drawings and words establish their role in relation to our subject.

Hill's article is followed by a series of counterpoints that allude to making's place in design: Mark Burry on our growing dependency on computation, Michael Stacey on craft, Phil Ayres on the nature of specificity in generic design, Nick Callicott on capturing the tacit through adaptive manufacturing techniques, and Sarah Chaplin on cultural diversity on notions of permanence and making, and distinction. Interspersed are a series of accounts

on built works that convey their unique character and purpose in respect of representation, behaviour and form.

TOOLING

In a speculative contribution on the nature of drawing instruments, Nat Chard develops critical insight into the methodology of drawing and prompts us to consider architectural practice as a reflective history of technological change. The invention of the blast furnace, the development of polymers, textiles and so on, were key events that radically altered the direction of design. Yet until quite recently the primary products of the architect, the drawing and the model, have remained relatively

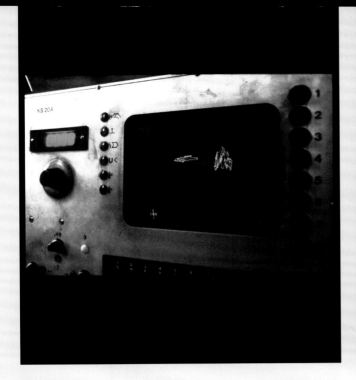

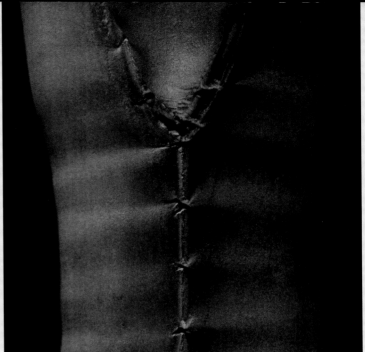

sixteen*(makers), Blusher project, Güsten, 2001
Components of the project awaiting digital fabrication momentarily appear on the CNC plasma-cutter's monitor; 45 minutes later, all 21 pieces were complete.

Mark West, Building a Way to Build, Winnipeg, 2005
Detail of concrete beam cast from fabric formwork, the work of Mark West, director of the Centre for Architectural Structures and Technology (CAST), University of Manitoba Faculty of Architecture.

consistent in character. Ideas and buildings have altered substantially, but design representations of the 20th century offered information much in the same way as those of the 19th. Such drawings required a particular expertise to ensure that the idea was understood and survived. They had to be efficient, clear, appropriate, skilful and expert, yet being transmitted into the tactile and physical world by a process that was subject to negotiation, they were reliant on translation.

Subsequently, making was at risk of becoming a responsive act, a demonstration of how effectively ideas were communicated by the information and read by the maker. The drawing instruments of Chard and his colleagues are a determined effort to challenge and reinvent the basic tools of the designer. The fabrication of specific tooling is a commonplace practice of manufacturing. In some instances, such as the torque ellipse forms by Richard Serra, the production of form is entirely dependent upon finding the right tool. Chard implies that in order to act as innovative designers, we must design appropriate tools as a continual by-product of the investigation.

ADAPTATION
By returning to the catalyst of change, digital fabrication implies that making drawings and making buildings are now inseparable entities – their interdependency has become a connected circumstance rather than a negotiable one. Designers, conventionally the makers of drawings and models, have in their grasp the opportunity to relocate to the centre of building production with a powerful array of tools to convey innovative propositions that are fused with the information to make them. Yet the more difficult question raised here is that which asks whether they are equipped with all the necessary knowledge and expertise to

By returning to the catalyst of change, digital fabrication implies that making drawings and making buildings are now inseparable entities – their interdependency has become a connected circumstance rather than a negotiable one. Designers, conventionally the makers of drawings and models, have in their grasp the opportunity to relocate to the centre of building production with a powerful array of tools to convey innovative propositions that are fused with the information to make them.

Tom McGlynn, Under Observation, Queen Elizabeth Hospital, London, 2004
Ambient lighting of redundant operating theatre.

Alastair McDonald, Eavesdropping, Queen Elizabeth Hospital, London, 2004
Handmade/hand-held modulated polymer 'clinical' surface.

Alastair McDonald, Eavesdropping installation.

Notes

1 I am therefore deeply grateful for this opportunity and must thank not only each contributor, but the commissioning editor, managing editor, copy-editor, book designer and publisher, who have offered nothing less than full support throughout the drawn-out process of putting this together.
2 Numerically controlled (NC) machinery was first developed in the 1950s for the US military. Its subsequent proliferation has largely occurred within the automobile and aeronautics industries where an automated, but inflexible manufacturing process realised the potential for rapid adaptation to change. With efficiency and development, NC became CNC as computer numeric-control systems centred upon factory-based manufacturing processes and successfully managed a speedy transition towards a system of devolved specialisation and greater specificity. The relatively recent breakthrough of CAD/CAM into architecture has been the result of having first to develop the advanced interface of CAD so that CAM processes are instigated via drawing techniques rather than a requirement to understand the necessary programming language. This aspect is expanded upon in greater detail later on in Nick Callicott's article 'Adaptive Architectural Design'.
3 Some of the images presented in this article are taken from recent work of Unit 23 at the Bartlett School of Architecture, carried out at an abandoned building in London. Further information can be found at www.bartlett.ucl.ac.uk/architecture/programmes/units/unit23.htm and www.bartlett.ucl.ac.uk/architecture/events/lobby/u23_snapshot.htm

Further Reading

N Callicott, Computer-Aided Manufacturing: The Pursuit of Novelty, Architectural Press (London), 2001.
S Groak, The Idea of Building: Thought and Action in the Design and Production of Buildings, Spon (London), 1992.
B Kolarevic, Architecture in the Digital Age: Design and Manufacturing, Spon London), 2004.
M McCullough, Abstracting Craft, MIT Press (Cambridge, MA), 1998.
N Potter, What Is a Designer: Things, Places, Messages, Hyphen Press (London), 1980.
D Pye, The Nature and Art of Workmanship, Herbert Press (London), 1968.
D Schodek, Digital Design and Manufacturing: CAD/CAM Applications in Architecture, in Chaszar, Blurring the lines, Wiley-Academy (London), 2005.
M Stacey, Component Design, Architectural Press (London), 2000.
Kieran Timberlake, Refabricating Architecture, McGraw-Hill Professional (New York), 2004.

do so? Do centuries of making information for the production of buildings form a sufficient basis on which to exploit this new opportunity? Should new skills be learned, should the design environment be redesigned?

It is clearly essential that all aspects of what is emerging from this shift are examined. Making is an immense resource for ideas, experimentation and research, but to reiterate the opening remarks, it requires expertise in the physical and the tactile – it is a tacit expertise. With it, designers may develop skills equal to their powerful repertoire of representational skills; without it, a great opportunity will be missed. If architectural designers do not grasp the centre of building production by taking command of the art and craft of construction, when now they are offered the chance, who will? ∆

The understanding and, consequently, the status of the terms architect, drawing and building, alter through context and time. Less recognised are the interdependencies that lie beneath their constituent parts; the drawing and the building, the designer and maker, the material and the immaterial. By reversing typical patterns of exchange, Jonathan Hill disrupts the security of the familiar and the certainty of the stable, and considers how drawing and building are both similar and different.

BUILDING THE DRAWING

Charlie De Bono, Urban Council Estate – Sustainable Picturesque Garden, 2004
The tenants' association proposes the evolution of their Victorian council estate to a more sustainable approach, simultaneously transforming their environment into a picturesque agrarian landscape and functioning garden, providing a model for the reconfiguration of existing urban housing stock.

Idea, No Matter

Architecture is expected to be solid and certain, offering both physical and psychological reassurance. Bound to each other, the architectural and the material are considered inseparable. However, the immaterial is a characteristic of architecture as important and influential as the material, if less recognised. The history of immaterial architecture is tied to the origins of the (Modern) architect in the Italian Renaissance, when drawing first became essential to architectural practice.[1] Dependent on the concept that ideas are superior to matter, the command of drawing underpins the status of architectural design as intellectual and artistic labour.

Associated with manual labour and dispersed authorship, the status of the architect was often low before the 15th century. In the Middle Ages, the three visual arts – painting, sculpture and architecture – were mechanical arts 'confined to the artisan's guilds, in which the painters were sometimes associated with the druggists who prepared their paints, the sculptors with the goldsmiths, and the architects with the masons and carpenters'.[2] First trained in one of the building crafts, the master mason was but one of many craftsmen and worked alongside them as a construction supervisor.

The Italian Renaissance offered the architect a new, much higher status due mainly to the command, not of building, but of drawing, which was previously only a minor part of building production, a means to copy information rather than generate ideas. The Renaissance introduced a fundamental change in perception, establishing the principle that the drawing is the truthful depiction of the three-dimensional world. For the first time, drawing became essential to architectural practice, focusing attention on vision to the detriment of those senses closer to the material, such as touch.

The architect, as we now understand the term, is largely an invention of the Italian Renaissance. The architect and the architectural drawing are twins. Interdependent, they are representative of the same idea – that architecture results not from the accumulated knowledge of a team of anonymous craftspeople working together on a construction site, but is the artistic creation of an individual architect in command of drawing who designs a building as a whole at a remove from construction.[3] From the 15th century to the 21st, the architect has made drawings, models and texts – not buildings.

The history and status of the architect and architectural drawing are interwoven with those of architectural design. The term 'design' comes from the Italian 'disegno', meaning drawing, suggesting both the drawing of lines on paper and the drawing forth of an idea from the mind into physical reality. Disegno implies a direct link between an idea and a thing. As Vilém Flusser remarks: 'The word is derived from the Latin signum, meaning "sign", and shares the same ancient root.'[4] The 16th-century painter and architect Giorgio Vasari was crucial to its promotion: 'One may conclude that this design is nothing but a visual expression and clarification of that concept which one has in the intellect, and that which one imagines in the mind.'[5] Disegno enabled the three visual arts to be recognised as liberal arts concerned with ideas, a position that previously they had rarely been accorded.

Disegno is dependent on Plato's assumption that ideas are superior to matter and, thus, that intellectual labour is superior to manual labour.[6] To justify the intellectual status of art, Italian Renaissance artists accepted the status that Plato ascribed to ideas, yet undermined his argument that the artwork is always inferior to the idea it depicts. Instead, they argued that it is possible to formulate an artistic idea in the mind, produce the direct visual expression of an idea, and that an artwork can depict 'an otherwise unknowable idea'.[7] Asserting the pre-eminence of the intellect, disegno is concerned with the idea of architecture, not the matter of building. Alberti notably states that: 'It is quite possible to project whole forms in the mind without recourse to the material.'[8]

Charlie De Bono, Urban Council Estate – Sustainable Picturesque Garden, 2004
Detail of vertical composting sleeves.

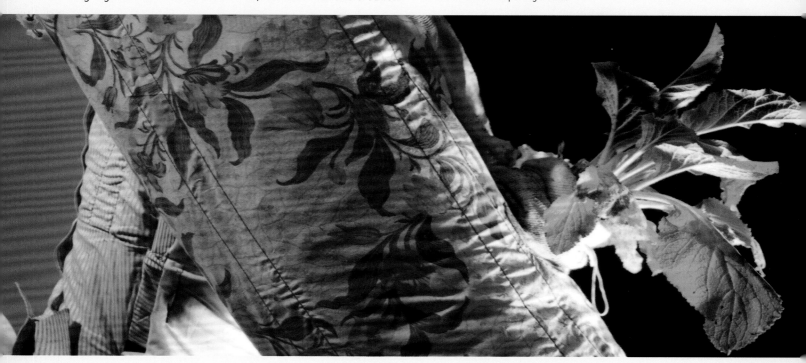

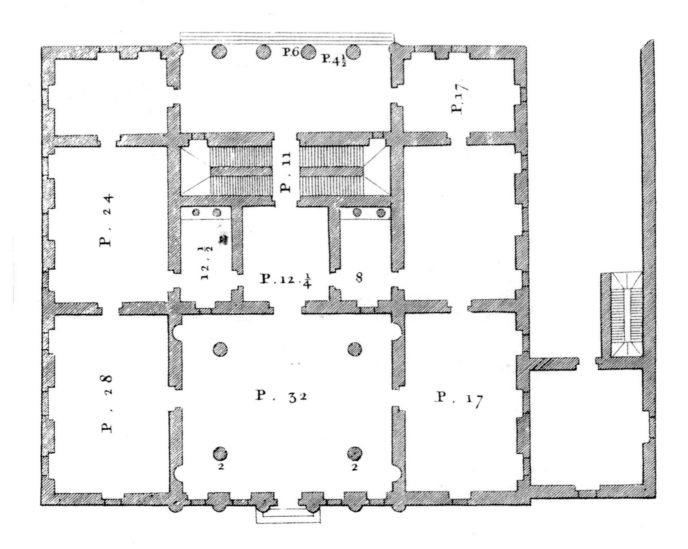

The concept of design established with the promotion of *disegno* during the Italian Renaissance, and dominant since, states that first an idea is conceived in the mind, second it is drawn on paper, and third it is built. To design is, therefore, to draw. From mind to matter.

Andrea Palladio, Palazzo Antonini, Udine, Italy, 1556
Plan indicating a matrix of geometrically proportioned rooms.

In 1563, Vasari founded the first art academy, the Accademia del Disegno in Florence. A model for later institutions in Italy and elsewhere, it enabled painters, sculptors and architects to converse independently of the craft guilds. As the academy replaced workshop instruction with education in drawing, and the architect nearly always first experiences a noted building as a representation, the architect standing before a building often sees not mass and matter, but form and proportion.

<u>Design Through Making</u>
The conception of design established with the promotion of *disegno* during the Italian Renaissance, and dominant since, states that first an idea is conceived in the mind, second it is drawn on paper, and third it is built. To design is, therefore, to draw. From mind to matter. Design is in actuality far more complicated, and most architects are known for their buildings not their drawings. But design through making fundamentally questions the basis of

the architect's status and practice because it includes manual as well as intellectual labour, and pulls the architect closer to construction. To consider the consequences of design through making, rather than discard drawing I will focus here on the further interdependence of drawing and immaterial architecture.

Redrawing Drawing

The architectural drawing depends on related but contradictory ideas. One indicates that design is an intellectual, artistic process distant from the grubby materiality of building. Another claims that the drawing is the truthful representation of the building, indicating the mastery of architects over building production and the seamless translation of idea into form. The architectural drawing is a projection in that invisible lines link a point on the drawing to one on the building. But the journey from one to the other is not direct. All representations omit as much as they include. The drawing, model, photograph and text provide ambiguous and elusive information – an uncomfortable thought for any architect. Rarely do marks on paper equate to marks on site. To transform the drawing into the building requires an act of translation and an intimate knowledge of the techniques and materials of drawing and building.

It is nearly impossible for an architect to build without drawing. Even if the architect begins to design without drawing, the drawing is the main means of communication in all phases of building. But the architect's focus on drawing is only a problem if it is unrecognised and the sole means of design. 'Transitional object' is a term used in psychoanalysis. For example, in the case of a child this may be a teddy bear. Its role is positive and 'a defence against separation from the mother', to be discarded when no longer needed. However, Elizabeth Wright adds that if a child is unable to make this transition, the result can be 'the fixed delusion which may turn the transitional object into that permanent security prop, the fetish, both in the Freudian sense (it disguises the actuality of lack) and in the Marxian sense (it functions as a commodity that supplies human want)'.[9] Like a child who cannot discard a teddy bear, the architect who chooses not to recognise the differences between the building and its representations also fails to notice how they can be similar and is unable to reach a level of mature self-awareness.

The architectural drawing has a positive role if these differences and similarities are acknowledged and used knowingly. All practices need an articulate language to develop complex ideas and propositions before or without their physical application. A sixfold investigation of the architectural drawing is necessary: first to consider how the architectural drawing and building are similar and different; second to look at drawings elsewhere, studying other disciplines that have developed articulate means to draw qualities relevant to architecture; third, to develop new ways to draw architectural qualities excluded from the architectural

Andrea Palladio, San Petronio, Bologna, Italy, 1572–9
Facade emphasising line and proportion, not matter.

Matthew Butcher, The Flood House, 2004
Since the formation of the Netherlands, the relationship of the land to the sea has informed the Dutch psyche. Set within the Rhine delta, the Flood House responds to the Dutch environment ministry's decision to counter tradition and return land to the sea. Analogous to the environment it inhabits, it expands and contracts, reconfigures and adapts according to the tides, seasons, weather and occupation.

drawing; fourth, if these qualities cannot be drawn, to find other ways to describe and discuss them; fifth, to focus on the architectural potential of the drawing; and, sixth, to bring drawing and building closer to each other.

The Drawing As Analogue

On the one hand, design through making suggests building without drawing, or at least that the importance of drawing is diminished. On the other – if to design is to draw – it means drawing through making. Traditionally, the architectural drawing is a representation, but it can also be an analogue, sharing some of the building's characteristics. When architects assume that the drawing is similar to the building, they often mean that the building looks like the drawing. But the drawing as analogue allows more subtle relations – of technique, material and process – to develop between drawing and building. A dialogue can exist between what is designed and how it is designed, between design intention and working medium, between thought, action and object – building the drawing rather than drawing the building. As a representation, the drawing can consider all the senses, but vision is usually its primary concern. As an analogue, a more direct engagement with the various senses is possible. As an analogue to building, the drawing can be cut, built, erased and demolished. If the building is to be made of artificial light, it can first be modelled in artificial light and drawn in photograms so that the techniques and materials of drawing are also those of building. In building the drawing, any instrument is a potential drawing tool that can question the techniques of familiar building construction and the assumed linearity of design, so that building and drawing may occur in conjunction rather than sequence.

Chee Kit Lai, A House for A House, 2004
'The occupant of the house is another house. The outer-public house is a house for my parents. The inner-private house is a house as a reflection of myself. I exist as the inner house in my parents' house, as every traditional Chinese boy is expected to live with his parents into their old age. The house is situated in the woods very far away, too far for any visitors.' (Chee Kit Lai, 'A House for A House', diploma, Bartlett School of Architecture, UCL, London, 2004)

Today, most architectural drawings are produced on the computer, for which significant claims are made. But often architects draw on the computer much as they draw on paper, as a means to visualise form. The conjunction of computer-aided design (CAD) and computer-aided manufacture (CAM) is quite different. CAD/CAM aligns thinking, drawing and making so that the architect can more accurately claim that to be in command of drawing is to be in command of building. In that it depicts actions in four dimensions rather than elevations in two, CAD/CAM investigates building as process, as well as the building as object. Bringing building closer to drawing and designing, it questions the 600-year history of the architect in a manner that recalls the 13th century as well as the 21st.

The construction of physical prototypes, building drawings with tangible architectural qualities and CAD/CAM are allies not alternatives, each valuable to the architect interested in the analogue as well as the representation. Particular pleasure and creative tension exist where representation and analogue overlap – drawing the building and building the drawing – one feeding the other.

Drawing the Immaterial

Building the drawing means the drawing that is a physical construction with tangible architectural qualities, and the building that is analogous to the drawing in terms of its production and perception. Conceiving the drawing as an analogue means that it can become more like the building, but it also enables the building to be more like the drawing. For example, a line drawing suggests an architecture of line not mass. Some of the most innovative architectural developments have arisen not from speculation in building, but through the translation of particular qualities of the drawing to the building. One important characteristic of the drawing – that it is associated with mind rather than matter, and is literally less material than the building – encourages architects to build with an equal lack of material, to try to make architecture immaterial. That the products of architects' daily endeavours – words and drawings – have limited physical presence, undoubtedly affects what they do and think, whether conscious or not.

In *The Ten Books on Architecture*, Vitruvius writes that knowledge of geometry, philosophy, music, medicine, law and astronomy are as important as expertise in building construction.[10] He adds, however, that 'architects who have aimed at acquiring manual skill without scholarship have never been able to reach a position of authority to correspond to their pains, while those who relied upon theories and scholarship were obviously hunting the shadow, not the substance'.[11] Vitruvius is correct in his assumption that some architects are hunting the shadow, but not one limited to, or by, theory. Hunting the shadow, hunting immaterial architecture, is an important and creative architectural tradition invigorated by theory. The highly influential concept that ideas are superior to materials is nothing but a prejudice. One option is to dismiss it, concluding that its effect on architecture is purely negative because it denies the solid materiality of architecture and encourages architects to chase after artistic status that they will never fully attain, may not need and should question. But the desire to make architecture immaterial should not be automatically denied, and has alternative motives and positive consequences.

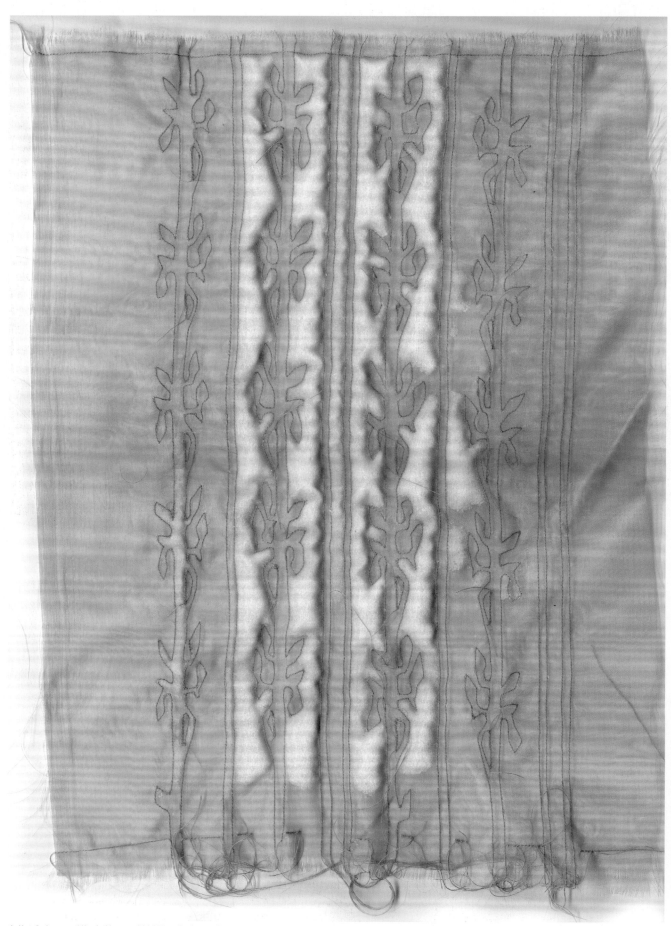

Juliet Quintero, Alice's House, 2004 Detail of curtain wall of crystallised sugar and nylon.

Juliet Quintero, Alice's House, 2004
The house explores the relations between the private Alice Liddell and her public but fictional other, Alice of Wonderland. Fusing electromagnetic technologies, crystallised sugar and Victorian furnishings, the gradual building of the house mirrors the identity of Alice as she frees herself from the confines of the narrative world, and returns to a reality where the architecture of the home breaks the grip of eternal childhood.

Immaterial Architecture

There are many ways to understand immaterial architecture: as an idea, a formless phenomenon, a technological development towards lightness, a representation of the sublime, a tabula rasa of a capitalist economy, a gradual loss of architecture's moral weight and certitude, or a programmatic focus on actions rather than forms. I recognise each of these models but emphasise another: the perception of architecture as immaterial, which can be achieved by either the absence of physical material, or physical material understood as immaterial. My main concern is less the absence of matter than the perceived absence of matter. Whether architecture is immaterial is dependent on the perception of the user, which relies on fiction rather than fact. Richard Gregory writes that 'visual and other perception is intelligent decision-taking from limited sensory evidence. The essential point is that sensory signals are not adequate for direct or certain perceptions, so intelligent guesswork is needed for seeing objects.'[12] Consequently, 'perceptions are hypotheses'.[13]

The appreciation of immaterial architecture is complex and a challenge to the familiar, habitual experience of architecture. The richness of the user's experience of any building depends on an awareness of all the senses, but immaterial architecture may trigger a sense more often associated with the immaterial, such as smell, and question one more often associated with the material, such as touch. The experience of immaterial architecture is based on the juxtaposition of contradictory sensations, and is appropriate to an active and creative engagement with architecture. The complexity of the whole experience depends on the user's awareness of the sensations both present and absent. To experience the full character of the juxtaposition therefore requires an understanding of the conflict, whether pleasurable or not, an attempted reconstruction of each of the absent elements, and the formation in the imagination of a new hybrid object formed from the sensations present. An example is Yves Klein's Fire Wall, a grid of flames, each flower-shaped, its six 'petals' whipped by the wind.[14]

Immaterial Home

A recurring theme in architectural discourse states that the house is the origin and archetype of architecture, the manifestation of its most important attributes. Home is supposedly the most secure and stable of environments, a vessel for the personal identity of its occupant(s), a container for, and mirror of, the self. However, the concept of home is also a response to the excluded, unknown, unclassified and inconsistent. Home must appear solid and stable because social norms and personal identity are shifting and slippery. Home is a metaphor for a threatened society and a threatened individual. The safety of the home is also the sign of its opposite, a certain nervousness, a fear of the tangible or intangible dangers outside and inside.

David Sibley argues that while the apparent stability of the home may provide gratification it can also, simultaneously, create anxiety because the security and spatial purification the home offers can never be fully achieved. Often the consequence is an increasingly intense need for stability, not an awareness of its limits: 'Generally, anxieties are expressed in the desire to erect and maintain spatial and temporal boundaries. Strong boundary consciousness can be interpreted as a desire to be in control and to exclude the unfamiliar because the unfamiliar is a source of unease rather than something to be celebrated.'[15] Referring to Sigmund Freud's 1919 essay on the uncanny, he

concludes that 'this striving for the safe, the familiar or *heimlich* fails to remove a sense of unease. I would argue that it makes it worse.'[16]

Whether insidious disorder inside or lurking danger outside, the immaterial is often associated with all that is perceived to be threatening to the home, architecture and society. But the threat of the immaterial is imagined as much as it is real. The desire for a stable architecture can never be fulfilled, increasing anxiety and furthering desire for a more stable architecture. Replacing a static and material architecture with one that is fluid and immaterial is no solution, however. Instead, compatibility between the spaces of a home and the habits of its occupants is desirable. A tightly structured group of people occupying a loose spatial configuration will create tension and anxiety, as will the opposite. However, matching users to spatial configurations is no answer because it fails to take account of changing users and changing needs. Instead, a home must have the potential to be both spatially tight and loose. To accommodate evolving conceptions of the individual and society, architecture must engage the material and the immaterial, the static and the fluid, the solid and the porous. An architecture that is immaterial and spatially porous, as well as solid and stable where necessary, will not change established habits. Rather it may offer those habits greater flexibility.

Max Dewdney, The Enigma of a House and its Furniture, London, 2004
Sited between 33 Surrey Street and 5 Strand Lane, the house can only be rented by two couples. Furniture such as the wax refrigeration table and steam dresser transform environmental conditions like moisture content and air temperature in response to the location of each individual and each piece of furniture.

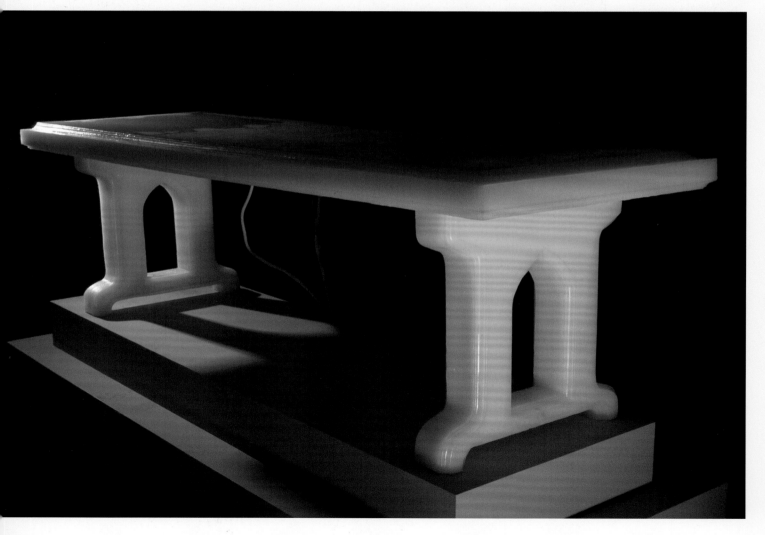

Rupert Scott, Linnaeus' Cabinet: the Conjoined House, 2004
The 18th-century Enlightenment scientist Carl Linnaeus initiated taxonomy, the classification of the natural world, which entered the home in the fashion for cabinets of curiosities. A cabinet made from objects rather than containing them, areas within the Conjoined House mutate and change according to particular taxonomies: the domestic, the architectonic and the botanic.

Immaterial Practice

The practice of architects is expected to be as solid as the buildings they design. With regard to immaterial architecture, therefore, architects are understandably cautious. An architect who persuades a client of the merits of an architecture that is insubstantial and unpredictable still faces numerous difficulties to see it built, such as building regulations and contractual liability. On a more fundamental note, immaterial architecture revels in qualities – the subjective, unpredictable and ephemeral – that are contrary to the solid, objective and respectable practice expected of a professional. However, the stability of architecture and architects' practice is already uncertain and illusory.

Mark Cousins suggests that the discipline of architecture is weak because it involves not just objects but relations between subjects and objects.[17] And if the discipline of architecture is weak, then so, too, is the practice of architects. But weak is not pejorative here. Rather it is the strength to be fluid, flexible and open to conflicting perceptions and opinions. The practice of architects needs to confidently reflect the nature of the architectural discipline. Architecture must be immaterial and spatially porous, as well as solid and stable where necessary, and so should be the practice of architects. Immaterial architecture is an especially poignant and rewarding challenge for architects as it forcefully confronts what they are expected to practise and produce.[18] ⌂

Notes

1 Manfredo Tafuri contends that the project of modernity began in the 15th century, not the 20th. M Tafuri, *Theories and History of Architecture*, trans G Verrecchia, Granada (London), 1980, p 16.
2 PO Kristeller, *Renaissance Thought and the Arts: Collected Essays*, Princeton University Press, 1990, p 176.
3 Architectural design is far more collaborative than this idea suggests.
4 V Flusser, *The Shape of Things: A Philosophy of Design*, Reaktion (London), 1999, p 17.
5 G Vasari, *Vasari On Technique*, trans LS Maclehose, Dover (New York), 1960, p 205. First published in *Le vite de' più eccelenti pittori, scultori e architettori* (The Lives of the Most Eminent Painters, Sculptors and Architects), 2nd edn, 1568.
6 Plato, *Timaeus*, trans F Cornford, The Liberal Arts Press (New York), 1959, p 54.
7 A Forty, *Words and Buildings: A Vocabulary of Modern Architecture*, Thames and Hudson (London), 2000, p 31.
8 LB Alberti, *On the Art of Building in Ten Books*, trans J Rykwert, N Leach and R Tavernor, MIT Press (Cambridge, MA, and London), 1988, p 7. First published as *De Re Aedifacitoria*, c 1450, trans J Leoni, as *The Architecture of Leon Battista Alberti in Ten Books*, 1726.
9 E Wright, *Psychoanalytic Criticism: Theory in Practice*, Routledge (London) 1984, p 93.
10 Vitruvius, *The Ten Books on Architecture*, trans MH Morgan, Dover (New York), 1960, pp 5–6. First published as *De Architectura* in the 1st century BC, it is a description of what Vitruvius thinks the architect should be and do, as much as a reflection of the actual practice and, in ancient Rome, low status of the architect.
11 Ibid, p 5.
12 R Gregory, *Eye and Brain: The Psychology of Seeing*, OUP, 1998, p 5.
13 Ibid, p 10.
14 Constructed for Klein's exhibition at the Museum Haus Lange, Krefeld, 1961.
15 D Sibley, 'Comfort, Anxiety and Space', in J Hill (ed), *Architecture – The Subject is Matter*, Routledge (London and New York), 2001, p 108.
16 Ibid, p 115; S Freud, 'The "Uncanny" ', *The Standard Edition of the Complete Psychological Works of Sigmund Freud*, Vol 17, ed J Strachey, trans A. Strachey, Clarke Irwin (Toronto), 1955, pp 217–52. First published in 1919.
17 M Cousins, 'Building an Architect', in J Hill (ed). *Occupying Architecture: Between the Architect and the User*, Routledge (London and New York), 1998, pp 13–22.
18 All the projects accompanying this text, for a Public Private House, were produced in Unit 12 at the Bartlett School of Architecture, University College London, and tutored by Jonathan Hill and Elizabeth Dow.

DRAWING INSTRUMENTS

Despite the obvious diversity in the ideology, materiality and character of architectural production, here it is argued that the way we (architects) draw is surprisingly uniform. One reason for this might be the limited range of materials and tools we draw with, and their generic qualities. Architect, researcher and maker **Nat Chard** reveals relationships between acts of drawing, making images and making ideas, by taking us through the design and manufacture of a series of analytical drawing instruments and contingent works.

Night-time drawing instrument
Drawing instrument showing picture plane (top left) and control surfaces.

We were talking yesterday at the studio about the picture plane, and to me there's some mysterious element about the plane. I can't rationalise it, I can't talk about it, but I know there's an existence on this imaginary plane which holds almost all the fascination of painting for me. As a matter of fact, I think the true image only comes out when it exists on this imaginary plane. — Philip Guston[1]

We draw for various reasons, and the tools we choose to work with have many capabilities. At one end of the scale we have the hope of a transparency between a thought and its projection on to a picture plane. In this case, the facility to draw and the capability of the tools must have some sympathy with the intention. Generic drawing tools for architecture try to establish this sympathy (through horizon and gravity, for instance in T-squares and set-squares) without prescribing too far what will be drawn. In the middle of the scale, the idea is not so complete before it meets the picture plane, and the media used offer some resistance (perhaps critical) allowing us to question or reflect on the intention. Greg Lynn's observation that in the work of certain architects the types of forms they design reveal the (different) software packages they draw with would suggest that even in the computer, which tries to be as ubiquitous as possible, the medium is in some way a contributory factor, not just a transparent translation.

The other end of the scale is where we know something about our concerns, but do not know how they are formed, and need the media we use to be more active in developing our ideas. It is here we come across an apparent paradox in the relationship between intention, facility and media, for it would seem that the simplest, most generic medium (let's say, pencil on paper) would offer us the widest range and most open means of expression. Though this appears to afford the most indeterminate condition within which to work, it is one that is at the same time very restricting. The medium is well known and has a deeply entrenched set of precedents, and every mark we make has to be understood from every aspect of this medium.

In a small retrospective at the Tate, an early sketch was accompanied by an explanation that Cy Twombly had difficulty in developing his early scribbles on account of his facility at drawing and his highly developed eye. To overcome this he had to first draw in darkness to free his drawing from his intuitive aesthetic concerns. Here, the familiarity with the medium and the reflective critical process of working through it made it less available for ideas outside its normal domain. If we were to make a drawing not with a pencil but with a stamp, for example, the figure's content in that stamp would load or prescribe some of the drawing's content, yet also allow the author to use it with great freedom, without having to worry about the aspect of the drawing covered by the figure in the stamp. Although the tools are more prescribed, perhaps the person drawing has the opportunity to work more spontaneously, knowing that some aspects of the content are inherently discussed in the stamp. It is this end of the scale that I would like to discuss here.

Architects' built work is very diverse, and made from many materials that are formed and assembled by many

Cold Bog camera
The curved film plane is an exact scale model of the diorama shell. The pinhole is (upside down) in the idealised viewing position. The winding mechanism prevents the film leaving the curved plane when winding on.

processes. Yet the way we draw is surprisingly uniform. This is in part due to the need to have generic notation that is understood in the same way by all of the agencies involved in the realisation of a project. However, the exploratory drawings that are made in order to establish what the building should be are not subject to this discipline, and yet remain surprisingly consistent with the work of other architects working with distinctly different ideas. One reason for this might be the limited range of materials and tools we draw with, and their generic qualities. At architectural school we learn how to use given tools, but I was inspired to learn from two of my cousins who undertook engineering apprenticeships that they started their education by making their tools themselves.

At first these tools were measures, a ruler and a square, followed by tools to assemble and then to manufacture. The pieces

Photograph of original site taken on 17 June 2001 with the Cold Bog camera. This image makes all the anamorphic corrections necessary to become the surface of the bog diorama. As a consequence, the horizon is horizontal rather than curving up at the edges, as is the case at the real place or when viewing the diorama.

Cold Bog camera photograph of the diorama – the left-hand image of a stereo pair – that effectively unpeels the painted background.

Right-hand image of stereoscopic pair.

were, I admit, generic, however they suggested the idea that we might both learn and practise through tools of our own making, related to our specific concerns. By making the tools, my cousins learnt about their capabilities and limits – for example, the tolerances of the square or ruler and how these relate to the materials and processes they use. For a number of years I have been testing the relationship between drawing tools[2] and what they draw, both in teaching and in practice. The aim of developing tools is to make the medium active in the design process; to provide something to think through (in its invention and use), and to provide a critical resistance that is particular to the concerns under discussion. One of the most important opportunities of this process is that in designing the tool to discuss an idea, the idea might be clarified or revealed.

Normally when we draw, an idea is projected on to a picture plane. The tools that are active are the ones that project, while the surface that receives tends to be more passive, often chosen for its ability to be submissive to the qualities of the tool that draws. The projection made by the tool is most often an intention that is collected by the picture plane. However, in the examples I will show and discuss here, it is the picture plane that is active – critical in the way that it accepts, modifies or rejects the projection upon it. When we draw with a pencil our hand movement is the same as the figure of the drawing. Our actions and intentions are tied to our image like a shadow. When we modify the picture plane our actions and intentions are reflected by the consequent image, but are not apparent in it. I could suggest that the act of drawing in this way can therefore be related to making the idea, more than making the image.

The picture plane has been the site of many attempts to make picturing empirical, and is the surface on which the silent structures of measured perspective are constructed. Since Leonardo, the imaginary plan of the picture plane has been under discussion, with many proofs and counter-proofs of the ideal surface. If the picture plane can be folded to make the image more true, then of course it can also be folded to question the image; the possibility of the folded picture plane is not restricted to perspectival projection. In my two examples below, the first is completely held by perspective, while in the second it is hardly present.

Pattern for Cold Bog diorama camera. The left-hand side is the top, and shows the plan of the film plane. The underside is on the right where the wind-on film-holding-mechanism pockets are visible.

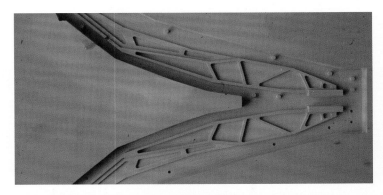

To illustrate some of the work we have done in this area I have included an example of a student project by Bernd Felsinger (see page 28), and will here cover two drawing instruments of my own in a little more depth. The first is a simple analytical tool that is particular to its subject matter. Apart from a few panoramic examples, most cameras have a flat picture plane; the lens is designed to resolve the image on a flat surface (the emulsion of the film or a light-sensitive chip), and this makes it difficult to manipulate. The camera does, however, provide the means for capturing a projection to work on. The pinhole (working as a lens) offers us much more than the glass optics of a typical camera lens, as the extensive depth of field allows us to form a picture plane and still capture a reasonably sharp image at many depths (subject to varying exposure times for different focal lengths). This makes it a favourite means to manipulate a projection and the first of my examples illustrates the control that is possible in using such a medium.

Cold Bog Camera

The Cold Bog camera is a reflexive tool, for the subject it studies is the spatial potential of the picture plane. In the middle of the 20th century, diorama painting reached its peak in natural history museums in the US. The most rigorous of these painters in projecting the geometry of the image from the site into the background painting was JP Wilson, who worked mainly at the American Museum of Natural History in New York and the Yale Peabody Museum of Natural History in New Haven, Connecticut. His work is interesting in this area for many reasons, but for the scope of this paper I will contain the discussion to his projection techniques.

Wilson trained as an architect at Columbia[3] and worked in the office of Bertum Goodhue making fastidious perspective drawings. When he became a diorama painter he transferred this attention to detail to the geometric problem of relating an image captured on site on flat picture planes (photographs and paintings) to the curved backdrop. His method involved oil paintings made on site to capture the colour and a series of Kodachrome slides taken as panoramas (as in join-ups).[4] These were taken at set angles either side of centre, one set horizontal and others above and below. If prints from these were assembled, they would make a faceted picture plane with the centre of each facet equidistant from the centre. His process of translating this image on to the curved backdrop so that it looks natural and in scale with the foreground to the observer is clever but also complicated. In trying to understand his method, I developed a camera that could make all the necessary transformations in a photograph of the site.

The Cold Bog camera is specific to the Cold Bog diorama at New Haven, chosen because Wilson scholar Michael Anderson from the Yale Peabody could arrange for access to the diorama and the original site, and could provide accurate drawings of the diorama shell. Three identical versions were manufactured, to allow steroscopic photography and also to provide a back-up. The picture plane in the camera is a scale model of the diorama shell, with the pinhole located at the ideal viewing position. The site is remote, so the cameras have wind-on mechanisms

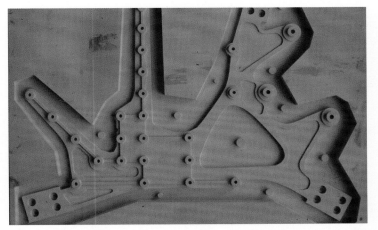

Night-time drawing instrument
Patterns for the drawing instrument. The parts shown here include the legs (top), subframe (above), main chassis top (below), and and underside of the main chassis (bottom). All are machined on a three-axis CNC mill.

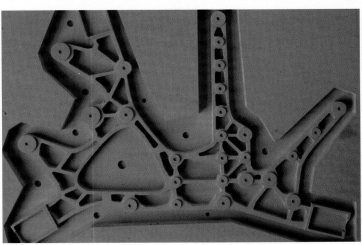

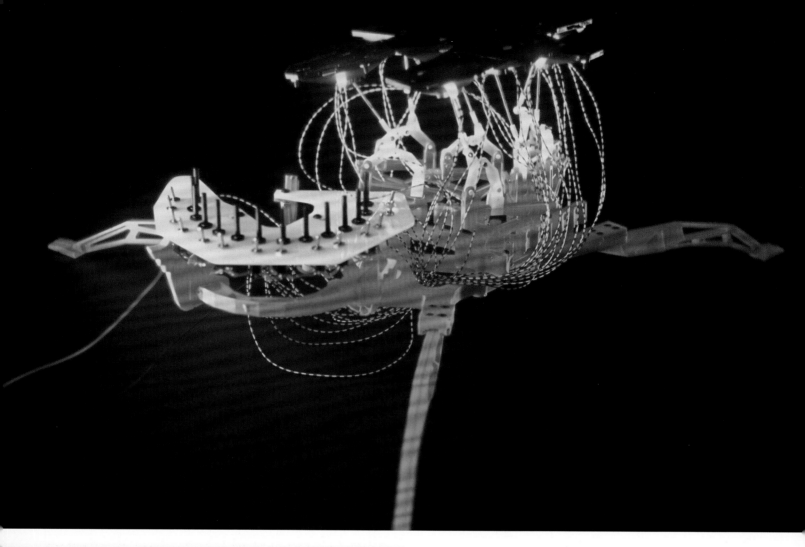

so that several shots can be made without reloading. As they have to work stereoscopically as a pair in front of the diorama (partly as a check on their accuracy but also related to Wilson's use of stereoscopy), the cameras had to be as narrow as possible to achieve a 65-millimetre separation between pinholes. As a consequence the roll film spools are located behind the picture plane. Three rollers pull back when winding on to keep the film on its intended curvature and ensure it does not pop out of its runners.

So the camera is specific to the content that it will photograph, yet also to the circumstances in which the photograph will be taken and the method of testing the results. The original survey was made on 17 June 1949 and my photographs were made on 17 June 2001. A normal camera was used to compare the results. In the stereoscopic pair of photographs of the diorama taken by a normal camera, the diorama shell appears curved as in reality. In the Cold Bog camera's stereoscopic versions the shell appears perfectly flat – confirmation of the accuracy of the tool.

As a tool, the Cold Bog camera is both particular to its task but also completely prescriptive as to its content. I learned almost everything I needed to know by designing and making the camera rather than using it (although this was revealing in other aspects of the work). However, it

A folding picture plane of the Night-time drawing instrument supports figures with variable colour and illumination. The variations in the folds change the nature of the image. The observer is implicated in the image by his or her position.

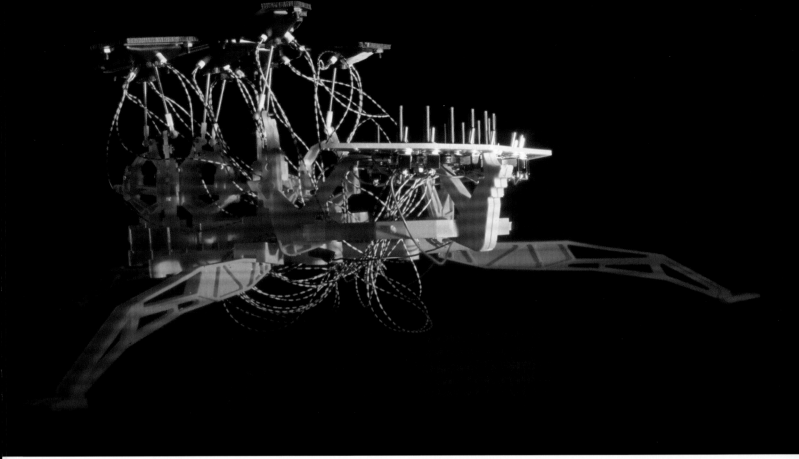

offers the means by which such a camera can also be more speculative, and several variations on this have been made in the studio.

Night-Time Drawing Instrument

The Night-time drawing instrument is much more speculative. It is made to draw the consequence of a project where there is a degree of separation between the apparatus and the architectural consequence. Asking questions about the programmatic relationship between architecture (or the city) and the body, new synthetic organs are added to our original ones to change our performance. The new apparatus[5] focuses on those sites where architecture claims to have the most straightforward relationship with us: for example, hygiene, waste disposal, digestion, heating and cooling. The new equipment modifies these so that if it is true that architecture and the city have such a tight relationship with our bodies, by changing our performance we should therefore change the city. By changing our performance in different ways we can change (or take possession of) the city for ourselves without changing it for others. Drawing such an apparatus for the body is quite straightforward, and to some extent so are other aspects of its consequence, but there is a problem with the project in that at night the programme of the city partly dissolves, or at least changes. The drawing instrument was made to find out about this condition where the consequence of the body apparatus fell between intention and more sublime spatial effects.

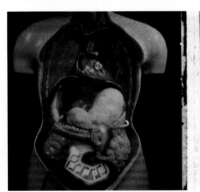
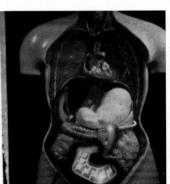
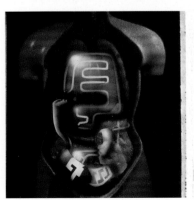

Layer 4 and layer 6: internal architecture project three. If it is true that architecture and the city provide a tight programmatic relationship to our bodies, then by modifying those performances of the body that are related to those programmes we should necessarily modify the city.

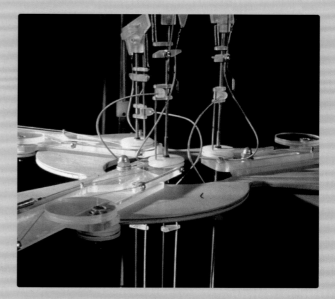

Detail of drawing and sensing elements.

The range of performance is always the same. It is how it is used and how much of it is used that modifies our experience. A set figure of dashes is cut in the picture plane to discuss this performance. The instrument is interested in discussing the periphery, as there is an inversion of interest from the focus of the programme of the day to the margins of the evening. Behind the slots (some of which can be blanked off just as some of the apparatus can be dormant), are pockets that contain two different-coloured light bulbs, each of which can be turned on or off or dimmed anywhere in between. The settings on the instrument relate to settings on the body apparatus. It is a night-time drawing instrument and it draws in light. Each pocket is held on a mechanism that can adjust its position with intention by a sliding element that raises or lowers the pocket and a rotation that is connected to a broader context (outside our intention), which also adjusts the attitude of the pocket due to the eccentric location of the support. The instrument is connected to a reader that translates the experience of the city when using the body apparatus.

Bernd Felsinger's Anticipation Navigator

The aim of the preliminary study at the Bartlett was to construct a 'drawing instrument' that operates as an interface between the observer and the city. The drawing instrument is essentially a recording device that constructs 'informed surfaces' on plaster casts by providing 'access' to a printing mechanism, which in turn produces the cast's surface condition. For each successive cast the previous plate is fed back into the production process and takes on the role of a latent memory, subject to re-evaluation by the user. As the observer filters through the city, 'recordings' in the form of plaster casts are produced along the journey. This journey through the city is finally drawn out in the form of a series of interrelated casts, unique to the location of where they were made and prescriptive of the journey once they are seen in relation to each other.

A normal camera takes photographs of the seven connected leaves of the picture plane. The obliqueness and position of the shot relates to the situation in the city. The nature of the image depends on the lighting of the slots and the folds in the picture plane with respect to the camera position. The wires that lead to the bulbs have stripes on them so that they register in the seams between some of the pockets. This noise is reminiscent of the internal experience of the apparatus as some slight difference between the natural and synthetic systems is perceived, for instance a temperature divergence as one system works more efficiently than the other. A series of photographs is taken for parts of the journey and then assembled on a picture plane that is particular to that journey or place. That picture plane is also folded so that the observer has a spatial relationship to the image.

Both of the drawing instruments described above were drawn using highly conventional drawing tools, a mixture of architectural drafting, 3-D modelling and CNC milling applications as the pieces were manufactured on CNC milling machines. To different extents they had known intentions that were translated with varying degrees of transparency on to the drawing. In using both of them, the act of drawing (or photography) concentrates on the precision of the idea rather than the construction of the image. ⌂

The drawing instrument ready to use. The cast from the previous site is seen at the bottom. The drawing instruments that register the current condition are in the middle and the casting plate is at the top.

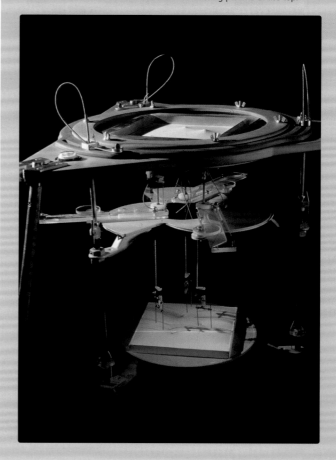

Notes
1 David Sylvester, *Interviews with American Artists*, Pimlico (Yale), 2001, p 87.
2 I use the word 'drawing' to cover the activity of proposing an idea on a flat or folded surface, and not just to include delineation. When we discuss architectural drawings we often refer to images constructed through various media and processes.
3 Michael Anderson, 'Raising Standards In Natural History Dioramas: The Background Paintings of James Perry Wilson', *Curator* 43/4, October 2000.
4 Ruth Morrill, 'A Dual Grid System For Diorama Layout', *Curator* 39/4, December 1996.
5 This project is a development of one described in Peter Cook and Neil Spiller (eds), *The Power of Contemporary Architecture*, Academy Editions (London), 1999, pp 28–31.

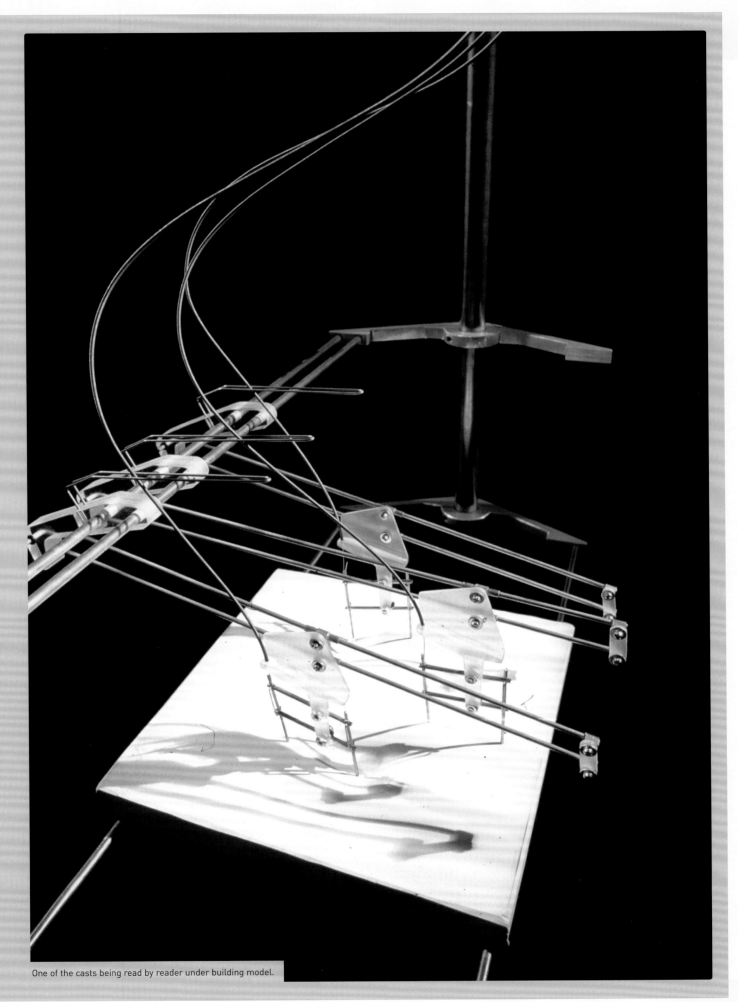

One of the casts being read by reader under building model.

HOMO FABER

During his final 12 years, Gaudí proposed that the surfaces of the Sagrada Família Church all be defined geometrically – he rejected freeform in his experiment in updating the Gothic for the postindustrial age. His plastic experimentation is revealed in his final models for the project, but it is a notoriously slow process. Using cartographic principles, his geometry requires mapping by his successors for the project. This 1980 drawing shows the component geometry for the nave screen-wall composed of a series of different-sized openings formed by intersecting hyperboloids. The task is to find the curves of intersection between adjacent geometry and, more particularly, the 3-D coordinates of the triple points – points in space where three curves of intersections intersect. This work is the intermediary phase between Gaudí's 1:10 plaster of Paris studies, and the construction of the screen itself.

Professor **Mark Burry**'s extraordinary and devoted work is nothing short of a measure by which standards for architectural research are set. Known for his investigative use of computational techniques to unravel the mysteries of Gaudí's Sagrada Família Church, he here takes a moment to reflect on where computational technologies in architecture are taking us. His experience suggests that before we abandon old tools for new, this is a good moment to put the brakes on. Hybrid activity, he remarks, demonstrates unequivocal benefits to the design process, and slow design has proven to be indispensable for success.

1995 student project for an art space
Half-size prototype for a section of the proposed building using a constrained set of timber sizes. The assignment included an investigation into the normally undisclosed potential of constituent materials. Intriguingly, in this example the project's author has used timber in tension to add strength and value to its contribution to the assembly. It is a predigital haptic experiment testing such potential through direct hands-on experience, and it is not certain that these tentative propositions would emerge in digital experimentation alone. (Credit: Colette Mullin)

Visitors to Jean Nouvel's Torre Agbar building in Barcelona during its construction phase will have noticed a large 1:1 3-D prototype constructed in the precinct of the actual building site. The project itself is radical in as many ways as possible – his use of colour and the building's second skin, plan and programme, profile, and its proximity to Gaudí's Sagrada Família Church less than a kilometre distant, apparently in some gesture of homage, though it might be regarded as in competition. In an age where airliners are digitally prototyped, built, then tested entirely from a digital design process, it may seem curious that crude, full-size 3-D prototypes are required during the construction phase of this innovative building, rather than as an essential precursor.

For me, it was one of the more heartening experiences of recent years, where, firmly seated within the context of ubiquitous computing and pervasive digital design,

homo faber – 'man the maker' – is required to experiment with the actual stuff of his or her endeavours, at full scale and regardless of all the automated design and building aids increasingly at our affordable disposal. Possibly this circumstance is evidence of a maturity in practice, where each tool and each modus operandi is evaluated independently for merit, and retained or adopted accordingly. Successful slow design married to the quicker pace that capitalism ordinarily ordains.

The debate surrounding the appropriateness of the computer in design has shifted away from direct and often unfavourable comparison with *Handwerkskunst* to a number of more intractable and problematic issues – the role of computation in design, apparent enfranchisement of the amateur, the 'art of the accident' elevated to legitimate design enquiry, and the formation of entirely new multidisciplinary creative teams mediated by the computer. New paradigms for practice through the previously impossible virtual collocation of designers and manufacturers, and the real effect of rapid prototyping, has yet to reach proportions that actually threaten time-honoured craft based firmly and exclusively within the discipline of architecture. When the affordability and ubiquity of rapid prototyping facilities attain levels similar to the

Full-size prototype of a modular fabric screen, predigital in all respects other than the frame, which is shaped in response to calculated bending stresses. The prototype is made from the proposed materials for the final product, including turned stainless-steel fittings, cast aluminium and canvas. (Credit: Chris Norman)

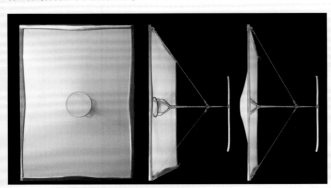

desktop computer and associated 3-D modelling software, however, will we see the end of the studio as we have known it since *homo faber* first experimented with the plastic formation of ideas? There are already indicators that we will have a similar period of the less thoughtful and zealous overproduction that comes with the ease of automation, typified by the increased use of paper precipitated by the arrival of the inkjet plotter.

The seed for CAD (computer-aided drafting to some, computer-aided design to others) was first sown within the education sectors of graphic representation and professional practice, thus beginning its life in relatively innocuous circumstances with regard to the status quo. CAD, after all, would be a significant labour-saver at the level of drafting, providing the designer with extra time to contemplate and reflect – increased time to hatch ideas rather than hatch drawings. The shock wave caused by the rapid and unplanned infiltration of CAD to wider architecture programmes worldwide during the 1990s, most notably design, has exacerbated the traditional generational gap that has always spiced up architectural educational programmes.

Formerly, during at least 150 years of institutionally based architectural education, programmes benefited from the frisson of the antler-locking between experienced world-weary senior practitioners and the young Turks not yet burdened with mortgages and family responsibilities and atypically willing to provide free labour in support of the project. A further predominant source of creative friction came from the competing agendas of theory and practice, further complicated by the debate between architectural historians (architects first, historians second) and their counterparts, historians of architecture who have never made a single building, still less designed one. In this context, during five years of study, contrasting often with contiguous part-time work in offices or the interregnum of a gap year, young architects could set their sails according to their own predilections formed from a clear and reasonable set of both contrasting and complementary priorities.

With the insurgency of new digital design tools to the design studio, new pressures and often irreconcilable differences have produced, in many cases, an unbridgeable gulf between the fuddy-duddies, whose currency is the sagacity born from

Sagrada Família Church
Gaudí's quest for form is plastic in its expression yet rational in its description. It emerges from a haptic process using setting plaster of Paris. In the 20 minutes it takes for the plaster to set, the rotating hyperbola profile shapes half a hyperboloid of revolution that acts in turn as the master form to provide any number of negative reproductions.

experience, and a generation of digitally adept school-leavers, who not only have to attempt to assimilate the priorities associated with a traditional way of practising that increasingly becomes irrelevant, but are also in the key position to point towards new ways of operating without the benefit of any meaningful apprenticeship in as yet untried modes of practice. Of course, in the world of exploring ideas this situation provides wonderful opportunities for truly innovative design enquiry, not least in the world of virtual space, and the spatial representation of information that is everything about intellectual engagement but may have nothing to do with a more tangible world of bricks and mortar.

In terms of being able to influence practice, the profession has now suffered for some while from an impasse that curiously affects architecture in ways other industries have been able to deal with quite successfully; most notably the aeronautical, nautical and car design industries, along with manufacturing. Rapid prototyping and the efficiency gains obtained thereby are regularly proselytised as the necessary technological advance required to lift the profession of architecture into the 21st century. My experience in both teaching and practice to date suggests that this is a good moment to apply the brakes to headlong adoption of all the new tools prior to figuring out how we will at least retain the skill base of traditional methods of design exploration and representation, especially in 3-D. It strikes me that an amalgam of both handcraft techniques that are currently threatened, and the digital tools that will increasingly proliferate at affordable price points, ought to be actively sustained for at least as long as we need to understand fully what we lose through a degree of abrogation of

The production of negative hyperboloids of revolution, which are the actual components sought for interaction with neighbouring forms.

Several of the individually produced forms are intersected by hand to provide the underlying rationality for the nave screen-window. The surfaces are all characterised by the fact that they are 'ruled' with an infinite array of 'non-coplanar' straight lines that intersect obliquely with the surfaces. This property aids construction and provides the clues for the decorative treatment.

Decorative overlay in detail for the nave screen-wall. The star-shaped decoration is set up by the straight lines that run obliquely along the surface. Any point on the surface has two such lines running either side of the opening 'collar'. Adjacent surfaces intersect usually as 3-D curves. These intersections themselves intersect, providing key points in space known as 'triple points'. In selecting these key points as the basis for the sculptural surface treatment, Gaudí introduced a decorative logic to the composition. This process involves excision from some of the surface areas, and addition of material to other areas, a handcraft process not easily emulated digitally.

The interior and exterior of the Sagrada Família Church clerestory windows, as proposed by Gaudí at a scale of 1:10.

To make the mould-masters for the full-size components, Gaudí's process is simply scaled up using the same process that he used for his 1:25 and 1:10 scaled prototypes, and uses the same materials.

Full-scale mould-master for part of the central nave ceiling vaults (inverted for convenient fabrication at ground level). This plaster of Paris mould-master is for the production of fibreglass production moulds for building components.

workload to the machine, while not necessarily being blind to what we stand to gain.

Currently, the relative expense of the rapid prototyping machinery and materials combined with the relative slowness of their operation ('rapid', sadly, is a relative term in this debate as a single 3-D print can tie a machine up for more than a day) limit use of such equipment to tasks of relative importance, so this seems a perfect time to ponder the best possible relationship between *homo faber* and the agency offered through the automated procedure. The three projects that follow variously span the 10 years that separate the pre- and postdigital eras, in the first case predating ubiquitous computing, and deliberately make use of the best aspects of both manual and machine-aided making. Together they provide some pointers on how hybrid activity demonstrates unequivocal benefits to the design process, where slow design has proven to be indispensable for the success of the project, despite the successful quest for the relative rapidity provided through adoption of the computer across all sectors of architectural design activity.

1 Student projects: 1:1 – predigital

In consolidating the association between idea and artefact, I have been running courses in 1:1 ideation-fabrication for senior students of architecture since 1990. At that time, the construction of buildings was much less interesting to the students than architectural theory, especially theory more inclined towards philosophical preoccupations. Buildings, it seemed, somehow managed to be built from loose sketches. Other people would effect this essential translation – 'they' would find a way with a minimum of prompting. This attitude is apparently still with us, as engineers, among others, regard part of their role as 'problem solvers', where the architect is seen as part of the problem.

Since commencing with full-scale projects, I have found that in working this way students observe forcefully that, in fact, what they design might be influenced in reverse, that is to say, considering built architecture in its possible fulfilments may work backwards to influence the ideation at a point where the physical manifestation of an idea is still hardly defined. Working at 1:1 essentially means working with real materials where practicable, and simulation only when absolutely necessary. This activity may provide students with interesting insights regarding the messiness of foundry work, the dangers of welding and the propensity for timber to be wayward. More critical, in my view, is the connection with scale, particularly pertinent in an era of CRT/LCD renditions that have no scale at all and the confrontation with materiality and its intellectual extension way beyond fitness for purpose.

The two examples shown here are from a five-week project: a three-week conceptual design for an artist's workshop and gallery within the platform area of a busy railway terminus, followed by a two-week 1:1 3-D *esquisse* of a single meaningful element. Neither project is digital, although one is influenced in shape by numerical calculation of forces. I believe that both projects, and the majority of those of other students at the time, would have

Positioning the fibreglass moulds above the ambulatory around the apse.

Not all the ceiling vaults are made from in-situ artificial stone. The central nave vaults are made from three layers of flat tile using the time-honoured 'bovedas Catalana' (Catalan vaulting) technique, recorded as being Gaudí's original intention. This image shows the first such use for this project in 1996, 70 years after his death: it has been made as a full-scale prototype, and in this image it is about to be lifted to its proposed location 45 metres above.

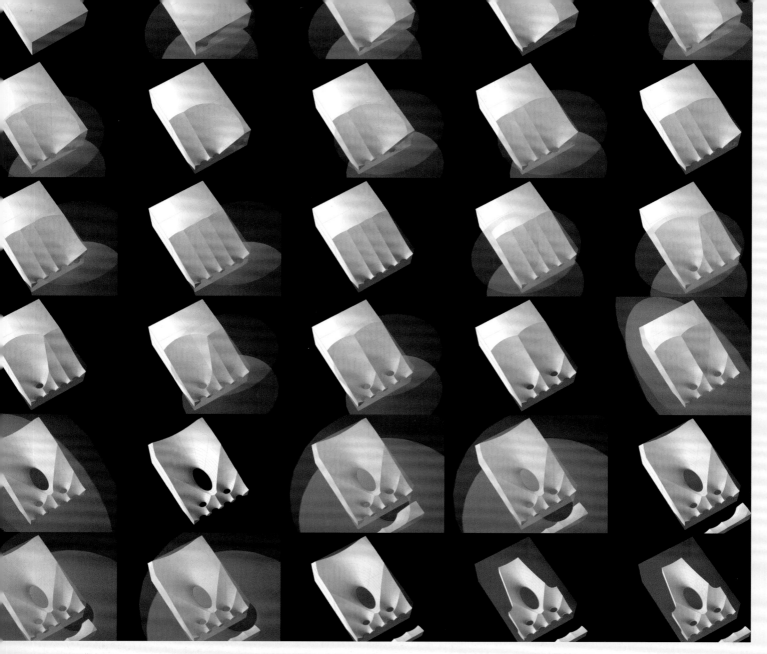

The introduction of the computer to the design office in 1989 was to further enhance an exceedingly slow process, whether by hand modelling or the subsequent analytical drawing. This image shows the series of subtractions required to produce the proposal for the nave clerestory.

missed many of the potentials and ironies that could only be played out by hand.

2 Sagrada Família: pre- and postdigital design development

Gaudí introduced a rationality to his work at all times, despite appearances to the contrary. He dedicated his final years (1914–26) exclusively to the Sagrada Família Church, and combined the Gothic Revival basis of the design – from an earlier architect's involvement prior to his own commission in 1883 – with a growing sense of a need for a system. The system was to ensure that his design had a legacy, as he realised the implications of his own physical frailty.

The work today is as complicated as it has been for the century and a quarter it has been on site, made more complicated still today by the two million visitors who come to see the building as a construction: the project has to use high-end modelling software aimed for the vehicle and aircraft design and manufacturing sector. Gaudí insisted that innovation must be in the design, not in the making, arguing that traditional methods should be used in order to keep risk to a minimum. In his final years, however, he began to realise through experimentation that new materials and methods would need to be introduced to the project, which can be seen with the construction of the finials on top of the first four towers, with his inevitable uptake of concrete having avoided its use from the first.

The accompanying images show the comprehensiveness of Gaudí's design modelling, and its posthumous translation to full-scale building operations. Especially appealing is that, despite the need for the introduction of software beyond the architectural sector's demands, and despite being one of the first projects ever to involve rapid prototyping of design and CNC automated material preparation, the modelling studio remains intact, and its workforce vibrant, as any visitor can witness. It would seem that not only was the Sagrada Família Church one of the first projects anywhere to have adopted the most sophisticated digital tools, it is also one of the first to enter a postdigital era as a leader, in circumstances where the

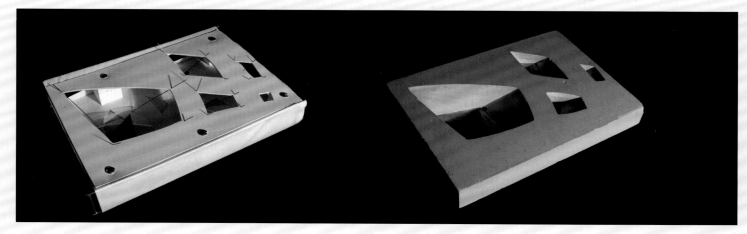

continued contribution of the craftsperson is judged as a crucial partner to the digital dialogue.

3 Student project: 10:1 postdigital

The final project shown here is part of a 2004 design studio where architecture and industrial design students worked together on a project based on water, working ultimately to a scale of 10:1. It is an extension to the 1:1 project referred to as predigital, but over a decade later this studio reflects a number of realities and opportunities. The enlarged academy, where student numbers have risen dramatically, means that it is now very difficult to offer them the material intimacy of one on one working at 1:1. We deal with this by asking them to work in groups. However, the use of the Internet not only provides incredible access to materials and construction information, but also allows students to work in different physical locations to each other if desired.

Further, the very nature of design authorship can now be questioned by asking a particular group to work on a project whose original author is not in their midst, he or she being located in a different group, also working on someone else's project. Encouragingly, the original authors have almost always been open enough to acknowledge that, in most cases, the design development has added considerable value to their original proposal. Equally, group members have not expressed any negative views about working as hard as they do on 'someone else's' design.

The final opportunity we are making the most of is the breakdown of discipline boundaries through the convergence of technology. Whereas going back to the guilds we see the emergence of protected materials and techniques, the digital era has brought in devices of common currency. Whether the students prefer to work using time-honoured manual techniques or not is hardly evidence of degree or lack of digitality, or a value judgement of either. That today's students are far more aware of other disciplines and their respective ways of working, combined with intimate association through sharing the same digital tools, points to a new era of design collaboration regardless of how 'digital' as individuals we are inclined to be. It is for this reason that I believe the academy should resist both any tendency for conservatism or a total rush into technology. Rather, it seems best that they seek to consolidate both traditional and digital design processes within teaching programmes lest we lose the skill to pass on skill – the malaise currently besetting some schools of fine art. ∆

Politics of Water design studio
1:10 scale model for the parametrically variable windows. The analogue parametric model shown to the left led to the 1:10 scale model on the right, cast in plaster of Paris. (2004 studio collaboration between architecture and industrial design students: Tatu Parssinen (concept), Sheree Danli Lai, Tony Josendal, Jakob Lange, Stephen Wallace (developed design), Mark Burry, Dominik Holzer, Malte Wagenfeld, Mark Taylor (studio directors)).

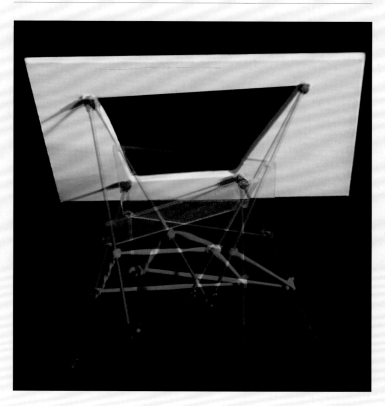

Working model of part of a swimming-pool facade 'parametrically' variable at a scale of 1:10. Although there are over 400 unique window openings for the swimming pool project, whose opening sizes respond to the required degrees of interior privacy, only five sizes of glass are proposed. The glass in this analogue parametric model swivels around the four pins fixed to the corners of the exterior surface (represented by the cardboard plane). These pins point to the interior surface. The glass panel is twisted until the interior opening (represented here by the rubber band) is deemed satisfactory. This overlaid image is indicative of two of an infinite range of possibilities.

Acknowledgements
Sagrada Família Church: pre- and postdigital design development. The research on the Sagrada Família Church reported here has been part-funded by the Australian Research Council. I acknowledge their support and that of the Junta Constructora of the Sagrada Família Church in Barcelona for the opportunities they provide for extending the work of Gaudí into contemporary architectural practice and research. Team: Jordi Bonet (architect director and coordinator), Jordi Faulí (project architect), Mark Burry (design architect), Jordi Cussó, Josep Talledes (model-makers).

IN MY CRAFT AND SULLEN ART
OR SKETCHING THE FUTURE BY DRAWING ON THE PAST

Brookes Stacey Randall, Ballingdon Bridge, Sudbury, Suffolk, 2003
Sectional digital model of the bridge revealing the use of an iterative
lofting technique.

The welsh poet Dylan Thomas in his poem *In My Craft and Sullen Art* writes about the remoteness of the poet or author, which starts:

> In my craft or sullen art
> Exercised in the still night
> When only the moon rages
> And lovers lie abed
> With all their griefs in their arms.[1]

Perhaps this poem reflects part of the dilemma of those who chose to create and engage with society by creative processes. It is all too easy to see contemporary architectural practice as a remote activity where concepts and creativity are encoded typically in drawings, and the process of constructing the building is left to others. In the late 20th century, the role of the architect had arguably been eroded by fragmentation and specialisation. Direct communication and dialogue in the construction process could be difficult. Although this was the beginning of the information age, modes of procurement and forms of contracts distanced the potential collaborates in the creative process of making a building.

Creating architecture is not just problem solving, it's about invention and interaction. Architecture is an art and, simultaneously, a science. It is in the materials, in the realisation of a project that the physics and the experiential come together. In the mathematics of architecture, 2+2 does not equal 4; two spaces plus two spaces can generate millions of possibilities.

In many ways I think of myself as a student of architecture. By instinct I am a design-maker, which has led to my involvement in digital design and digital fabrication. My interest in materials, manufacturing processes and details came from concepts, from the desire to extend the boundaries of the possible – to move from a world of ideas to the public realm. Rem Koolhaas asserts his approach as 'no budget, no details, just concept'. Why deny the considerable skill devoted to the realisation of his projects? Ludwig Mies van der Rohe famously suggested that 'God is in the detail', and many a builder that the devil is in the detail! Both expressions place too much emphasis on the 'supernatural'; the key is mankind's amazing ability to invent and to create.

The craft tradition, essentially an oral tradition, was in danger of being lost after the Second World War, particularly in Britain and America. In the 1950s and 1960s in particular, science was seen as a 'universal' and preferable replacement for craft. This approach characterises ARJP Ubbelohde's chapter of *A History of Technology* (Volume IV),[2] published in 1958, and entitled 'The Beginnings of the Change from Craft Mystery to Science as a Basis for Technology', which traces his perception of the role of science in the development of technology from the age of enlightenment to the late 19th century. The objectivity claimed for science is portrayed as of universal benefit, and oral continuity is viewed as a mystery. The potential for continuity of skills and innovation was overlooked in the 'white heat of technology'.

Contemporary society still suffers from a false dichotomy between the academic and the practical. The role of precision and close observation in making or craft processes, the linking of hand and eye, and the use of one's intellect to control a physical outcome, should be honoured and rewarded. John Harrison, the 18th-century carpenter who over his lifetime developed precision chronometers and transformed navigation, is an excellent example of a maker who developed a very sophisticated understanding of materials.

Whether made digitally or by hand, remotely or locally, realisation of architecture is still reliant on the agency of dialogue from a practice that stems from oral exchange. Professor **Michael Stacey,** a global figure in the development of digital fabrication in architecture, and author of *Component Design*, draws from his broad experience in manufacturing, practice and research. This grounded text is a prompt for architectural practice to adopt digital fabrication technologies with clear reference and understanding of their origins and, thus, redefine itself as a form of live research.

It is revealing to examine the roots of the words 'technology' and 'craft'. 'Technology' is defined in the *Oxford English Dictionary* as the study or use of the mechanical arts and applied sciences, and originates from the Greek *tekhnologia*, or 'systematic treatment', whereas 'craft' is defined as a skill, especially in practical arts, and a craftsperson as a skilled and usually time-served worker. The origins of the word 'craft' lie in Old English. Technology is often discussed within contemporary society as if an entity or a force itself. It is vital to remember that all technology is made by people, for people.[3] Technology is not deterministic; the decision-making is in the hands of the designers and users. Almost all technologies can be used for war or peace, to denude or enhance the planet! There is a real and present danger in contemporary society; as we enjoy the fruits of technological progress, we may lose some of the best means and methods of the past – even the recent past. This is not to suggest nostalgia or an obsession with heritage, but more an active use of history, precedent and traditions.

My design practice is based on a detailed knowledge of materials and process combined with a direct engagement with the making of a component-based architecture. It has proved vital that in the UK and Europe sufficient 'remnants' of the Industrial Revolution remain, and it has always been possible to find an appropriate manufacturer and, often, craftspeople who can help realise a design. Although science is vital in the computation of a structure or in the chemistry of a polymer or casting, the craft 'mysteries' remain; for example, the sizing of a sand mould for a metal casting depends on the skill and experience of the foundryman. In part, this can be replaced by computational fluid dynamics (CFD), a transfer from experience to computation that is being driven by skill shortages due to a lack of investment in apprentices. The trade secret remains a vital tool of competitiveness.

The 'complexity' of contemporary technology is a myth in itself; the essence of successful technology is always in essence simple – it needs to be reliable and repeatable. The design of a die to produce an aluminium extrusion is 'relatively' simple, whereas the design of dies for PVCU remains a black art. I became interested in extrusions in part because they are a direct realisation of the drawing, and I discovered whilst working within manufacturing that it is possible to go from a section drawing to an extruded component in two to three weeks. The drawing is not a representation, it is a component, the architecture. This experience was used later in practice to design the mullions for the bespoke glazing system of East Croydon railway station. When working with polymers and, particularly, elastomers, the drawing, which is five or 10 times the full size, starts and ends the making process. In addition, whilst developing the tubular gasket for Aspect 2 (with Alan Brookes and Varnamo Rubber), an integrated system of interchangeable composite panels, windows and doors, it became clear that the design of a gasket is not an exact science and is, in fact, more a product of experience, trial and error; it is a process of design, testing and development.

Development of Aspect 2 primary gasket

Four dies were needed to produce the final production run of the primary gasket for Aspect 2, which is still in use in Aspect 3, a further development of the system. The first gasket had two engineered hinge points, which resulted in too little elastomeric pressure. This gasket was also too 'fine' for the range of joint sizes resulting from component and site assembly tolerances. The second gasket had a modified hinge point intended to provide a 'set' of the gaskets to ensure a successful compressed form. However, this proved not to be the case. The form of the third die resulted from close examination of the material properties of the ethylene propylene diene monomer (EPDM). The profiles of the next six gaskets resulted from modifying the way the same steel die plate is used in the extrusion process, by varying the ram pressure, the vacuum calibration and the speed at which the gasket is pulled from the extruder. The final production die was necessary to ensure that the successful gasket profile could be produced regularly and at economic speeds. The section of a gasket is usually checked by a small cross-section of, say, 2 to 3 millimetres deep being placed on an epidiascope and compared to a 10 times full-size drawing of the gasket profile.

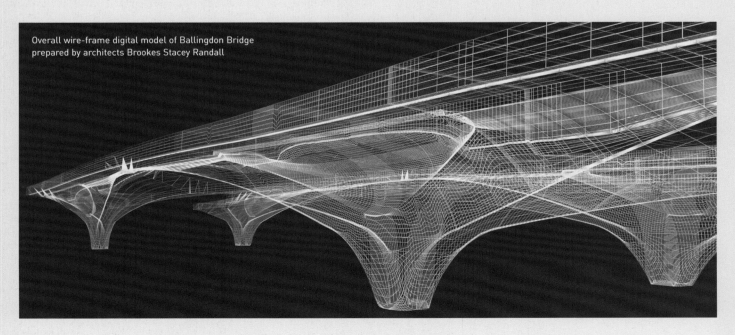

Overall wire-frame digital model of Ballingdon Bridge prepared by architects Brookes Stacey Randall

Testing

The importance of physical testing cannot be overstated; although we now have access to very sophisticated computational analysis, it is vital for architects, engineers and designers to remain grounded by physical reality. Testing full-scale prototypes is a relatively expensive process, and some engineers argue that we can 'jump' scales in testing, from coupon tests of small samples to establish the properties of a new material straight into the full-size assembly, by using finite element analysis.

It is sobering to remember the impact on the 19th century of David Kirkaldy's Testing Works, Southwark South, London, when it opened in 1866. The provision of precise data on material properties exposed failings in contemporary constructional practice. Nor was his influence limited to London; the Kirkaldy Testing Works received orders from many continental manufacturers including Krupp in Germany, and Westanfors and Fagersta in Sweden.

The organising and witnessing of physical testing is a source of confidence for the architect or engineer. Seeing a cladding system or curtain walling survive the load or wind and weather test takes one beyond the abstract, theoretical or debatable. Steve Groák in *The Idea of Building* (1992) writes eloquently on the need for robust technology in construction. Having presented the case for the decline in robust technology, he states: 'One of the implications is that all building projects will have to be treated as innovative ... This will lead to a greater need for research literacy on the part of all practitioners throughout the professional building industries – they will evolve a role I call "the research practitioner".' He continues: 'I suggest that the paradigm of R&D inherited from the nineteenth century scientific research, via the early paradigm of engineering research, by itself is inadequate for the design and production of buildings,' and proposes a new research paradigm based on 'the process of making things, from the concept of "know-how". It will use design and production methods as the cutting edge.'[4]

Design by Collaboration

The design and delivery of modern buildings is in essence a collaborative process between the client and the architect, the architect with the structural engineers, mechanical and electrical engineers, and the quantity surveyors. Initially just within the office of the design team, this process then reaches out to site, workshops and factories, establishing a creative dialogue with the specialist subcontractors who will ultimately make the components of the project. The Japanese industrial designer Sori Yanagi puts it very clearly: 'Design is not something achieved by an individual working alone. If three put their heads together, goes a Japanese proverb, the wisdom of Manjusri Bodhisattva can be theirs. A designer cannot have too many gifted collaborators.[5] I include the software engineers who have created the CAD/CAM programs we use as gifted collaborators who should be chosen with care. Even or particularly when engaged in a process of direct manufacture using a unitary project model, the need for close dialogue is essential and is facilitated by the common model data.

One of the precast-concrete models of Ballingdon Bridge under construction at Buchan's works in the West Midlands.

The design and delivery of modern buildings is in essence a collaborative process between the client and the architect, the architect with the structural engineers, mechanical and electrical engineers, and the quantity surveyors. Initially just within the office of the design team, this process then reaches out to site, workshops and factories, establishing a creative dialogue with the specialist subcontractors who will ultimately make the components of the project.

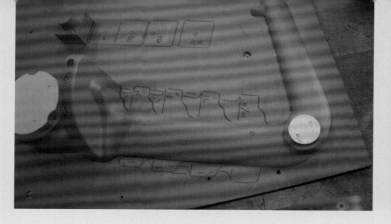

Timber pattern of the stainless-steel castings of the Ballingdon Bridge balustrade showing, by drawing, the variation in the casting length responding to the curved form of the precast-concrete superstructure

The 'foot' of the Ballingdon Bridge pier mould split at Buchan's works in Lancashire, ready for installation of the reinforcement.

The use of digital design tools has the potential to position the architect in the centre of the construction process, controlling the flow of information and, critically, the generative geometry.

James Timberlake and Stephen Kieran, in their book *Refabricating Architecture*,[6] contrast the current conventions of the construction industry and architectural practice with limited communication between the architect and the contractor, with typically no dialogue with manufacturers, material scientist and product engineers. Worse than this, there are many forces in contemporary society, including specialisation and fragmentation, that tend to marginalise the role of the architect. Compare this to the potential of digital fabrication and electronic information management. Timberlake and Kieran's second diagram (see below) shows a model of the construction process that is multidisciplinary and highly interactive, yet it is the architect who provides and controls the vision and physical outcomes on site. To some this is a renaissance of the architect as master builder; to others it offers the architect the possibility of becoming a designer maker.

The architect no longer needs to be remote from the manufacturing process; the digital 3-D model can become the building and all of its component parts. This places a significant emphasis on the skills employed and the interrelationship of 'global' and 'local' modelling techniques. The set for the opera *The Girl with No Door on Her Mouth,* designed by architects Philip Beesley and Derek Revington, is an example of direct manufacturing. The set comprises laser-cut Mylar film, which was cut at the Integrated Center for Design, Visualisation and Manufacture (ICDVM) of the University of Waterloo, Ontario.

Digital fabrication and the management of electronic information can place architects at the centre of the construction process. Comparative diagrams: the current isolated conventions of recent construction and the potential of digital fabrication, prepared by James Timberlake and Stephen Kieran.

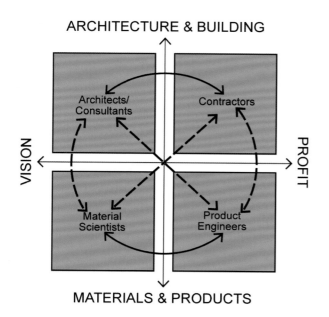

The Ballingdon Bridge pier mould showing the formwork of the scoops.

Ballingdon Bridge from the Sudbury bank.

The filigree and translucent screens are the direct combination of the laser-cut design drawings and the material qualities of the Mylar.

The terms 'standard' and 'nonstandard' are becoming obsolete. The rhetoric of 20th-century architecture was dominated by a call for standardisation and the deployment of mass production. In essence, in the built environment mass production was never successfully mobilised. The manufacturers almost always manufactured batches or series. Thus the potential for mass customisation or personal production in construction has been nascent for the past 70 years. The key issue today is not whether a component is standard or nonstandard, but whether or not the part can be manufactured and can be manufactured affordably.

Ballingdon Bridge

The setting is a wonderful combination of the water meadow that surrounds Sudbury and the listed buildings that form a conservation area, including the village of Ballingdon. There have been bridges on this site since the 12th century. The previous bridge, built in 1911, could not sustain heavy traffic, and closure would have resulted in a 35-mile diversion. The new Ballingdon Bridge, designed by Brookes Stacey Randall and Arup, is an integral reinforced-concrete structure that carries the A131 over the River Stour, replacing the existing bridge, which could no longer sustain 42-tonne articulated lorries. With the RIBA, Suffolk County Council organised an architect-led design competition for the new bridge, partly because of the large number of stakeholders involved, ranging from English Heritage to the River Stour Trust. Consultation with the local residents was particularly important as the competition resulted from 150 residents protesting at the town hall demanding a bridge of a new quality that could rapidly be constructed.

The design of the new bridge is visually calm, respecting the historic context; however, the structure has a dynamically 3-D soffit. Designed using an evolutionary technique, there is an ever-changing and site-specific geometry. Its feet appear to lightly touch the surface of the water. Its primary structure is formed from precast concrete, with the mix selected to match the local limestone of the 12th-century Norman church. The precast units were manufactured by Buchan in timber models, which were beautifully crafted from Brookes Stacey

Randall's digital geometry. By careful study of the construction and phasing of the bridge, and extensive prefabrication, disruption to Ballingdon was minimised and two-way traffic on the bridge was maximised during reconstruction. Ballingdon Bridge is an example of fast construction – slow architecture.[7] The bridge was rebuilt in 18 months and has a design life of 120 years. Brookes Stacey Randall sought to uphold the rich architectural traditions and construction quality of Suffolk – Sudbury was the home of Gainsborough, and the landscape of the Stour is set in Constable country.

Morphed Geometry

Brookes Stacey Randall's design for Ballingdon Bridge has a gently curvilinear profile and a dynamically morphed soffit. Within this ever-changing geometry, no two adjacent sections are the same. The geometry morphs from slice to slice, and at the pier feet the architects prepared sections at 47-millimetre centres, a section under every 2 inches. An interesting comparison is the in-situ formwork constructed for Eero Saarinen's TWA Terminal, for which construction company Grove Shepherd Wilson & Krudge built the formwork based on sections at 1-foot (305-millimetre) intervals. Antonio Román notes in *Eero Saarinen, Architecture of Multiplicity,* that: 'By 1960, about midway through construction, the intricacies of the site work required the builders to turn in part to computer generated computations.'[8] Thus, the TWA Terminal is both visually and technically a precursor of a digitally based architecture, though it is the physicality of the many physical models used by Saarinen that was key to the design process.

The morphing of the bridge superstructure developed out of the apparently conflicting criteria required for the bridge and its setting: the desire to create a fine edge, yet provide the robustness of a road bridge, combined with the need to maintain the wetted area in the course of the river. As project architect Laura Irving noted during the competition: 'Quickly we realised the potential that morphing brought to this project – transcending the constraints forming a gently beautiful bridge.'[9]

Considerable design endeavour and discussion have gone into when to introduce a point of contraflection or when to have smooth transitions, or when to generate a definite line or elevation. Visualising those subtle differences and modifying the end product as a result is the essence of this design development process; an architecture that is akin to product design, where every inflection in the form is critical. During the design of Ballingdon Bridge, Brookes Stacey Randall evolved a design process in which there was continuous iteration between 2-D delineation of form and 3-D modelling of the form. Klavs Helweg-Larsen, the architect of the KTAS telephone booth, noted that: 'There are no fixed rules on how to achieve harmonic proportions. Yet the difference between good and bad can be a question of a few millimetres.'[10] Visualising those subtle differences and modifying the end product as a result is therefore the essence of the design development process.

The smooth transitions in space have been achieved by a dedicated iteration, a design process targeted to extend the possible, not a simple explosion or implosion of space and form. This design process created geometry closer to the evolutionary geometry characteristic of nature, yet was delivered within a realistic human timescale. It was not a simple question of morphing the major sections together as we consciously sculpted the form of the bridge. The lighting scoops are a major example; however, there are also many inflections and nuances introduced into the form of the bridge: expressions of the line of forces spring from the pier foot, a memory of the existing bridge in the use of arched form.

The scoops provide distinct hollows in the daytime, with well-defined shadows, and at night gentle, glowing focused light. Once the overall form had been determined, the joint locations of the precast units were carefully considered to ensure they did not interrupt the flow of the form

The final form of the superstructure has been 'tested' by rapid prototyping at the ICDVM at the University of Waterloo. The rapid prototypes have been produced directly from Brookes Stacey Randall's 3-D digital files. To date, the key outcome from this process has been the rigorous checking of 2-D and 3-D data, seeking physical feedback on the design decisions. The potential role of rapid prototyping to assist form finding in architecture has been explored further by Jonathan Friedman, who fabricated a 1:33 CNC-machined model of Ballingdon Bridge (exhibited at the 'Digital Fabricators Exhibition' in Birmingham, London, and Cambridge, Ontario), using a flatbed CNC router to produce a full 3-D representation of the concrete structure.

The bridge has been designed to be asymmetrical, not purely symmetrical – a more 'natural' form with a site-specific extended tail to the Sudbury bank. Many pier locations were considered and tested, and the most expressive buildable options implemented. The precast units forming the bridge have been designed, by careful tuning of the profile and resultant levels, to have diagonal symmetry. Thus, six moulds are required to produce the 12 units of the bridge superstructure.

Design Development: Delivering the Morphed Geometry

Ballingdon Bridge was designed using an iterative lofting technique. The design files were a common digital resource for the whole of the design team. Without the common resource of the digital geometry generated by the architects, it would not have been possible to realise such a project. Although the design of the bridge takes inspiration from nature, it does not take a specific precedent from the natural world. The form development process can be described as evolutionary, yet carried out within a humanly realistic timescale. The confidence to deliver its geometric diversity comes from the use of digital data – both 2-D and 3-D computer modelling. The time spent and dedication of the design team, however, is the critical component in this design development process.

Balustrade

The balustrade has been designed to be visually open so that the views of the landscape are as uninterrupted as possible. This 'P2 Low Containment' balustrade, in combination with the bollards, is capable of arresting a 42-tonne truck, yet appears to be an elegant pedestrian handrail. The traffic and pedestrian functions of the bridge have been safely separated, the pavement being protected by bollards that also house light fittings. The enlarged walkways create a generous provision for pedestrians to enjoy the views of the river and meadows – a priority within the design of this road bridge.

The visually open, yet robust, balustrade was achieved by the combination of purpose-made aluminium extrusions, stainless-steel wires and stainless-steel castings. On impact, all the components work together to form a 'ribbon' that will arrest the vehicle. The top rail is a combination of extruded aluminium and English oak. This point of human contact is key to the design; to a pedestrian, the vehicular safety role is intended to be an unseen quality.

Even once the geometry and all of the details have been agreed upon, the drawing does not stop. The project architect then marks up the castings in the foundry, highlighting areas where the peened[11] finish is not yet satisfactory. Although the architect did not administer the contact, direct contact with the specialist subcontractors was facilitated by Suffolk County Council highway engineers, who delegated responsibility to their architect.

Canonbury Canopy

Schools or departments of architecture have enormous potential to work directly with the local community. This project, a canopy for a local primary school in Islington, London (2004) came indirectly from a summer school for Islington schoolchildren held at London Metropolitan University's Department of Architecture and Spatial Design. Canonbury School, built in the late 19th century, needed an outdoor classroom for four- to five-year-old pupils to extend their teaching curriculum outside. The shelter also forms part of the school's sustainable transport policy, encouraging parents and children to walk or cycle to school. My second-year architecture students at London

Ballingdon Bridge showing the illuminated scoops at twilight.

Metropolitan consulted with governors, teachers, children and the schoolkeeper on a wide range of designs; however, the priorities of pupils and teachers were not necessarily the same.

The final design is a collaboration between the students, the tutors, the client and the end users, ably facilitated by structural engineer Tim Lucas of Price and Myers 3D Engineering. The design comprised three semi-monocoque units prefabricated in the London Metropolitan University department and transported to site. The semi-monocoque units comprise bulk heads on 18-millimetre ply with two skins of 12-millimetre ply. The birch veneer ply was sourced from eastern Europe, and its supply sponsored by timber merchants James Latham. The canopy cantilevers in all directions, and the cantilever to the front is 3.6 metres. The canopy is located to gain maximum benefit from the existing brick wall, its purpose to shelter children from the sun as well as the rain.

London Metropolitan University took on the role of architect, project manager, main contractor and specialist subcontractor for the joinery. Trade contractors installed

---

Detail of Ballingdon Bridge from the Sudbury bank.

The in-situ reinforced concrete soffit of Ballingdon Bridge, including bat boxes. The in-situ concrete ties the precast concrete unit together to form an integral structure.

concrete foundations, steel columns and the single-ply waterproof membrane. The students and staff fabricated the plywood units. The design was transferred from microstation to the plywood by the use of full-scale templates to enable the curved profile to be accurately and consistently achieved. The steelworker, Michael Wilson, proved invaluable on site, lending his experience to enthusiastic architecture students. This was essential as the steelwork and the plywood units structurally work together with tight tolerances. The canopy was completed by the application of the single-ply waterproof membrane and simply detailed translucent polycarbonate rooflights. It has been designed as a permanent structure that can be readily maintained by the schoolkeeper. The physical excitement of realising the canopy proved to be a unique learning experience for those involved, providing a respect for the artisans and a confidence in their own decision-making that hopefully will remain with them throughout their careers. In addition, the schoolchildren now enjoy the shelter of the canopy, confident in their own imaginations.

The success of this and other 'live projects' has led to the formation of a projects office within the Department of Architecture. In essence, this is a collaborative practice that enables architects and other disciplines to work together to deliver projects particularly in the public realm. Thomas Fisher observes in *In the Scheme of Things: Alternative Thinking on the Practice of Architecture*, that: 'There was once a troubled profession. Its members had relatively modest incomes that were slow to grow. Its schools focused on the "art" of the discipline, with relatively little time or money spent on research.' He continues: 'The profession I am talking about is not architecture at the end of the twentieth century, but medicine in the second half of the nineteenth century.'[12] Medicine turned itself around in the 20th century; architecture should in the 21st century, by engaging with society, taking on responsibilities and forging a new collaborative approach. Architects should also be confident of their own subjective value judgements; the directness of design through making is one route to that position of purposefulness and responsibility. △

Notes
1 Written and published in 1946.
2 C Singer, EJ Holmyard, AR Hall & TI Williams (eds), *A History of Technology* (Volume IV), Oxford University Press, 1958, pp 663–81.
3 This is a conscious echo of John Wycliffe's introduction to the first bible in English (1382) in which he states: 'This Bible is for the Government of the People, by the People, and for the People,' and Abraham Lincoln's Gettysburg Address, 1863.
4 Steve Groák, *The Idea of Building*, Spons (London), 1992, pp 180–1.
5 Sori Yanagi, *Sori Yanagi's Work and Philosophy*, Yobisha, 1983.
6 J Timberlake and S Kieran, *Refabricating Architecture*, McGraw-Hill (New York), 2004.
7 Before the 20th century, the construction of a building was seen as an act of continuity. It is now possible to combine robust, rapidly deployable contemporary technology and the immutable qualities of architecture to create slow architecture analogous to the slow food of the slow food movement – an architecture of fine ingredients designed to be purposeful, savoured and enjoyed.
8 A Román, Eerö Saarinen, Architecture of Multiplicity, Laurence King (London), 2002, pp 118–23.
9 In coversation with the author during the competition.
10 P Ammitzboll *et al*, *DD Casebook 1: KTAS i Gadebilledet Street Signal KTAS*, Danish Design Council (Copenhagen), 1985, p 76.
11 Peening is a cold working process where the surface of a metal is blasted with shot pellets. For stainless steel it is essential that stainless-steel shot is used.
12 T Fisher, *In the Scheme of Things: Alternative Thinking on the Practice of Architecture*, University of Minnesota Press, 2000, p 115.

ORGONE
REEF

Making architecture may be considered
a conscious endeavour to imagine and
investigate the physical and psychological
aspects of human experience. Fed by an
insatiable urge to understand and explore
his environment, **Philip Beesley** constructs
exquisite thresholds that mediate between
craft and manufacture, meaning and
behaviour, physicality and psychology.
His works Orgone Reef and Orpheus Filter
invite us to imagine and touch the
extraordinary.

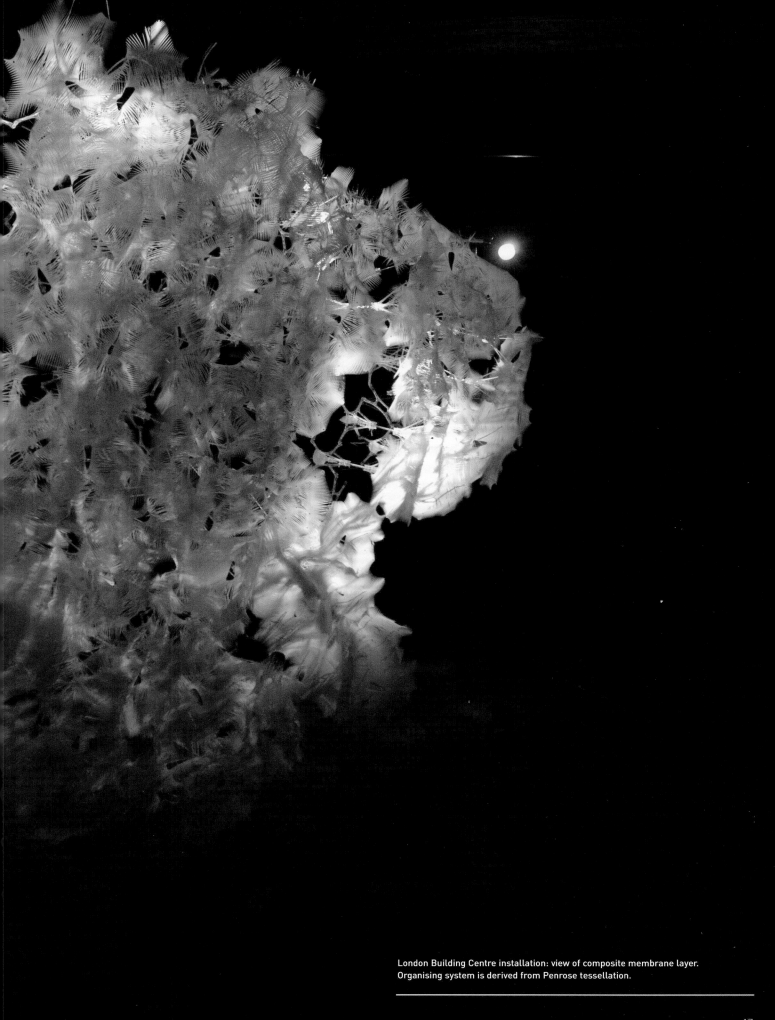

London Building Centre installation: view of composite membrane layer.
Organising system is derived from Penrose tessellation.

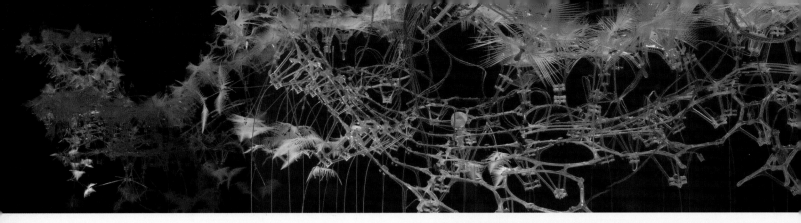

Panoramic view of Orgone Reef, showing exposed layer of whisker actuators positioned below upper injection and collector matrix. The pillowed structure is derived from isolated vertical bonding between layers.

Orgone Reef is in part a technical exercise in construction and fabrication. The project is a hybrid geotextile, a new class of materials used for reinforcing landscapes and buildings.

Penelope was stained darkest moss-green and black-red. Artemis bubbling with one thousand flowing breasts. Her bodice a garland cover of countless more: tangled fields of pendant vires cut from ripe fathers, overflowing testicles making a cornucopia. Remus had skin the same colour, black-blood crust that rimmed the pit inside the sanctuary on the hill. Bull after bull, bleeding into the earth.[1]

The Orgone Reef series of installations are speculations of what the surface of a building could be like. In 2004 projects in Birmingham and London, and most recently in Cambridge, near Toronto, Canada, lightweight expanded meshworks are installed within large rooms making an immersive lining. The structure in the gallery responds to the viewer, hovering and vibrating in response to air currents within the room. This structure acts like an artificial reef that could support a turf-like surface of natural material. The project probes the possibilities of combining artificial and natural processes to form an uncanny, hybrid ecology.

Cupped filters and valve-forms in this collection array derive from selective warping of flat-sheet fabrications. One-way passive valve details induce transfers through the assembly.

Penrose tessellation assembly rules: alternate configurations for rhombic structural units with corresponding decagonal membrane tiles.

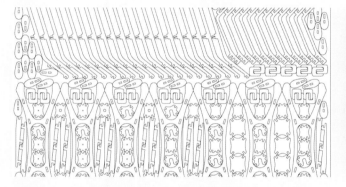

Nested laser-cutting production layout, showing cutting paths for snap-fit assembly elements.

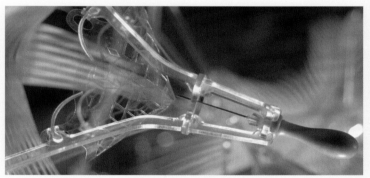

Orgone Reef injection-unit needle with bladder reservoir fitted to growth-matrix clamping cone. Units are positioned within the membrane filter layer.

Microprocessor nodes in the upper layer of Orgone Reef control clusters of sensing whiskers suspended from the lower layer. When proximity is sensed, oscillating waves transmit throughout the assembly.

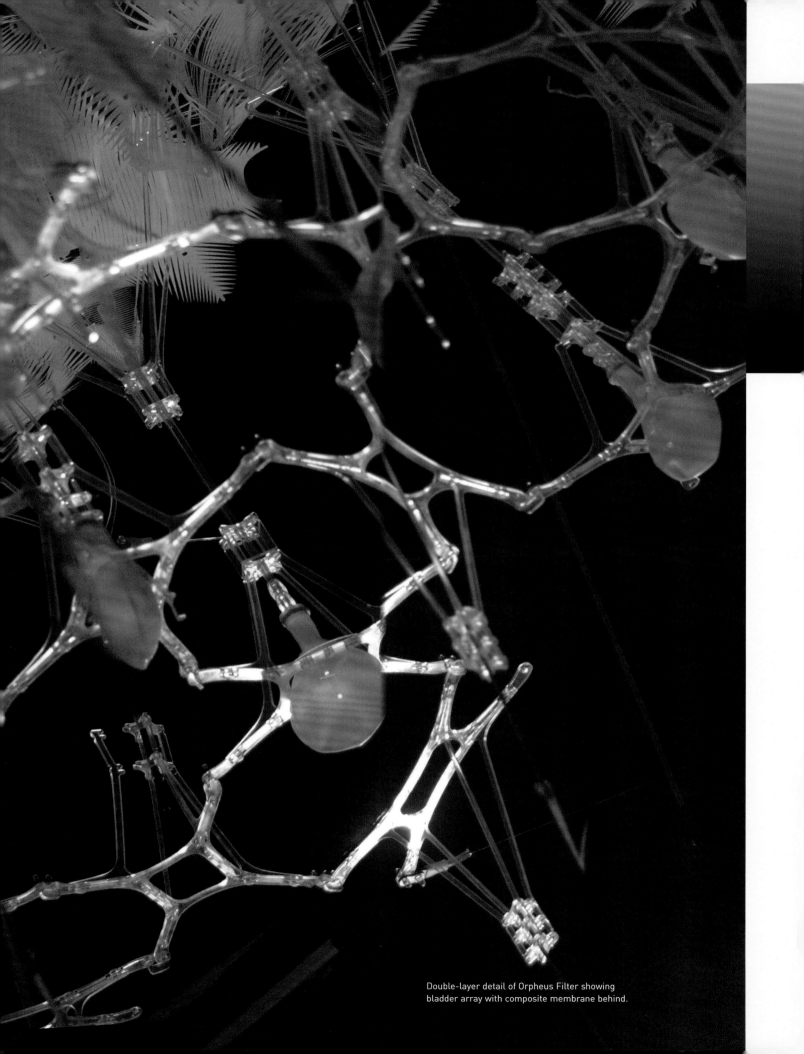

Double-layer detail of Orpheus Filter showing
bladder array with composite membrane behind.

> The installations are dense interlinking matrices made of thousands of plastic and latex pieces manufactured using automated laser-cutters working directly from digital models. Individual elements can be produced at low cost and with quick cycles of refinement. The small scale of the production suggests the possibility of a new cottage-industry-based economy.

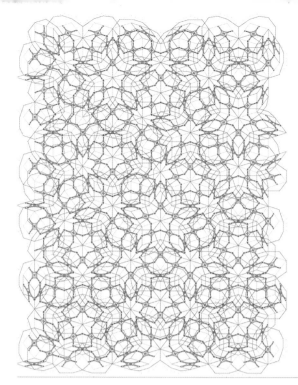

Unfolded layout for Orpheus Filter meshwork structure showing a self-generating pattern of interlinked rhombic units.

Orgone Reef is in part a technical exercise in construction and fabrication. A minimal amount of raw material is expanded to form a network, producing a large, porous volume. A Penrose tessellation, a nonrepeating geometrical system, is used to organise this fabric. The installations are dense interlinking matrices made of thousands of plastic and latex pieces manufactured using automated laser-cutters working directly from digital models. Individual elements can be produced at low cost and with quick cycles of refinement. The small scale of the production suggests the possibility of a new cottage-industry-based economy.

The project invites us to question our own relationship with the world. The actions in this project are subtle and occur over long stretches of time. Trembling vibrations and visual oscillation provide a general undercurrent. Osmotic action that pulls moisture and floating matter through the pores of outer membranes is created within intermeshing valves detailed into the outer surfaces. Clamping, injection and digestion functions would occur in reaction to the intrusion of larger organisms within the structure. These processes would encourage a living turf to accumulate, intermeshed within the lightweight matrix. The structure would eventually decay and be replaced by this growth.

Each link of the fabric net receives special details. Inside is an anatomy of bladders cushioned by sprung tendons and terminated

Side view of Orgone Reef strata with collection layer above, and activation meshwork fitted with microprocessor controls below.

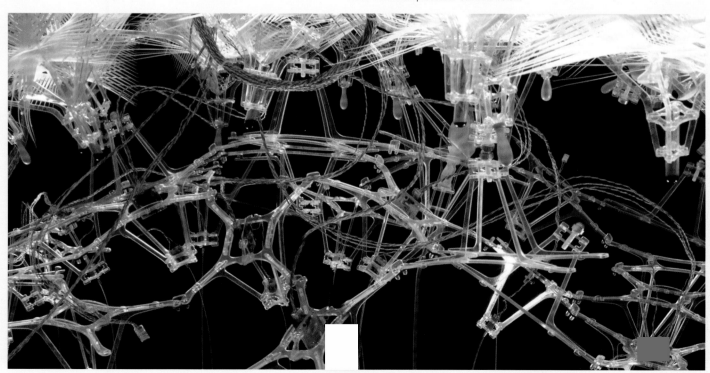

Detail of Cambridge installation showing lower strata with activation system suspended below membrane assembly. Microprocessor clusters control whisker sensors and actuators, interspersed with clamping units.

by hollow needles to puncture and drain. Towards the outside, angled crampons bent back for springing and grasping are set up with hair-trigger antennae. Around, a spread of open joints with outflung guides to catch and link with neighbours. Each of these protozoan cells is thin and meagre, but by linking and clumping together they make mass and thickness. At first a bare latticework controlled by the geometry of its elements, then increasingly formless and growing darker as it ingests decomposing matter. Thicker, and fertile, enveloping the implants and making a complete turf. This cover is finally dense, redolent with growth. And within that vital new earth, a convulsion glimmers – a poise telegraphing through from the sprung armature deep within.

Implication

The term 'Orgone' was coined by Wilhelm Reich, a psychologist working alongside Freud, to suggest a fertile life force encircling the world. Reich, whose work was tinged by obsession, saw the world as an evolving entity dominated by primordial energies.[2] His visions offer a poignant alternative to the Modern version of progress.

The physical nets constructed in these projects are a class of geotextiles, structural materials developed to reinforce and sustain natural landscapes. Engineered fabric systems are a common technology for shaping terrain. These nets use physical detailing, encouraging self-assembly. Their pursuit of artificial life is an extension of modern landscape architecture.

At the same time, the projects tend to question boundaries of psyche. Their large-scale field structures offer immersion, rendering our physical bodies porous and offering wide-flung dispersal of identity. Two prevailing qualities root this within a Romantic tradition. First is a vertigo that comes with immersion within the

fluctuating hollow ground of the installation; a lurching release from ordinary gravity. A second quality is a version of the oceanic. Teilhard de Chardin, writing in the past century, described this in optimistic terms as 'a stage of active sympathy in which each separate human element, breaking out of its insulated state under the impulse of the high tensions generated in the Noosphere, will emerge into a field of prodigious affinities ... Humanity, as I have said, is building its composite brain beneath our eyes.'[3]

I acknowledge de Chardin's confidence in tangible ways: the caress of this installation induces little bundles of sensation – in the joints of my elbows, at the backs of knees; between eyebrows, in sternum; in whole-skin reactions – projecting and hesitantly encountering things that lie outside. The caress of Orgone Reef offers a mechanical empathy. ◬

Notes
1 Author's journal entry, conception of Orgone Reef installation 2004.
2 Wilhelm Reich, *Selected Writings: An Introduction to Orgonomy*, Farrar, Straus and Giroux (New York), 1961.
3 Pierre Teilhard de Chardin, *The Future of Man*, Fontana Religious Books, 1964, p 184.

Credits
Author: Philip Beesley
Computing Systems Design: Steven Wood
Design Assistants: Michael Bentley, Jordan Darnell, Kirsten Douglas, Will Elsworthy, Nancy Gibson, Daniel Hall, Vincent Hui, Alex Josephson, Coryn Kempster, Thomas-Bernard Kenniff, Luanna Lam, Alex Lukachko, Farid Noufaily, Jonathan Tyrrell, Desmond Shum
Prototyping: Integrated Centre for Visualization, Design and Manufacturing, University of Waterloo, Ontario
Consultants: Thomas Seebohm, Diane Willow
Supported by the Daniel Langlois Foundation for Art and Technology; the Building Centre Trust, London; Michael Stacey/Digital Fabricators Research Group; and Cambridge Galleries. Installation assisted by students of University of Waterloo School of Architecture and London Metropolitan University.

HOOKE PARK

As a New AA Initiative in Education

Architectural education is passing another milestone. Whilst the reverberation of the 20th-century avant-garde can still be registered, a barrage of questions and choices is facing the next generation of graduates and their educators. Mark Prizeman argues a case to nourish designing by making as a passionate, cultural, intellectual and human activity. Through making, he concludes, three stages of building a confident architecture are found.

The intellectual superiority that architects forged over master builders was the act of observational drawing. Robert Adam built his career on the publication of *Ruins of the Palace of the Emperor Diocletian at Spalato in Dalmatia* in 1764, a condensed version of his 'grand tour', which followed five weeks' intense study on site. Adam touted the book around London in a carriage drawn by 'two of the finest greys' he could lay his hands on. This thesis is much expanded upon in Baynes and Pugh's 1981 *Art of the Engineer*, which chronicles the development of production drafting and the airs of boat-builders, amongst others, who had conquered the mysteries of constructed perspective.

'Design with Beauty, Build in Truth,' the motto of London's Architectural Association (AA) School of Architecture, positions the architect's contribution to society at the level of a moral obligation rather than as mere compliance to an agenda. The AA was established in 1847 by a group of independently minded architectural assistants who wished to further their education by inviting particular intelligences of their choice to lecture them. It still attempts to fulfil these liberal desires for the furtherance of architectural education.

The School of Forestry at Hooke Park, set deep in rural Dorset, was established in the 1980s by the furniture maker John Makepeace with the particular vision and agenda of giving an economic future to sustainable forestry by adding the value of design to timber. Furniture students were trained in a strong mixture of business studies along with their design development. The school was established as an addition to the furniture school at Parnham, and was intended to encapsulate a completely new way of thinking about the means of producing timber-based products from furniture to buildings. Set in a restored plantation of varied stands of commercial timber, it also generated an income from forestry. Since John Makepeace's retirement, the facilities at Hooke Park have become part of the AA.

The Hooke Park thesis began by looking at how the materials for making furniture were produced, and questioning the use of exotic imports. This introduced students to the realities of the woodland industries – over 50 per cent of the UK's trade deficit is from timber imported for the construction industry, whilst domestic woodland is left to decay as being uneconomic to harvest. It was realised that in the process of growing a crop of timber there is an enormous wastage of material in the thinning process. Trees are planted close together to make them grow straight, with some being thinned after 10 to 15 years to allow the best specimens to reach maturity unobstructed. These thinnings – trees of between 50 millimetres and 150 millimetres in diameter – are a worthless material that cannot even be sold as firewood. The objective of giving an added 'value' to waste wood by 'design', thus providing a commercial return for forest thinnings, would create a commercial incentive to manage woodland, improve the remaining timber resource and reduce carbon dioxide production from burn-off.

It was this by-product of the timber industry that inspired the School of Forestry at Hooke Park, which not only uses this forgotten resource of the coppice, but also uses timber in the most efficient way structurally. The buildings use timber in tension and compression, and include a prototype house built like a tent, a large arched workshop with studio space, and an accommodation block using a lattice mesh for the roof. Designed variously by the architects Richard Burton of ABK and Edward Cullinan in close collaboration with the engineering skills of Buro Happold and Frei Otto, they are unique experimental exemplars of a vision of how to make buildings in a manner that potentially could solve many problems. Compared with building the same structure in laminated timber, the thinnings method uses less than 20 per cent of the forest and far less synthetic resin glue.

Technology transfer is about taking a particular way of making things and applying it to an apparently completely incompatible environment. The *Mosquito* aircraft was the fastest production aircraft for the first half of the Second World War; known as the 'wooden wonder', it was conceived as a way of bringing the underused industry of furniture-makers into the war effort. Made of plywood and balsa, it was regarded with deep suspicion until, on its maiden flight, it managed twice the expected speed. Another unexpected benefit was its resilience to structural damage and the ease of repair by mechanics of average skill.

Wood remaining in the 'round' – that is, not being sawn down which severs the fibres that give timber its strength and its resistance to decay – gives a far higher strength-to-weight ratio. Traditional splitting and cleaving have the same benefits. And in certain situations, timber can be stronger than steel. For instance, take a match and try to pull it apart – you can't. If you then try to break it by pressing hard on both ends, you might. But if you simply snap it in half by holding either end, then you have discovered why conventional methods of timber construction use the material in its weakest form.

The use of 'green' and 'round' wood are ancient techniques. The novelty of the Hooke Park buildings lies in a 'worthless' material being jointed with technologically advanced joints; resin splices and stainless-steel rods with fibreglass bandages stopping the material from fraying, all carefully tested and worked out. Using green wood is the art of working wood whilst it still has a high sap content and is relatively much easier to split and fashion using the adze or

saw; the important factor here is that less energy (animal) is used and blade life is conserved. The timber then dries in situ and locks the structure together. Round wood is used in this fashion to make baskets, a technique that a cursory study of Egyptian architecture reveals to be the first building method used by mankind.

These days, the culture of making is very 'undernourished', our postindustrial consumer culture does not educate its children for a career in making things as of yore. Schools first disposed of their workshop equipment and then their playing fields. Yet as architects we are still expected to know how to control a group of people in the articulate task of making a building. How does one reinvent a passion for making within tertiary education?

The addition of the workshop, accommodation units and working woodland at Hooke Park to the AA's current facilities provides a unique opportunity to develop a fresh agenda for the teaching of architecture through the medium of making. It is a consideration of the possibilities engendered by the space, distant location and local resources, and the discipline of the agenda inherited from the Hooke Park Trust, that makes a re-evaluation of the role of learning to design by making so opportune. By working at one-to-one, the appreciation of scale and the limits of material manipulation become decisive aids to furthering architecture beyond the mere discussion of form and intellectual process.

The Cullinan-designed accommodation block at Hooke Park. Adjacent are the footings for a fourth building that will be used to erect the first of the AA-commissioned structures.

The concrete jig used to make the De Havilland *Mosquito*. Sections of wood held in the grooves were skinned in a sandwich of aero-ply and balsa wood.

The simple structure shielding the circular saw at Hooke Park. Designed by students from the furniture school, it uses the material agenda of green round wood with intelligent simple joints to make a small, exemplary, useful building.

The interior of the workshop at Hooke Park, a structure based on a concept by Frei Otto and engineered by Buro Happold. The basket-like arches are composed of three sections of round wood, resin-spliced and bent into position whilst still 'green'. A concrete ring beam around the floor slab constrains the structure.

Making things allows the imagination to observe the possible improvements and future development of the idea.

Good design is, like drawing, a question of how hard one looks at something. The act of drawing an object makes one understand it better; army snipers are trained by sketching tracts of woodland to locate carefully concealed squaddies, so increasing their powers of observation. Designing by making takes observation to a greater emotional and intellectual involvement with the developing product of one's musing than the distancing of a drafting process. It is part of the reason why models are so important in the design of buildings, as they bring in to play various other faculties of judgement and involve binocular vision. Assessing a physical model is totally different to assessing a 3-D electronic model for the simple reason that we have two eyes. Beyond any discussion as to the validity of the theories, aesthetics and economics that have informed the design process, one is still left with the reality that the thing has to be made. As master builders we should have an ingrained passion for putting stuff together in order to realise whatever ideas we wish to satisfy. The more you make the better you get, or does practice not make perfect?

Recently, what an architectural student gets taught in order to fulfil whatever role society sees fit to give him or her has shifted from providing a creative working knowledge of the classical orders with a foundation in building details, to the stylistic exercises of Modernism with its opportunities to build on a scale never seen before or since. Further on, through the advent of 'paper architecture' during the recent cycles of building recession, one now finds the architect is intellectually divorced from the contemporary mass provision of buildings worldwide. Now we are embroiled in 'art school'-like debates about the ephemeral, philosophical nature of building, and seem quite happy to let someone spend five years never designing a building only to emerge with the dubious CAD skills that will allow them to slip unobserved into a corporate firm to do competitions like a battery chicken. This may give the external examiners some titbits of modern culture to mull over at dinner, or allow invited jurors to keep the work firmly under their conceptual control, but is the pain really justifiable? The ambition for realising a structure, an evaluation of material behaviour and the search for a way to make it within one's limited means involves the disciplines of physical observation and a personal goal.

Conventional instruction in basic building construction does not now take place in architectural education, as the subject is too vast. It is rather by learning how to learn that technology is transferred into the realm of detailing a proposal. Students are taught about construction primarily through the preparation of case studies, an onerous research task that, as a teacher, makes one wonder whether the subject has really been understood. Reading and writing about how things are made means precisely nothing if the author has not physically worked with a material directly, to understand the possibilities and limitations of a material – any material. It is perhaps also in the realm of giving materials and methods a value, within an agreed hierarchy or morality, that concepts such as 'sustainability' are unravelled. These are used as a label and not as a quality, as in heavy or light, loud or quiet. Yet it is only by evaluating the full consequences of using a material or construction system that one can build with responsibility. Asbestos, PVC and concrete all do their jobs admirably, but from certain perspectives are catastrophic.

Models have their limitations, and it is only at full size that a model can begin to operate fully, as the history of the Morris Minor, produced from 1948 until 1972, shows. The drawings for the pressings had been done: one drawing for the inner face of a pressed piece of steel, and one for the outer, hand-drafted 3-D curves with a radial difference of the thickness of a steel sheet. After testing, the designer, Alec Issigonis, decided the prototype was too narrow: 'So I went to the shop one evening and I told my mechanics to cut the car in half. Then I went in the morning and we moved it apart – ah, too much; ah; too little; no, a bit more that way – that's it!'[1] The right proportion left a 4-inch gap that was filled with a flat insertion to the pressing drawings. This strip can be best seen on the bonnet of the production vehicle.

Typically, the full-size model for an architectural student has been a 'tent' structure or prototype shelter, perhaps a full-size detail of the student's own design or as part of a case study – in musical terms a cover version. This at best gives a balance between time, resources and ambition that

A mobile home following the attentions of a tornado in Alabama, US. The loss of life and property from the use of unsuitable and unsustainable timber structures is endemic. The economic calculations involved in making houses in the cheapest and fastest manner, using the minimum of labour and materials, are formidable. It is difficult to redirect this economic leviathan towards another way to produce human habitation.

The abstract sculptor Henry Moore (1898–1986) used this reliquary of forms and objects to inform and inspire his work. The translation of hand-to-eye coordination in the production of his sculptures relied emphatically on physical assessment in three dimensions.

can produce interesting results. Installation and model-making really only represent things, and never are themselves for the sake of themselves. The disciples of Detmar Blow followed the Arts and Crafts tradition of being true to their product by physically involving themselves in the building of their own buildings, Blow having done an apprenticeship in stoneworking. The architect Geoffrey Lupton, working at Bedales School in Hampshire with the furniture-maker Ernest Gimson, personally split the green-oak beams for the library and hall.

Working with materials at full size is one thing; working with studying the effects of the elements and time quite another. The inventive technical preoccupations of the Architectural Association allow an independent and not prescriptive exploration of the realisation of built form and programme. It is one capable of becoming an advanced research facility into the making of buildings. The addition of an 'artificial sky', a wind tunnel and a climate chamber with exemplary experiments would allow the inventive lateral thinking so advocated by the agenda of Hooke. The aircraft designer Donald W Douglas Senior was renowned for his use of a cigarette in the wind tunnel, developing the streamlined DC-3, an aircraft that made commercial aviation viable.

An analogue model of the entire Mississippi basin made by German POWs (mostly generals from the Afrika Korps) at a scale of 1 foot:1 mile horizontally, 1:800 vertically and 5 minutes for a day. It was used until computers took over in the early 1990s to simulate storm bursts as they happened and thus predict the priority of relief provision.

Simulation programs never quite capture the simple nuances of real air, yet this combination of digital control and measurement with physical investigation would be unique for students of architecture.

The material agenda of the School of Forestry at Hooke Park was particular and, whilst firmly placing itself in the furniture industry world of design awards and commissions from clients, it also positioned itself away from the rural bodger and his contemporary successors. By allowing an architectural student to observe the unfamiliar world of woodland crafts, many clues to the current architectural obsessions will be found. Traditionally, until the 1960s, woodland crafts supplied a vast array of everyday objects in all shapes and sizes. A revival of interest in this area of human endeavour has yet to be taken to the full implications of building, and many ecological, conservation and environmental answers lie waiting to be discovered.

The potential resource that Hooke Park could give the AA as a hands-on laboratory is yet to be realised. The AA was founded by a group of articled pupils who wished to arrange their own education. Facilitating the birth of the inner skills of a student is the fragile responsibility of a teacher, not by the imposition of a preconceived prescriptive regime, but by a mutually negotiated positioning. Ultimately, it is the responsibility of students to educate themselves by putting themselves in situations that best facilitate this. How will the desires of the international student body for an informed position within the architectural arcana be helped by inviting an informed body of little-known technical skills into their education?

Many of the original Hooke Park graduates now work from former agricultural buildings in the region; one can imagine a dialogue that will develop a vibrant local culture that can then export its ideas. How does one teach this flavour? First, by engaging the designer to produce pleasing designs which, thanks to the research inherent within the technology used, cannot rely on pastiche as a shortfall. And second, by aiming to develop a range of thoughts on building types and their architectural/social relationships as poignant as the legacy of the exemplary buildings at Hooke. It is by encouraging students to learn to understand by looking and making that Hooke will generate a new culture. The three stages in building a confidence in making are first providing a problem to be solved, then a comprehensible range of techniques and, finally, the chance to test that confidence to destruction. ∆

Note
1 Paul Skilleter, *Morris Minor: The World's Supreme Small Car*, Osprey Publishing (London), 1981.

GETTING
SPECIFIC

The Art and Architecture Partnership, known for commissioning public works such as Softroom's Belvedere and James Turrell's Skyspace, has recently awarded its first architectural residency at Kielder to sixteen*(makers). Here, **Phil Ayres** introduces initial questions for an evolutionary design process that the practice has begun to explore and will execute as a series of interventions on the landscape.

Expressions of the Generic

In 1998, a thousand hybrid walnut tree plantlets of the Paradox variety were exhibited in San Francisco. They had been grown from the same genetic material, cloned to make a thousand equivalent instances.

It was already evident at this early stage of growth that environmental influence, rather than genetic determinism, was the key driver of specific formal expression. Local variations were exhibiting themselves through different leaf numbers, internodal lengths and branching patterns. The clones have since been planted in the San Francisco Bay area, being sited in diverse microclimatic and social environments, acting as material witnesses to the influence of their specific locations.

Natalie Jeremijenko's OneTrees project is a powerful demonstration of how the same genetic starting point will result in unique and specific expressions determined through each instance's particular engagement with an environment.

The emergence of the specific from the generic over time is a compelling process to consider. Could we imagine a piece of artifice that might develop local specificity in a similar manner? Could notions of 'growth' and 'adaptation' extend beyond metaphor and actually become processes embedded in, and actually driving the design, manufacture and life cycle of fragments, or larger parts, of the built environment?

This article will examine these questions by presenting a collection of ideas drawn from previous work by sixteen*(makers) to inform a methodology that will be investigated and tested as part of a two-year residency programme in the Kielder forest, Northumberland.

A Methodology

An abstract generic model digitally encoding a collection of architectural attributes defines our genetic material – an architectural seed. This can be planted into a computer and replicated to provide a population of possible outcomes. Over time (measured in gigahertz and generations), individuals of that population are grown, driven by environmental data and their own imperative. Suitable individuals are then selected for synthesis. The means of synthesis is computer-numerically controlled (CNC) machinery. The designer need not interfere as the specific individuals have grown from the generic with all the necessary descriptions to be manufactured.

The constructs are then sited and sensors placed, the data from which provide a record of actual performance in relation to environmental conditions. This data set drives further generations in a process of reiteration.

Two parallel worlds are being described here, connected to each other to form a circular system with both positive and negative feedback loops. One connection acts as a data input bridge from the world of the analogue and into the world of the

sixteen*(makers), Shorting the Automation Circuit, installation at Fixed Dome Observatory, UCL Quadrangle, London, 2000
This was both an exploration into the formal possibilities of the fused-deposition process and the development of a system by which local environmental data could directly inform a 3-D CAD model in real time. Sequential lateral and transverse sections of the sensing object were generated by the Deposition Modeller software by analysis of the CAD model, and indicate deposition areas of object material (fine hatching) and support material (coarse hatching).

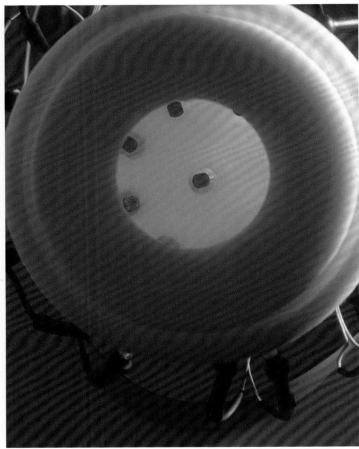

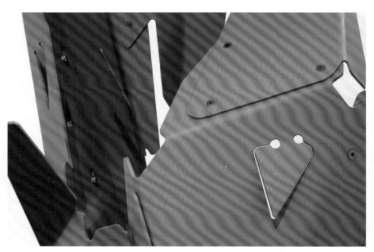

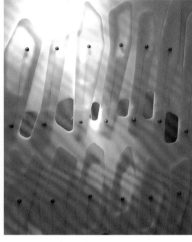

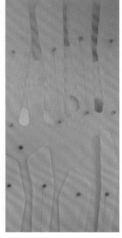

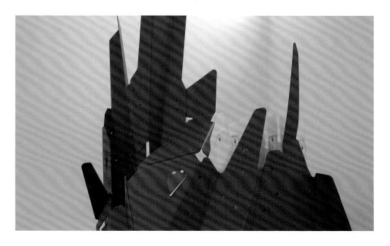

sixteen*(makers), Blusher, 2001
Comprising folded steel-plate sections, actuatable surfaces and sensors defining invisible thresholds surrounding the construct, Blusher explored the notion of a system that could suggest reconfigurations of its component parts in relation to histories of occupancy and new sites. It was reconfigured for six sites over the course of a year as part of the Craft Council's 'Making Buildings' exhibition.

digital, and the other acts as a data output bridge direct to CNC facilities and back into the world of the analogue. This cycle need not be broken, resulting in an architecture that is in continual transformation – the design designing itself.

With the route to manufacturing now directly within the grasp of the designer through the advent of computer-aided design and computer-aided manufacturing technologies (CAD/CAM), the opportunity exists to recast the design process in relation to the making of physical output. The use of computer-aided manufacturing is generally predicated upon the definition of a digital design model. In the majority of cases the digital representation is defined through the use of proprietary CAD packages that encode processes of geometry creation and geometry removal through the application of tools on the model. The CAD operator draws from a palette including lofting, extruding, sweeping, drafting, boolean subtraction, boolean addition and boolean intersection, among many others, to encode specific design intent.

The methodology outlined above offers an alternative approach to the generation and iteration of design model data. Explorations into this territory cross boundaries of design, computer science, mathematics and engineering, and belong to an emerging paradigm – computer-generated design (CGD).

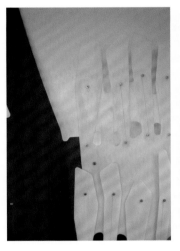

Siting the Seeds

Moving though the Kielder landscape, histories of use, redundancy, reuse, appropriation and exploitation reveal themselves through marks and conditions to a backdrop of temperate climatic conditions fairly typical for the northern UK. The landscape possesses witnesses to most processes one can inflict upon a ground condition: turned, planted, eaten, harvested, parcelled, cut, excavated, relocated, detonated, burned, flooded, laid upon.

Some marks are left to entropic forces, being consumed by the persistence of gorse, grasses and goats, until they are virtually homogenised with their surroundings. These are the gashes of 19th- and early 20th-century open-pit mining and quarrying. And some conditions are layered in the severest of ways, the edges where they meet becoming thresholds between polarised conditions: dry/wet, hard/soft, enclosure/exposure, proximity/distance.

Amongst the most enduring traces are those that exist through representations of the landscape, and in the minds of those familiar with it. Wind Hill, Devil's Lapful, Creamy Rigg, Hunger Edge and Jock's Pike – the names of places carefully preserved through numerous surveys and which have survived most transformations of the landscape.

Some of the latest marks belie a complex set of interdependencies between use of landscape, landownership, social responsibility, business, tourism, economics and cultural awareness. These include Minotaur, the contemporary maze by Nick Coombe and Shona Kitchen; the Kielder Belvedere by Softroom; and James Turrell's Skyspace.

A glance across Explorer™ OL42 ordnance survey map (Kielder Water and Forest, scale 1:25,000) presents three dominant conditions; reservoir, forest, moor. Of these, the forest covers the greatest area. Kielder is one of Europe's largest man-made forests, with 150 million trees standing within its boundary. The dominant species is the sitka spruce. Lying well outside its native range of west coast North America, it accounts for approximately 75 per cent of the planting, with Norway spruce, lodgepole and Scots pine, and broadleaf appearing in diminishing proportions. This canopy acts as habitat to a wide variety of inhabitants, including the rare goshawk, crossbills, eider ducks, otters and the red squirrel, exiled to a few pockets of the British mainland by the grey.

But this is a working landscape operating to a strict temporal model – the 50-year cycle. This temporal measure defines a complete period of growth, harvesting and preparation for regrowth. The myth of the bucolic landscape is quickly dispelled upon seeing the mappings, predictions, calculations, simulations, strategies and computational models used by those involved in the management of the land to relate the forest as resource to demand over time. From the introduction of nonindigenous species to the determining of harvesting parcel boundaries in irregular geometries, so as to appear more natural in perspective to the observer, this landscape is contrived from a mix of hard economics and notions of the romantic. It is a complex piece of biomass accounting. Current demand requires the production of 1,300 tonnes of timber daily, which is used for paper production and feeding the construction industry. Annually, over 1,200 hectares are subject to harvesting and replanting programmes. It is a 62,000-hectare transient landscape. For sixteen*(makers), this transience of conditions over varying time scales is one of the territory's most compelling attributes.

Drivers and Registers

Chapter 2 of W Ross Ashby's *Introduction to Cybernetics* is entitled 'Change', and begins by stating that: 'The most fundamental concept in cybernetics is that of "difference", either that two things are recognisably different or that one thing has changed with time.'[1]

Change, or difference, are obviously key to processes that transform the generic into the specific and can be attributable to drivers and registers. But implied in these definitions is the

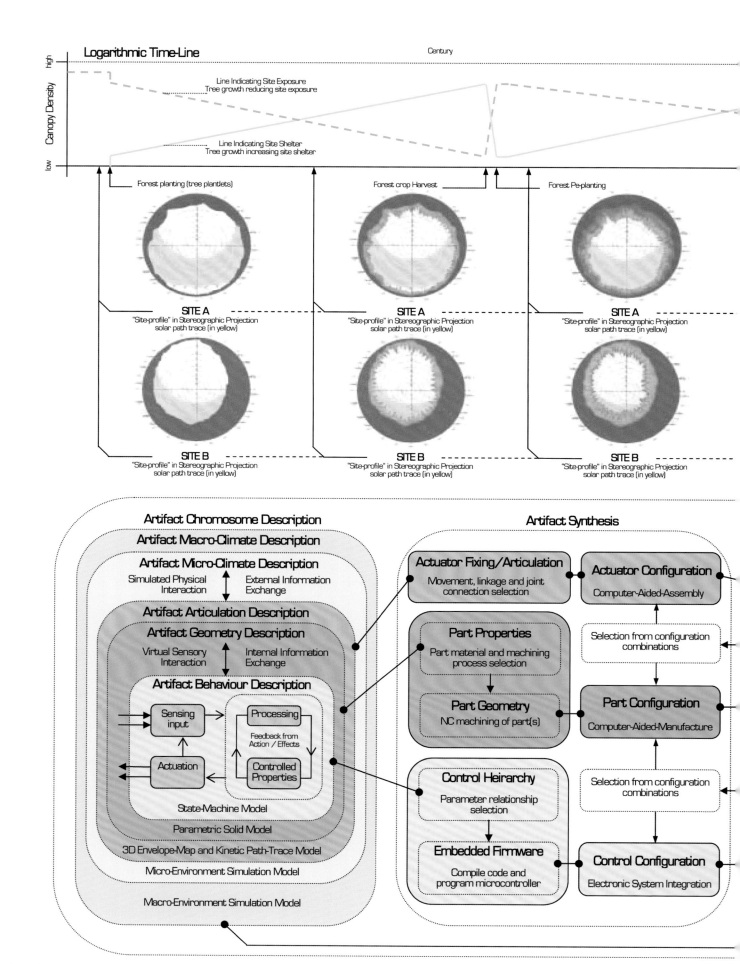

Logarithmic Time-Line

Century

Canopy Density (high / low)

Line Indicating Site Exposure
Tree growth reducing site exposure

Line Indicating Site Shelter
Tree growth increasing site shelter

Forest planting (tree plantlets)

Forest crop Harvest

Forest Pe-planting

SITE A
"Site-profile" in Stereographic Projection
solar path trace (in yellow)

SITE A
"Site-profile" in Stereographic Projection
solar path trace (in yellow)

SITE A
"Site-profile" in Stereographic Projection
solar path trace (in yellow)

SITE B
"Site-profile" in Stereographic Projection
solar path trace (in yellow)

SITE B
"Site-profile" in Stereographic Projection
solar path trace (in yellow)

SITE B
"Site-profile" in Stereographic Projection
solar path trace (in yellow)

Artifact Chromosome Description

Artifact Macro-Climate Description

Artifact Micro-Climate Description

Simulated Physical Interaction — External Information Exchange

Artifact Articulation Description

Artifact Geometry Description

Virtual Sensory Interaction — Internal Information Exchange

Artifact Behaviour Description

Sensing input
Processing
Feedback from Action / Effects
Actuation
Controlled Properties

State-Machine Model

Parametric Solid Model

3D Envelope-Map and Kinetic Path-Trace Model

Micro-Environment Simulation Model

Macro-Environment Simulation Model

Artifact Synthesis

Actuator Fixing/Articulation
Movement, linkage and joint connection selection

Actuator Configuration
Computer-Aided-Assembly

Selection from configuration combinations

Part Properties
Part material and machining process selection

Part Geometry
NC machining of part(s)

Part Configuration
Computer-Aided-Manufacture

Selection from configuration combinations

Control Heirarchy
Parameter relationship selection

Embedded Firmware
Compile code and program microcontroller

Control Configuration
Electronic System Integration

sixteen*(makers), Kielder National Park, Northumberland, 2004–
Kielder process schematic integrating data-gathering, analysis and
synthesis related to candidate sites over time.

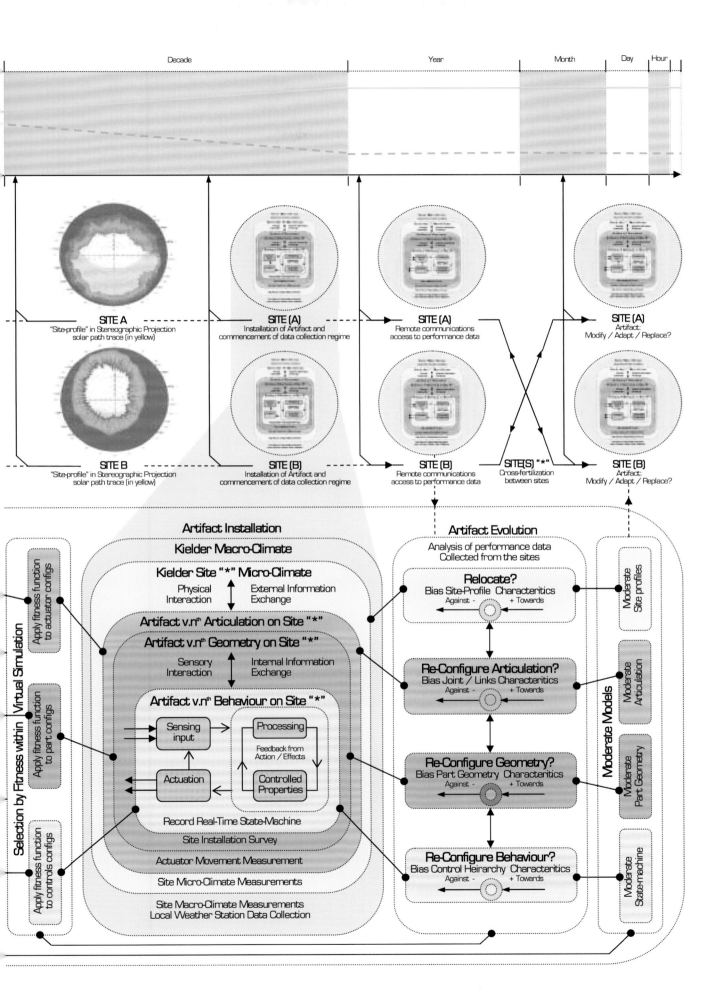

Decade | Year | Month | Day | Hour

SITE A
"Site-profile" in Stereographic Projection
solar path trace (in yellow)

SITE B
"Site-profile" in Stereographic Projection
solar path trace (in yellow)

SITE [A]
Installation of Artifact and
commencement of data collection regime

SITE [B]
Installation of Artifact and
commencement of data collection regime

SITE [A]
Remote communications
access to performance data

SITE [B]
Remote communications
access to performance data

SITE[S] "*"
Cross-fertilization
between sites

SITE [A]
Artifact:
Modify / Adapt / Replace?

SITE [B]
Artifact:
Modify / Adapt / Replace?

Artifact Installation

Kielder Macro-Climate

Kielder Site "*" Micro-Climate

Physical Interaction — External Information Exchange

Artifact v.nᵗʰ Articulation on Site "*"

Artifact v.nᵗʰ Geometry on Site "*"

Sensory Interaction — Internal Information Exchange

Artifact v.nᵗʰ Behaviour on Site "*"

Sensing input → Processing
Feedback from Action / Effects
Actuation ← Controlled Properties

Record Real-Time State-Machine
Site Installation Survey
Actuator Movement Measurement
Site Micro-Climate Measurements
Site Macro-Climate Measurements
Local Weather Station Data Collection

Artifact Evolution
Analysis of performance data
Collected from the sites

Relocate?
Bias Site-Profile Characteritics
Against - + Towards

Re-Configure Articulation?
Bias Joint / Links Characteritics
Against - + Towards

Re-Configure Geometry?
Bias Part Geometry Characteritics
Against - + Towards

Re-Configure Behaviour?
Bias Control Heirarchy Characteritics
Against - + Towards

Moderate Site profiles

Moderate Articulation

Moderate Part Geometry

Moderate State-machine

Moderate Models

Selection by Fitness within | Virtual Simulation

Apply fitness function to actuator configs

Apply fitness function to part configs

Apply fitness function to controls configs

63

observer who is able to do the recognising (drawing distinctions) of difference between entities, or in one entity over time.

The collective expression of attributes of an entity at a point in time, as observed by an observer, can be described as a state. This is the register. We can subsequently describe the mechanisms by which an entity shifts from one state to another as behaviour.

If there are mechanisms of feedback so that the entity can sense its own state, then a regulation between internal state and external influence can occur, assuming a palette of suitable behaviours. The entity now has the capacity to deal with change in an effort to maintain equilibrium between the two conditions. There are now internal drivers possessed by the entity and external drivers that act upon the entity, their relationship to each other being circular. The ability to generate new behaviours in the face of novel situations is known as adaptation. Adaptation also requires some form of memory through which

A recently harvested section of forest to the south of Kielder Water. This is a possible candidate survey site, due to its currently exposed condition and the promise of replanting and gradual growth towards mature canopy and shelter over the next 50 years.

a history of responses to stimuli can inform current and future behaviours.

The adaptive system intrigues us. Of those described it is the one that has the potential to surprise in its search for specificity. We have been exploring adaptive systems in an architectural context for some time – for example in our Shorting the Automation Circuit and Blusher investigations – and the Kielder residency offers us the opportunity to further this work in a landscape context.

The Specific Generic

We propose to begin the residency with a survey. It will be a time-based survey across a number of geographically dispersed sites with varying conditions. Orientation, elevation, current conditions and anticipated conditions will inform the selection of the candidate sites with a view that the initial starting conditions should be as diverse as possible. Each site will be initially planted with a small construct that has an interior. The enclosure defining the interior will be thermally driven so that increases in temperature into the actuation range will cause the enclosure to open to the ambient conditions, using technologies similar to those for driving passively actuated greenhouses. Our initial construct therefore already possesses mechanisms of feedback through which it tries to maintain equilibrium between internal and external conditions.

Digital temperature dataloggers will be used to record external temperature (shade and exposed) and the internal temperature of the enclosure. Other devices for gathering pyranometric data are also being considered. This data set will grow at a rate of one sample per sensor per hour, recording specific information about ambient conditions and the modulated condition in the interior from which inferences about the site and behaviour of the construct can be made. The collected data set from each site acts a fingerprint for each location, and this will be used to drive our digitally encoded generic instances towards specificity, resulting in a more substantial expression to replace the initial construct.

The receding edge of Kielder Water during an exceptionally dry summer (2004).

The process of generating a specific response to each site requires an adequately defined environmental simulation to test evolved instances and determine their appropriateness. The evolving of instances requires the definition of the genetic material, together with the necessary mechanisms for breeding and acting upon expressions such as reproduction, crossover and mutation. Both of these processes require quantifiable and measurable attributes by which assessments of fitness can be made. The design challenge is being able to adequately describe the criteria for assessment, and determining the nature of the genetic material.

The genetic material encodes parameters for the formal and behavioural attributes of a construct. In genetic terms, the chromosome defines the complete encoding. Within the chromosome, individual genes map to individual parameters of attributes, and the value of the attribute – its expression – is described by the allele. For example, in our genetic make-up there is a gene that controls the parameter for eye colour, and the expression of the blue allele defines the specific.

Every member of the population has to be tested at each generation. The fittest pair are selected and become the parents of the next generation through a process akin to reproduction, in which the chromosomes are recombined to create new offspring. The process balances the inevitable drive towards optimisation through selection of the fittest by generating a population that competes amongst itself and with its environment to maintain diversity. Once sufficiently optimised, the selected representation can then be manufactured and sited, the representation cloned to repopulate the search space, and the simulation redriven. Environmental data from the ambient conditions together with the modulated conditions (those created by the construct) provide the data set for redriving the simulation, and through this feedback a performance assessment can be determined. This assessment is not limited to the construct but to the entire set of definitions comprising the simulation. It is difficult to argue against empirical data, and so any disparity between it and the simulation will tend towards redefining the model.

Each site will be considered as its own problem space. However, we are assuming that there will be common characteristics between sites, and over time certain solutions developed for one site may be useful as a reference to another. This requires a degree of collective knowledge-sharing and may lead to the cross-fertilisation of genetic material between sites.

Over time, trends will start to appear in the data set of each site – diurnal and nocturnal fluctuations, seasonal variations and yearly rhythms. We also anticipate occasional sudden shifts in these trends. For example, a construct located on a south-facing incline under mature canopy is likely to be subject to very little solar gain during the day and exposure at night. Once harvested (a process that is guaranteed for almost all sites at some point in the 50-year cycle), this new condition of exposure will alter the thermal characteristics of the site and subsequently the passive behaviour of the current construct.

As new conditions begin to reveal themselves through changes in the trends of the data sets, we anticipate adaptive responses from our models. With this iterative adaptive cycle implicitly retaining an embedded history and supporting progressive development, the adaptations will be directly related to the existing structure, allowing the addition, replacement or removal of components and thus altering its formal characteristics and behavioural potentials.

There remain a number of conceptual and practical issues to be addressed regarding the implementation of such a process. Two immediate issues are:

1 The encoding of interaction rules between developed geometries and the tools and processes used to synthesise them.
2 The interfacing or coding of a simulation that understands basic concepts such as gravity, load distribution and solar geometry with our breeding environment to allow the direct testing of instances.

What we have described here is our working brief, the synthesis of which will result in an architecture that is driven both by its immediate context and its own requirements. It will be an architecture that has the potential to continually reinvent itself formally and behaviourally in relation to a particular context and to its own history. It will certainly be described as responsive. And some observers might even attribute it with intent. It will simultaneously exist locally and remotely – geographically and in substance. It will be an architecture that continually transforms in an effort to become specific to purpose and to location.

We hope it will be both strange and magical. ⌂

Note
1 W Ross Ashby, *An Introduction to Cybernetics*, Chapman & Hall (London), 1957, p 9.

ADAPTIVE ARCHITECTURAL DESIGN

Prototype house, Blankenburg, 2004
Designers and makers Nick Callicott and Kris Ehlert assemble the first
component in collaboration with the workforce of Ehlert GmbH, Gusten, Germany.

Fuelled by their passion for design, manufacturing and industrial production,
Nick Callicott and partner Kris Ehlert have boldly stepped away from the
London architecture scene and set up shop in new factory premises in
Wienerode, Germany. Here Nick, author of *Computer Aided Manufacture in
Architecture*, takes time to position their practice amongst the considerable
expertise and knowledge of advanced fabrication techniques with illustrations
of recent prototypes made for a future dwelling.

Over the past decade or so, computer-aided manufacturing has
begun to be absorbed into the collective consciousness of
architects through a series of generic encounters and populist
images, by which its physical capability – to realise unique and
complex environments – has finally begun to displace the iconic
after image of 20th-century mass production. Many opportunities
are suggested here, not least of which is the proposition that
complexity and variety in architecture can be explored beyond
the prior bounds of standardisation, yet within an economic
framework increasingly favourable to the unique. The realisation
of many complex proposals has also demonstrated revitalised
collaborative partnerships between architecture and engineering,
as innovation is developed within a changing medium of
representation and production.

It is clear also that our role as architects is being transformed
by subscription to these techniques. However, we must remember
that our roles may equally be transformed by a lack of
participation – particularly when CAD/CAM techniques are becoming
widespread throughout the wider construction team. The nature

of this change is not a determined automatic effect; the
outcome depends on how architects define a methodology
for the use of contemporary production with respect to the
practice of design. So, as we experiment with contemporary
production, we are going to have to reconsider what it is
that architects do.

The plain truth is, of course, that there is a dimension
to our knowledge and activity as designers that is, by
definition, unspeakable. There is, as philosopher Michael
Polanyi has described, a tacit dimension to much of human
activity and knowledge. It is most readily understood in
manual abilities; it is evident in the ability of musicians
to play their instruments, and potters to throw their pots.
These are abilities that cannot be easily translated to
another individual except through a prolonged process of
practice and learning. The possession of tacit knowledge
is personal, and to distribute any part of it requires it to be
translated into a host of other means: text, drawing, image,
physical and mathematical models. This process is one of

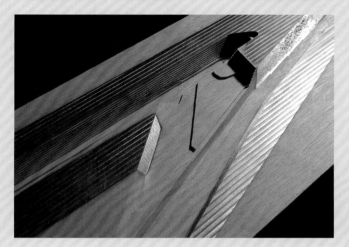

The tacit component and the numerically controlled model. Forming and postforming experiments by the author on the use of CAM as an incremental and interrogative method within an iterative design process. Alloy cast within hardwood section and milled.

conventional drawing by enlisting a temporal dimension to structure a specific choreography of making. Since architecture has been definable as a profession, the conventional drawing has comprised one of the essential protocols that separate the maker from the architect, a device of status and demarcation, whose information alone cannot be translated into building without a host of tacit and explicit contributions from a wider group of participants. The drawing has traditionally been a significant site of negotiation in design convergence, and dictates a collaborative protocol for its translation into the real. Record/playback marks a moment of departure from this convention in that it creates a representational mode that suggests a direct equivalence between description and object never before attained within conventional graphical modes of description.

The incongruous relationship between reliance and redundancy in the system was ultimately to prevent its widespread dissemination and, although record/playback developed into a working system, it was never utilised to any extent in industry. The social-historian David Noble cites the system's key weakness as a continued reliance on a skilled workforce, which made the enactment of Fordist or Taylorist management strategies on the workforce extremely difficult. But this reliance also embedded a further technical weakness in that the complexity and geometry of the objects was fundamentally limited by human dexterity.

This reliance was addressed in parallel research, initially in the aircraft industry and later at MIT, which resulted in the development of the type of computer control that still forms the basis of many CAM systems today. Numerical control was conceived as a system by which complete separation from the tacit

Tactile and numeric representation. Physical and computational site-analysis modelling.

the architect's most important functions and is central to design activity.

It is this process of distribution that fascinates me, in particular how design information – which itself comprises many tacit components – is made explicit through representation and production. Intriguingly, the development of computer control illustrates some important changes in the nature and value of tacit knowledge within the entire production process, and I am convinced that a consideration of this tacit dimension is a necessary step in the re-creation of our identity as architects.

Capturing the Tacit
One of the early attempts to control machine tools, the record/playback system developed up to 1947 by the General Electric Company, sought to capture and translate the tacit component of making – the manual skill, experience and intuition that embody the skilled act – into a numerical transcription. The system allowed the actions of a machinist operating a modified machine tool, initially a lathe, to be recorded on magnetic tape as a sample part was made. Once a specific tape was created, the machinist could, in theory, be dispensed with for a lesser-skilled operator, as further identical parts were created.

The recording's value appears to be founded on an essential paradox, in that the uniqueness of the event is enlisted to realise the repetition of standardisation. It was an attempt, like the use of a pattern for a complex mould, to capture the skill of the individual and translate it into a repeatable, permanent and geometric event. The tape highlights the incompleteness of information content within

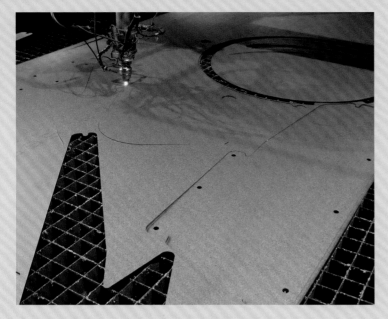

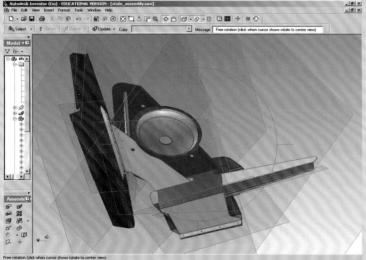

Making in the machine. Computer-aided design – a preview of fabrication. Computer-aided manufacturing – design by fabrication.

Modernism's defining desire to collaborate with the manufacturing industry. Fundamental differences in the nature of the manufacturing and construction industry notwithstanding, the architectural profession's inability to enlist computer control in the first four decades of its use is also linked directly to the broad disparity between numerical methods of representation within manufacturing and an unevolving allegiance to conventional drawing methods before the widespread introduction of CAD.

The Visual Domain

Whereas the manufacturing industry considered three-dimensional and process modelling the essential rationale for CAD use from the outset, architectural practice has more typically used CAD to increase the efficiency with which traditional two-dimensional visualisations are created. Whilst CAD use initially changed the manner in which information is produced, through an industrialisation of drawing production, it is only through consideration of multidimensional modelling that the nature of the proposals has begun to be affected by the medium within which it is created. More recently, this opportunity has become further expanded into the physical domain with the use of CAM software that enables the authoring and simulation of the actual machining operation specific to a virtually modelled form. The creation of the numeric G-code – still a necessary part of the control process – is undertaken automatically as part of a postprocessing operation that compiles the geometry of tool paths and other machining parameters into industry-standard protocols.

It is clear that this capability transforms the programming of the machining process into a domain where visual and graphic representation becomes the primary medium of communication, allowing the information of the virtual to affect more than just the further processing of information and instead become part of a process of 'making' that demands redefinition with respect to traditional experience. It seems that the visual has attained a momentary primacy over material, not through any inherent beauty or its potential status as a form of legal document, but rather through its ability to interface the geometric and numerical component of the model with the conventions of graphic communication associated with practice.

When we use CAM software to create a time-based simulation that reveals the sequence of subtraction or addition by which form is realised, we are in a sense neither making nor drawing, but are engaged only in an active reading of an authored function that differentiates surplus matter from our unique form. In contrast to existing definitions, making is no longer identified through that which is made alone, but becomes inseparable from the combined acts of its description and viewing. Making, therefore, has become dependent on the author, object (architecture) and observer existing within a cybernetic condition, within which a continuous and changing dialogue between form and observer is maintained. CAM has altered the process of describing architecture as much as the process by which it is made.

dimension of making could be achieved. Through the development of new numerically based programming languages, each of the operations of a manufacturing process could be described through an original scripting, rather than through a replication of a moment past. The resulting numerical model requires that each of the variables, both of the process and the geometry, are made explicit in the script. It effectively circumvents the opportunity for a tacit contribution by corporal means, and indeed has no syntax within its script to allow such an input. These characteristics and a general trend towards specialisation reduced access and opportunity for nonengineering disciplines to exploit the technology within a wider practice of design.

The development of CNC machine tools can arguably be considered to be one of the most significant changes in production, beginning a transformation of mass production into mass customisation, and radically redefining the professional demarcations, and the nature of the information, by which the physical world is brought into being. By comparison, though, the technological development of architectural production over this period initially fails to reflect these changes, and instead becomes characterised more by the widespread adoption of industrialised building products and systems than by a radical revision of

Test assembly and site assembly, the site of fabrication and the site of future adaptation. The first component designates and provides the hearth of the prototype house.

Prototypes in CAM

It has been argued that architects make drawings not buildings, that the relationship to the drawing and the image defines not only their professional status, but their identity. Inherent in the conversation pencilled above is the notion that this tradition can be turned on its head. By developing a practice of design centred on the capabilities of CAD/CAM, two short exercises have explored how I might begin to build a small dwelling in a manner that allows representation to become transparent.

First, in comparison with conventional architectural practice, this work required a reassociation of knowledge and skill, and the need to operate in a wholly collaborative manner with engineers, fabricators and users. Second, description and representation would become implicit only

through a process of cumulative building; that is, the architecture is never fully described before sequential parts are assembled.

The first phase of activity, the making of a model, has been concerned with exploring the boundaries between visual practice as it is understood in architecture, and visual practice as it is understood in the domains of manufacturing. Its reading is dependent on memory of the site, and of other design decisions (some of which are events). Its information is typically ambiguous; it seeks to identify potential. It develops a description of the site that goes beyond abstracted architectural space explored by purely visual means, into an information-rich dialogue, where the information could subsequently be used as an input to the design process.

The second phase of project activity acknowledges that the proposal involves two sites: the landscape of settlement and the artifice of the factory. The design is intended to be a reflection of the conditions of each, so there was a need to work directly with the manufacturing process, at full scale, as early as possible. This would provide an immediate counterpoint to the earlier representations and a necessary part of exploring the manufacturing medium in the context of architectural design.

It was decided, then, to begin a cumulative process of building, where the site is inhabited gradually over the duration of the project, and where each successive installation becomes a reflection of prior use or experience. It is also a means by which the explicit numeric representation required for manufacture is applied in a fragmented manner, reducing the necessity to describe the complete entity.

A Settlement Rather Than a Landscape

The construction itself is one corner of an exterior terrace, and incorporates one of the most distinctive elements of life on the existing and surrounding site – a fire. Interior and exterior occupation on the wider site is always centred on such an element, reflecting cyclical changes in environment and momentous occasions. It is a means of constructing an event and a destination in a part of the site that has never been used. (Indeed, it has no history, being landfill.)

This proposal seeks to define a collaborative model of design as part of system of adaptive computer-controlled manufacture. This will search for a means that not only allows us to physically realise the virtually described, but allows the reconciliation of authored intent both with a physical context (of a site, material properties or process characteristics) and the dynamic reality of occupation and use. The term 'adaptive manufacture' is intended to suggest the aim that the very manipulation of material becomes a means by which response is generated, modified and, ultimately, understood as part of the design process. ⚙

Further Reading
N Callicott, *Computer-aided Manufacture in Architecture: The Pursuit of Novelty*, Architectural Press (Oxford), 2002.
S Groak, *The Idea of Building*, E & FN Spon (London), 1992.
R Evans, *The Projective Cast: Architecture and Its Three Geometrics*, MIT Press (London), 2000.
D Noble, 'Social choice in machine design: the case of automatically controlled machine tools', in D MacKenzie and J Wajcman (eds) *The Social Shaping of Technology*, Open University Press (Milton Keynes), 1985.
G Pask, *An Approach to Cybernetics*, Hutchinson and Co (London), 1961.
CF Sabel, 'Turning the page in industrial districts', in CF Sabel and A Bagnasco (eds), *Small and Medium-Sized Enterprises in Western Europe*, Thomas Learning (London), 1995.
K Vonnegut, *Player Piano*, Scribner (New York), 1952.
D Willis, *The Emerald City*, Princeton (New York), 1999.

Making a bang

'Design is a performance and a process, a form of seeking, a journey where the caravan expands and contracts.' Guest-editor **Bob Sheil** describes the extraordinary make-up and approach of the studio of the accomplished maker Thomas Heatherwick. With **Ron Packman**, he also describes how this translates into physical form in the making of the sculpture The B of Big Bang.

Diversity

At Thomas Heatherwick Studios, ideas and make-ability go hand in hand. They are inseparable twins in a home of invention, strategic thinking, problem solving and material manipulation. The studio's work, incorporating furniture, public sculpture, architecture, urban design, product design and fashion, is generated by a small but unusually diverse team: a workshop fabricator, two architects, a theatre designer, a product designer, a psychologist, a furniture designer, a project manager, a civil engineer, an office administrator, a structural engineer from consultants Packman Lucas (stationed full-time), and Tom Heatherwick.

All 12 or so core staff squeeze into a wedge-shaped building overhanging the Circle Line tube tracks near London's King's Cross. From the hub of the studio's sky-lit central meeting table spin a series of compact spaces for making, drawing, storing, talking and showing. From this compact environment of expertise and enthusiasm (which is infectious), the methodology of the studio emphasises, amongst others things, the importance of task rotation in the design process. A well-equipped workshop is within a few easy steps of a 3-D digital scanning arm (the new toy) and several CAD stations. A kitchen and library snug are nearby. 'Strategic thinking,' insists Heatherwick, best describes the nature of this interdisciplinary practice; whether it is a blade, a pen, a camera or a swatch of materials, an inquisitive urge motivates whatever tool is in hand.

Although parallels are made with practices of architecture, art and urban design, the projected attitude of the studio is refreshingly dismissive of notions of tagging the work or boxing staff into specialist fields. Its work is driven by doing where the overwhelming force that guides project after project is the act of making. Boundaries that

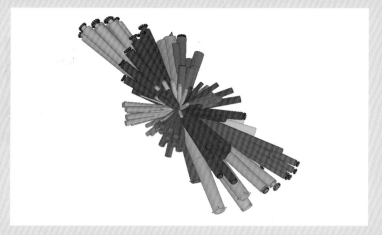

The B of the Bang (BotB): 3-D visualisation of the core sets.

are usually impassable for other disciplines get trampled upon by a multiskilled and highly motivated team who not only design and make prototypes and finished works, but also install them on site at all hours of the day and night. Design is a performance and a process, a form of seeking, a journey where the caravan expands and contracts. Bits get taken on, others get left behind.

An accomplished maker himself, Heatherwick is acutely aware of metamorphosis in the realisation of ideas, giving him the confidence to treat every project as a fresh experiment. This of course brings an element of uncertainty to the work in the early stages. Will it stand up? Will materials perform equally at full scale on site as they did in the studio? The studio is surrounded with objects of curious interest; perhaps it is the way it was press formed, injected or how the edge was cut. When he was a student, Tom was told how slow passing a high-pressure water jet would be the best way to cut through a 50-millimetre chunk of steel plate; it would produce the straightest smoothest edge, but it

The contorted geometry of the core required bespoke tooling and dexterous hands.

would not be cheap. Short of cash and willing to take a chance, he politely ignored the advice and discovered that cutting at maximum speed produced a beautiful, staggered uneven edge. This is an attitude he transmits on visiting manufacturing workshops early on in the fabrication process. He looks for the limits of their fabrication techniques, and then imagines what is possible if they are stretched. Heatherwick's work can be read as a series of such investigations. The more difficult it is to make something, the more he seems to want to make it.

Without at least partial involvement in the process of making, Heatherwick believes design is disengaged from a wealth of opportunities, of incidents that challenge direction, and of implementations that can influence outcomes. Design is a form of risk taking, including risks based on challenging convention and those based on tacit knowledge.

The diverse and practised experience with making that comes from the rich background of Heatherwick's staff raises questions of make-ability very early on in design development. Make-ability is both knowledge- and resource-based. What triggers innovation in make-ability is an instinct to deduce possibilities from previous experience, observation and curiosity. Heatherwick not only treasures his visits to industrial workshops, but also to supermarkets, DIY stores, pharmacies and airports too. Mental note is made of thousands of visual and tactile experiences that generate a personal reservoir of ideas, curiosities and questions. Whilst inspecting the work on one project, he might catch sight of a new machine in the corner of his eye and ask himself, 'What can I make with that?' He might chance upon an oddly shaped component or form and wonder, 'If they can make that, what else can they make?'

In addition to the full-time engineering support within the studio is the creative and technical expertise of consultancy director Ron Packman, an acquaintance of Heatherwick's from his days at the RCA. Packman offers what every risk-taking designer wants – unflinching confidence in structurally innovative ideas. He is also an accomplished and dedicated maker, whose knowledge and practice of manipulating material is constantly under experiment in his south London workshop, where he also lives. Below, Packman gives an account of their recent collaboration on designing and making Britain's largest public sculpture. He begins with a few key facts:
• There are 180 spikes including the five legs.
• The total steel weight is 165 tonnes (core = 60 tonnes, legs = 55 tonnes, spikes = 50 tonnes.
• The maximum force in any leg is around 300 tonnes.
• There are about 1,000 tonnes of concrete in the foundations.
• The highest point is 55.965 metres (184 feet) above the foundations; around 20 storeys.
• The longest spike is 35 metres (115 feet).
• The shortest spike is 2.9 metres (9 feet 6 inches).
• All the spikes have exactly the same external geometry in proportion to their length.
• If the spikes were laid end-to-end they would stretch 3,072 metres (10,105 feet). This is slightly under two miles, or seven times the height of the Empire State Building.
• It is made from weathering steel – a steel with a little copper added to it to form a stable and protective patina, so it will never need painting.
• It leans over at approximately 30 degrees to the vertical; the Leaning Tower of Pisa leans at about 4 or 5 degrees.

Figure 1: Preview of fabrication 1. 3-D visualisation identifies the 'cone' formations into which the subsets of spikes are grouped.

Making the B of the Bang

The B of the Bang comprises three main components: the core, the legs and the spikes. There are 175 spikes and five legs between 3 metres and 35 metres in length, all emanating from a single point 22 metres above the ground. All visible steel is weathering steel. The core is defined as the central part of the sculpture, where the spikes and legs converge. Each spike or leg is part of the core until the point at which it is no longer touching any of its neighbours. The core thus has an irregular, lumpy form defined by the density and orientation of the spikes and legs radiating from it. The legs are effectively those spikes that hit the ground and are made from much thicker steel, but are wrapped with weathering steel to give the same external appearance as the spikes. All of the spikes, regardless of length, are generated from the same rule; that is, they start at a 50-millimetre-diameter tip and taper outwards at the same rate towards the core. They are made as light as possible. The spikes and the legs are tapered hollow tubes, each with 18 facets so as to be almost circular in cross-section. Each spike is individually designed to account for its angle in relation to the horizontal; vertical spikes have no 'self weight' bending moment, horizontal spikes have maximum, and thus for all angles in between the structural duty, and hence wall thickness, may be calculated.

A further elaboration of the design is that, although seemingly random in their orientation, the spikes are in fact clustered in 25 groups. Each group is assembled as a perfect cone, and the tips of the spikes in each cluster lie on the perimeter of an ellipse (Figure 1). This comes into perception from certain angles, and rewards deeper inspection.

Designing and Making the Core

First thoughts on the core revolved around introducing a sphere or other similar shape into the centre to which the spikes could be attached. However, it was soon realised that whatever shape was chosen there would always be 'bald' spots visible between spikes, which would detract from the intricacy and interest of its form. It was therefore decided that the core had to be the consequence of the convergence of the 180 spikes and legs. In order to solve this, a rapid wax prototype of the core at 1:50 scale was commissioned (Figure 2). Although extremely fragile, this allowed us to view and understand how the spikes and legs come together, and how we could best control the forces and guide them into the foundations.

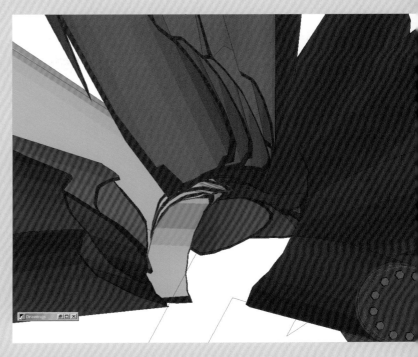

Figure 4: **Preview of fabrication 3.** 3-D visualisation groups the plating arrangements for the various layers of the spikes as they are added to the core.

Figure 2: **Preview of fabrication 2.** 3-D wax print of the complex core alignment.

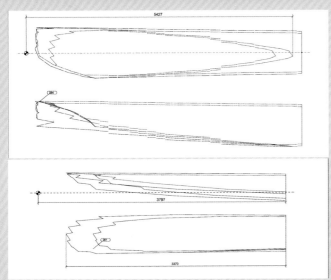

Figure 3: **Drawing as an instruction to make.** Cutting pattern for spike ends where they connect with the core.

The order of assembly of the core was critical; the earlier in the sequence a spike is installed, the more spikes will be welded to it, either directly, or indirectly through other spikes, and hence the more complex and higher the stresses it will be subjected to. In the end it was decided to let the considerations of the construction process determine the order, and then design the spikes to accommodate this. The construction process started with the section of the most highly loaded leg in the core before cutting the second leg to fit around this and fully welding it where it touched. The third leg was then fitted around the first two and welded in, and so on, until all five leg sections in the core were attached. We then moved on to the spikes, according to the order described above.

Before welding a spike to the core, the end had to be profiled to the correct shape to fit up against the spikes already installed. Had the spikes been circular rather than faceted, and not tapered, this profiling could have been performed automatically on computer-controlled machines. However, as this was not possible, a more traditional method was used. Each spike was prepared for installation by printing a paper template (Figure 3) at 1:1 scale from the 3-D computer model (Figure 4). The template was physically wrapped around the spike and transferred by punching through the profile on to the paper, but there were practical issues to overcome. Where a spike merges with its neighbours, sometimes it is the outer surface of the spike that first touches another spike, and sometimes it is the inner surface.

A second, larger issue was something over which we had no control. As each core section was added, sometimes requiring a significant amount of welding and, therefore, heat input, the core heated up and cooled down, expanding and shrinking as it did so. Because the heat input and cooling is never symmetrical about the core (there is no symmetry to the core), this leads to differential cooling and the whole core distorts slightly with each spike section that is added. The consequence of this is that no matter how

Figure 5: **It fits where it touches.** Prepared ends of the spikes prior to being interlocked and built as the core.

Figure 6: **Specials.** Some of the welds required left-handed welders using modified welding equipment, simply to get at the more 'embedded' welds.

accurately each spike section is positioned and installed, the core is never exactly the same as the model in the computer from which the templates are being produced. The result of these two effects is that in many cases the spike sections had to be carefully fettled to obtain the good fit essential for achieving the weld standard and also to avoid errors in the core shape accumulating as each spike was added (Figure 5). This fettling called for a high level of craftsmanship and patience from the workers assembling the core, with some spike sections being offered up eight times or more before finally being deemed acceptable (Figure 6).

The practicality of the assembly process was daunting. We used the computer model to determine the *x*, *y* and *z* coordinates of two predetermined target points on each spike, ideally separated by the maximum practical distance for maximum accuracy. A laser theodolite was then used to get the two points as close as possible to their actual positions. Once steadied, the spike was then adjusted to bring one of the two targets into exact register, and one end of the spike was tack welded. The remaining target was then brought into exact register and tack welded before the full welding process could begin.

Designing and Making the Legs

The legs are designed to appear similar to the spikes whilst also being sufficiently strong and stiff to support the 165-tonne sculpture. To achieve the required strength, each leg is made from 40-millimetre-thick steel rolled to the same shape as the spikes. Bending such thick steel to small diameters presents difficulties. The forces required to form the steel limit the length of section that can be produced to 3 metres near the top of the legs, where the leg diameter is larger, and only 1 metre near the foot of the legs, where the leg diameter is tighter. In practice, any diameter below 240 millimetres proved impossible to form without the risk of permanently damaging the material. For this reason, the bottom of each leg is made from a solid bar of steel machined to the correct shape.

Even for diameters above 240 millimetres, forcing the steel to shape has consequences. Deforming steel will result in an amount

of 'work hardening' in which the microstructure of the steel is altered and the material can become less ductile. Steel in this condition can be at risk of sudden failure in cold conditions when subjected to tension. The solution for restoring the former properties of the steel is a heat treatment in which the steel is heated and held at an elevated temperature. This allows the microstructure to rearrange itself and return to a ductile phase. Using samples, tests were first performed on 'stress relieving' the legs. This involved heating the steel to 650°C and holding it there for some hours. Though this helped, we were looking for a greater recovery of ductility. Further tests were undertaken on samples to 'normalise' the steel at the much higher temperature of 900°C (Figure 7). The results of these tests showed that the properties of the steel were restored to acceptable levels. The legs were therefore taken, each in two halves to suit the furnace size, to be normalised.

Designing and Making the Spikes

The spikes are designed to be as light as possible. This means that the thinnest steel possible, allowing for the loss expected due to corrosion, was used. The consequence of this is that the spikes, especially the longer ones, are quite flexible and will be seen to slowly move in the wind. Some spikes may also respond to local wind effects and gently vibrate. As the wind speed varies, different spikes begin to move and others will become still again. In order to make the spikes as economically as possible, we linked up with a company that specialises in the production of lighting masts. This is an industry where lightweight, hollow, tapered-steel columns are commonplace. Each spike was made in 7-metre-long sections, with the thickness of the steel adjusted in each section to accommodate the forces entailed.

Wind Analysis

To assess the response of the structure to wind, a model of the sculpture was tested in a wind tunnel. This validated

Figure 7: Manipulation of material property. Primary leg elements undergoing heat treatment.

Detail of the core showing how the subsets of the spikes are grouped.

some assumptions that had been made about the behaviour of the sculpture in various wind conditions. It also laid to rest a concern about the response of the structure that had existed since the completion of the first architectural model of the sculpture – namely the torsional mode of vibration about its primary longitudinal axis. Because there is no triangulation (bracing) between the legs of the sculpture, they are quite flexible when the sculpture twists on this axis. This can lead to a theoretical resonance occurring if the wind forces on the sculpture match the frequency of vibration in this mode. We had calculated the natural period of the sculpture to be around four seconds, and were concerned to establish that there were no excitation effects that might operate in a similar spectrum.

What the wind tunnel tests established, however, was in direct agreement with our assumptions. In order to produce significant torsional movement on the structure it is necessary for the wind

to act on parts of the structure remote from the core. Because the sculpture is very porous away from the core, it is not possible for the wind to contribute sufficient energy to the sculpture to promote resonance. In addition, it was established that the multiplicity of spikes acted as a damper to vibration because of the viscosity of the air itself, thus any global vibrations will rapidly decay.

Another phenomenon investigated was the potential for the individual spikes to gallop. Galloping is a large amplitude vibration that can quickly lead to structural failure. The concern with the spikes was that the longitudinal welds that joined the two half-pressings of the spikes together were machine welded and left as laid. There were thus two small beads of weld proud of the general spike surface running down the length of each spike. Depending on the orientation of the spike and the incident angle of the wind, this could cause the wind to behave differently on one side of the spike to the other, which could induce a cross-wind force in the spike. If the

effect occurred over a long enough section of spike and was sustained, it could lead to galloping.

Wind-tunnel tests on actual spike sections highlighted several ranges of angle of wind incidence that could cause galloping, and although the obvious solution to this scenario would have been to grind the longitudinal weld beads flush with the surface of the spikes, this would have required 5,000 metres of weld to be removed by hand – a costly undertaking.

An alternative strategy for dealing with the possibility of galloping was therefore investigated, focusing on ways to blur the point at which the wind hit a raised seam of weld. By intermittently welding additional beads of welds, either side of both longitudinal welds, the effect is blunted by smearing the point at which the wind encounters a weld bead over a wider area. Going back to the wind tunnel showed this approach to be effective and also allowed the

particular spike's risk to be identified so that intermittent welds only needed to be applied to some spikes.

Wind tunnel tests on actual spike sections highlighted the possibility of galloping in some of the spikes under very particular conditions, and the wind consultants are now in the process of resolving these, the final aspects of the design process.

For any red-blooded designer who welcomes a challenge and enjoys making something amazing, this project has had it all. The spirit of collaboration within the team has been a model of teamwork, from planning and financial issues right through to the complexities of welding and installation. It has been an exhilarating three years.

Finally, it is rare to find a city council with the vision and courage to commission such a radical and structurally implausible work of art. I have no doubt that the visual shock from the B of the Bang will fuse an icon into the world's perception of Manchester that will become an integral part of the city's unique persona. ⌂

SOME REFLECTIONS ON
JAPANESE DESIGN SENSIBILITY

Toyo Ito & Associates, Tod's Store, Omotesando, Tokyo, 2004.

By constructing a series of prologues on preconditions of making across cultural and industrial traditions, **Sarah Chaplin** describes the embedded condition of uncertainty that lies within the very human act of making. 'Makeshift' recognises the impermanent and the imperfect, the ritualistic and the indeterminate. From a question of meaning, this text argues that in Japanese culture at least, 'things are never fully designed, but are always in a state of being designed'.

In making for ourselves a place to live, we first spread a parasol to throw a shadow on the earth, and in the pale light of the shadow we put together a house.'
— Jun'ichiro Tanizaki[1]

As a typology of making, to the Western mindset the word 'makeshift' has connotations of improvisation and convenience, a making-do until there is time or money, or a change of circumstance, to permit a proper realisation of the item in question. It implies something inherently less than fit for purpose, approximate, something that has an expediency in relation to the ideal solution that is desired. It is a peremptory calling into being of something that can assume the role of a proxy, a stand-in, thrown together with materials that are to hand, where the quality of its realisation is less important than would ordinarily be acceptable. To give an example that grounds my discussion of the makeshift in relation to Japan, one Western visitor to the country in 1968 commented that he could not understand why, despite the opportunities for wholesale reorganisation of Tokyo, firstly after the massive earthquake in 1923 and secondly after the destruction wrought by the Second World War, Tokyo was still 'makeshift and confused'.[2]

What I want to put forward here, through a series of Japanese examples and with reference to Japanese aesthetic precepts, is a rereading of makeshift that establishes a different perception of the term, one less defined by its limitations and better able to capture all of the positive qualities associated with the temporary, the impermanent, the imperfect, the irregular, the perishable. Makeshift in these terms becomes fleeting yet potent, conditioned by aesthetic values that favour its necessary transitoriness. In so doing, what I hope to throw up is a different relation to the process of making and to the suppositions that drive design.

At the start of each new stage of their history, the Japanese entered into a makeshift period with respect to any given new technology, which afforded new techniques or materials an experimental looseness in relation to their gradual integration into the repertoire of making. To this day, the Japanese are more inclined to approach design in terms of releasing a trickle of new products to market, where each one is an incremental improvement on the last, in effect a process of continual variation on the initial theme. The designer exists in a developmental engagement with that which is designed. Things are never fully designed, but are always in a state of being designed. With this in mind, I will now work through six observations about

a Japanese design sensibility evident in architecture, literature, diet, product design, graphics and urbanism, each of which captures a the notion of makeshift within Japanese culture.

Makeshift 1

In many forms of Japanese literary expression there is a tendency to focus on gradual transitions, or shifts, in the movement from one state of being towards another. Literary theorist Yoshihiko Ikegami talks about 'the Japanese predilection for expressions with semantically blurred edges'.[3] Classic haiku poems often try to capture a makeshift moment, and invest it with intense poignancy that strives also to be devoid of sentimentality. They are simple, understated observations about a change in nature and our connection to it:

An autumn evening –
An hour of leisure
In a fleeting life
(Yosa Buson)

Against the bright full moon
A hilltop pine tree
Is the image of my rebirth
(Oshima Ryota)

A fallen camellia
On a rock
In the rapids
(Miura Yazuru)

The last of these three haiku has a poignancy that conjures up a range of specific sensory contrasts: the pastel-coloured petals that are slightly bruised from the fall, against a rough yet defined surface, with the sound of water rushing past, and the implicit risk that the flower will not be there for long, as the water is bound to wash it away soon. Between them, these three lines construct a makeshift situation that has the power to convey something quite ordinary, yet at the same time profound and memorable.

David Pye, in his seminal text *The Nature and Art of Workmanship,* seeks to differentiate between design and making by suggesting that 'design is what, for practical purposes, can be conveyed in words and by drawing: workmanship is what, for practical purposes, can not.'[4] He elaborates on the notion of craft by discussing the difference between the workmanship of certainty (afforded by mass production and industrial replication) and the workmanship of risk, which involves dexterity, care and judgement. The workmanship of risk is about accepting a makeshift approach to design, in the sense that in the actual act of fabrication there is

Toyo Ito & Associates, Omotesando, Tokyo, 2004
In designing this flagship store, Ito chose to emphasise the idea of design as making that he noticed in Tod's goods: 'I realised that all Tod's products are handcrafted with great attention to the natural quality of the leathers. The production steps strongly reflect a love of nature.' Here, the notion of makeshift is about working with the parameters of a natural material with all its inherent variations, and led Ito to a facade design that celebrates the shifting patterns of the surrounding trees.

every possibility that imperfection will occur, that the outcome could easily be less than satisfactory when measured against a desired outcome that in the West privileges predictability.

Makeshift 2

The Shinto temple at Ise in Japan is ritually reconstructed every 20 years. Each time, the site alternates, and the one lying next to the current temple lies empty, with only a small marker to indicate its future and past status. This periodic rebuilding is often cited as a way of drawing attention to the Japanese tendency to venerate the sacredness of the location itself, as opposed to venerating the longevity of built form, as is often the case in the West. The act of making celebrates the holiness of Ise through participatory means, and the craftspeople employed to do this are regarded as special cultural assets in their own right: national living treasures. With each reconstruction, the design of the temple subtly mutates, owing to the idiosyncrasies of the timber that has been sourced and the minor differences in technique that are used. In its ritualised remaking, subtle shifts thus occur: in other words, it belongs to the realms of the makeshift.

Lacfidio Hearn, who some hail as 'Japan's Great Interpreter', commented that 'generally speaking, we construct for endurance, the Japanese for impermanency. Few things for common use are made in Japan with a view to durability. The straw sandals worn out and replaced at each stage of a journey; the robe consisting of a few simple widths loosely stitched together for wearing, and unstitched again for washing; the fresh chopsticks served to each new guest at a hotel; the light shoji frames serving at once as windows and walls, and repapered twice a year; the matting renewed every autumn.'[5]

Hearn regards this preponderance of all things impermanent as being consistent with qualities of the Japanese landscape and its shifting substrata and seismic activity, but also with the adoption of a Buddhist orientation to life, as well as with the nomadic origins of the Japanese people. It is the 'extreme fluidity' of the Japanese that Hearn chooses to foreground, marvelling at the way in which a Japanese artisan can take an extraordinarily makeshift attitude to life: 'If he desires to travel a thousand miles, he can get ready for his journey in five minutes. His whole outfit need not cost more than seventy-five cents and all his baggage can be put into a handkerchief ... You may reply that any savage can do the same thing. Yes, but any civilised man cannot; and the Japanese has been a highly civilised man for at least a thousand years.'[6]

Arata Isozaki said in a recent interview: 'Architecture is not the fixing of images; in the design process we have to realise that architecture is always growing or decaying ... materialisation is the beginning of a new life, and if the lives

Frei Otto and Shigeru Ban, Japan Pavilion, Hanover Expo, 2000
In keeping with the 'Environment' theme of the expo, Frei Otto and Shigeru Ban's concept for the Japan Pavilion was to create a structure where the materials used could be recycled once it was dismantled. Ban wanted to make the construction as low-tech as possible, and its makeshift qualities are beautifully revealed in the joints, which were foxed together with tape.

of buildings move in the same direction that people's do, they will surely encounter change and eventually their end.'[7] He qualifies this culturally by saying: 'In the Orient there is an easier attitude towards deterioration and destruction, particularly in Japan.'[8] Why make something to last, when it simply will not. And, moreover, when a more powerful means of expression can be obtained from its impermanence?

Makeshift 3

Kenji Ekuan, eminent product designer and author of *The Aesthetics of the Japanese Lunchbox*, points out that 'the average lunchbox is a makeshift device, a resource in emergency situations, a temporary stopgap measure. This requisite application in accordance with circumstance is an "invisible system" pervading all levels of form-creation sensitivity in Japan. This brisk meeting of conditions such as deadline, place, difficulty of obtaining materials, cost adjustment, and timing – all contingent in terms of time, quality and quantity – might justly be termed an Applied Technology of Circumstance. The lunchbox (or *makunouchi bento*, literally "intermission lunch") was originally a meal to be consumed at the theatre. Thus it was born out of just such a technology.'[9]

Ekuan is at pains to point out that the designer of the contemporary lunchbox, such as can be bought at every railway station in Japan, is actually the merchant who improvises a meal from what is available and tries to make it as attractive and appetising as possible, to as many people as possible, with few basic ingredients. Ekuan notes 'the makunouchi lunchbox did not begin as a makeshift measure merely to satisfy hunger in a work situation where no other food was available, but rather as a picnic cuisine for outings and celebrations. Typical occasions were related to the annual calendar of Japan's agrarian society. The most popular is still cherry-blossom viewing (*hanami*).'[10] Thus, like the haiku, the lunchbox marks a moment in time; its makeshift quality has to do with observing and celebrating a seasonal event.

Japanese cities during the Edo period anticipated the fires, and built in fire breaks which were swathes of unbuilt land that frequently became the site of makeshift parties. The Low City was particularly prone to fires, and the lower classes living there kept emergency fire baskets hung at the ready in conspicuous places. These were described by Tanizaki as 'oblong and woven of bamboo, about the size of a small trunk, and they were kept where everyone could see them, awaiting an emergency'.

Makeshift 4

In his book *Low City, High City,* Edward Seidenstecker discusses the frequency with which fire rampaged through Tokyo in the Meiji period, commenting that the emperor spent 'more than a third of his reign in the Tokugawa mansion where the Akasaka Palace now stands',[11] owing to the fact that there were fires in 1871, 1873, 1891 and 1911. Japanese cities during the Edo period anticipated the fires, and built in fire breaks which were swathes of unbuilt land that frequently became the site of makeshift parties. The Low City was particularly prone to fires, and the lower classes living there kept emergency fire baskets hung at the ready in conspicuous places. These were described by Tanizaki as 'oblong and woven of bamboo, about the size of a small trunk, and they were kept where everyone could see them, awaiting an emergency'. As a makeshift measure, the fire basket enabled a few possessions to be gathered up quickly so a family could evacuate the home and flee to safety with sufficient means to continue their lives in the interim.

By contrast, those who lived in the 'high city' often had a small fireproof storehouse called a *kura* as part of their property, which could contain all the family heirlooms and items that were not currently in use. Edward Morse describes the traditional *kura* as being 'generally two storeys in height, with walls eighteen inches to two feet in thickness, composed of mud plastered to a framework of great strength and solidity'.[12] Morse reports that, remarkably, in contrast to the speed with which a timber dwelling was erected, 'two years or more are required in the proper construction of one of these fire-proof buildings'. In this way, day-to-day life can be seen to favour makeshift conditions over the sepulchral permanence of the *kura.* Morse evokes a powerful image of their durability after a conflagration: 'When all the surrounding territory is absolutely flat – these black, grimy *kura* stand conspicuous in the general ruin.'[13] In different ways, both the fire baskets of the low city and the *kura* of the high city represent an accommodation of natural disaster and illustrate the inherently makeshift nature of human existence.

The Kobe earthquake of 1995 caused architect Shigeru Ban to consider what it meant to design makeshift accommodation in the aftermath of a natural disaster. Appropriately enough, he chose cardboard tubes, a makeshift material, and managed to produce shelter that served its practical purpose and yet projected a dignity and a resonance about its particular circumstance. Ban is quoted as saying: 'Refugee shelter has to be beautiful. Psychologically, refugees are damaged. They have to stay in nice places.'[14] Among other more recent projects, a day-care centre for children in Odate provides a space made of plywood lining, an external stressed skin of fibre-reinforced plastic and ribbed metal sheeting. The interior is designed for a makeshift occupation of space and the possibilities of improvised play.

Similarly, a well-published house by Ban involved a large single volume that contained a number of mobile room/ furniture elements mounted on castors, so the inhabitants could manoeuvre them at will into different positions. This project therefore can also be seen to accommodate a need to appropriate and participate in space in such a way as to produce makeshift conditions of living. The work stems from Ban's observation that it is invariably the furniture that safeguards survival in natural disasters, and these 'furniture houses' are designed so that the furniture elements will support a collapsing roof. They are also designed to be put up very quickly – typically in two or three days – without the need for specialised carpentry, which highlights a further makeshift attitude in relation to constructional means in Ban's work.

Makeshift 5

Haga Koshiro, in an essay entitled 'The Wabi Aesthetic Through the Ages', surveys what has been an important

precept in Japanese design since the Zen tea masters of the 16th century who circumscribed the rituals of *chanoyu*. One master, the author of 'Zen-cha Roku', wrote: '*Wabi* means lacking things, having things run entirely contrary to our desires, being frustrated in our wishes.'[15] Koshiro quotes further from this text, in which Roku elaborates: '*Wabi* involves not regarding incapacities as incapacitating, not feeling that lacking something is deprivation, not thinking that what is not provided is deficiency.' From this, Koshiro surmises that: '*Wabi* means to transform material insufficiency so that one discovers in it a world of spiritual freedom unbounded by material things.'[16] As such, the makeshift is elevated from a context of a temporary making-do to a 'richness of spirit, a nobility, and purity within what may appear to be a rough exterior'. Over time, not only were things that were lacking perceived as being *wabi*, but also 'a preference for warped and irregular forms developed'.[17] The teachings of Rikyu in the sacred text 'Samporoku' record the attitudinal shift that is necessary to follow the way of tea: 'It is sufficient if the dwelling one uses does not leak water and the food served suffices to stave off hunger.'[18] Thus, makeshift epitomises the prerequisites of a tea ceremony.

American artist, architect and author Leonard Koren published a modest book on *wabi-sabi* in 1994, in which he admitted: '*Wabi-sabi* resolved my artistic dilemma about how to create beautiful things without getting caught up in the dispiriting materialism that usually surrounds such creative acts ... *wabi-sabi* appeared the perfect antidote to the pervasively slick, saccharine, corporate style of beauty that I felt was desensitising American society.'[19]

In the last chapter, Koren ascribes the material qualities of *wabi-sabi*: the suggestion of natural process; irregular; intimate; unpretentious; earthy; murky and simple. He then attempts to locate contemporary examples of the *wabi* aesthetic: a sweater by Comme des Garçons from 1982–3,

'supposedly created by programming the loom to create a fabric with randomly placed holes',[20] and an expanded metal chair by Shiro Kuramata called 'How High the Moon' (1986), which Koren thinks is 'a good example of the fusion of modernism (the industrial process, precision execution, geometric forms) and *wabi-sabi* (sense of nothingness and non-materiality, murky colour, subordinate importance of utility).'[21] Koren's notes reveal a critique of modern production methods and the qualities of finish they favour: 'Things in process, like buildings under construction, are often more imagistic than the finished thing itself. Poetic irregularity and variability are difficult to mass produce however.'[22] Nevertheless, he is concerned to find ways of prescribing material qualities such as 'grainy, tangled, wispy, wrinkled, and the like'.

Koren refers to a Japanese art movement dating from the late 1960s/early 1970s called *mono-ha*, or school of things. Toshiaka Minemura defines their intent as being 'to bring out some artistic language from "things" as they stood, bare and undisguised, by letting them appear on the stage of artistic expression, no longer as mere materials, but allowing them a leading part'.[23] Minemura attributes the emergence of this school of thought to several factors, including 'an ambivalent feeling of both fascination and repulsion towards the products of our industrialized society'.[24] The work of *Mono-ha* artists might include using a material in a way that foregrounds its transformative potential: Narita simply made charcoal from wood, so that 'the subject was the "qualitative metamorphosis of an object of the same genus"'.[25]

Interestingly, Minemura contextualises the impact of *mono-ha* as being makeshift in its own right: 'If one looks at the *Mono-has* with synchronic eyes and sees in them only a transient group phenomenon, one may regard them as ... air pockets, rather similar to the violence of war, [which] while ruining plenty of things history has built up, or was about to build up, modify

Jun Aoki, Louis Vuitton store, Tokyo, 2002
Makeshift as movement and transient effects is what characterises Jun Aoki's Louis Vuitton Store on Omotensando Avenue, Tokyo. The use of two different high-tech German mesh materials creates the impression of layers of 'suitcases' that have been wrapped in stainless-steel mesh. Coloured glass shimmers through the mesh during the day, and at night the mesh changes its level of apparent transparency to create a more dramatic effect.

completely the relationship between things by bringing about a revolution within people's awareness'.[26]

Makeshift 6

Toyo Ito has always emphasised the constant state of flux and the consequent need for architecture to respond by being in some way makeshift. In an interview with Christophe Knabe and Joerg Rainer Noennig in 1997, Ito said of Tokyo: 'It is an image that is incomplete ... I think that as a city [it] is further advanced than the individual pieces of architecture which comprise it and that it is in a perpetual state of revision.'[27] Ito's intentions as a designer correlate with the approach of a haiku poet, who is not trying to isolate the object of study from its context, but conceive it as part of a momentary totality. Yet he acknowledges that this is, in fact, difficult to achieve: 'Once you have started the construction however, it slips out of that relationship [to its context] and establishes a way of isolating itself and this is simply difficult to avoid.'[28]

Ito's privileging of the nomad during the 1980s introduced a new figurative makeshift element in relation to the city: instead of a 'walking city', the human being was transient and the environment had to respond appropriately to this new state of existence. Ito reflects that this concept emerged for him when 'consumer culture was at its climax and when people's mobility was also at its height. These modern nomads are probably fewer in number now.'[29] What is important to Ito is that his architecture is capable of 'mastering the now'. This focus is very similar to that taken by the haiku poet or the Zen master, for whom living in the

Jun Aoki, Louis Vuitton store, Tokyo, 2002.

introduction to the new millennium, it will not last forever.'[31] Thus he acknowledges that the term itself is inherently makeshift – a response to a transitional phase in history that is being experienced on many levels.

Conclusion

Roland Barthes conveys his perception of a profoundly makeshift space in *Empire of Signs*: 'In the ideal Japanese house, stripped of furniture, there is no site which designates the slightest propriety in the strict sense of the word – ownership: neither seat nor bed nor table out of which the body might constitute itself as the subject (or master) of a space: the centre is rejected ... whether we pass by, cross it, or sit down on the floor (or the ceiling if you reverse the image), there is nothing to *grasp*.'[32] This is revealing of a Western need to pin down the trappings of a designed environment in order to achieve a sense of mastery over the space. These entrenched assumptions serve to preclude a more makeshift design sensibility that celebrates risk, temporariness and, ultimately, life. ∆

moment carries a special significance. This often translates in Ito's work as a fascination with qualities of light and a palette of materials that mediate or emit light, whether daylight or artificial. This gives his work a makeshift character that is much to do with the layering of materials and the attention he pays to the borderlines and interactions between materials as we experience them.

Of Ito's protégés, Kazuo Seijima's and Jun Aoki's recent work maximises the layering of light and movement to produce a kind of architecture that Taro Igarashi describes as 'especially distinguished by its focus on the expressive possibilities of the building's skin, as opposed to its volume – the exploration of what might be called the 2.5 dimensional'.[30] Aoki's design for a Louis Vuitton shop in Nagoya (1998) and Seijima's retail emporium for Dior in Tokyo are both designed to be experienced in motion, the former rewarding the passer-by with a wonderful moiré display of surface interplay, the Dior project a milky glimpse into another space-time continuum.

The appellation 'superflat' has been used to describe the work of both architects, and is thought by Igarashi to derive from the subcultural world of *manga*, itself a makeshift phenomenon that exemplifies the state of play of Japanese culture in general. Igarashi concludes: 'Japan at beginning of the 21st century is undergoing rapid upheaval. Its economy is slowing down, class distinctions and public unrest are increasing, traditional administrative and educational systems are tiring, the population is aging, and its political structure is shifting towards a bureaucratic right-wing administration. Many elements of the superflat society are in need of overhaul. Thus, while the concept of the superflat may serve as an

Notes
1 Jun'ichiro Tanizaki, *In Praise of Shadows*, Leete's Island Books (New Haven, CT), 1977, p 17.
2 Hal Porter, *The Actors*, Angus and Robertson (Sydney), 1968.
3 Yoshihiko Ikegami, 'Do-language and become-language: two contrasting types of linguistic representation', in Yoshihiko Ikegami (ed), *Empire of Signs*, John Benjamin's Publishing Company (Philadelphia, PA), 1991, p 294.
4 David Pye, *The Nature and Art of Workmanship*, Cambridge University Press, 1968, p 1.
5 Lacfidio Hearn, *Japan's Great Interpreter: A New Anthology of His Writings, 1894–1904*, Louis Allen and Jean Wilson (eds), Japan Library Limited (Folkestone), 1992, p 83.
6 Ibid, p 87.
7 Arata Isozaki, interview in *Shaking the Foundations: Japanese Architects in Dialogue*, Christophe Knabe and Joerg Rainer Noennig (eds), Prestel (Munich), 1999, p 112.
8 Ibid, p 113.
9 Kenji Ekuan, *The Aesthetics of the Japanese Lunchbox*, MIT Press (Cambridge, MA), 2000, p 5.
10 Ibid, p 6.
11 Edward Seidenstecker, Low City, HIgh City, Tokyo from Edo to the Earthquake, 1867–1923, Penguin Books (Harmondsworth), 1983, p 63.
12 Edward Morse, *Japanese Homes and Their Surroundings*, Dover Publications (New York), 1961, p 33.
13 Ibid, p 35.
14 Shigeru Ban, in Belinda Luscombe, *He Builds With a Really Tough Material: Paper*, taken from www.time.com/time/innovators/design/profile_ban.html.
15 Haga Koshiro, 'The Wabi Aesthetic Through the Ages', in Nancy Hume (ed), *Japanese Aesthetics and Culture: A Reader*, State University of New York Press, 1995, p 246.
16 Ibid, p 246.
17 Ibid, p 248.
18 Ibid, p 272.
19 Leonard Koren, *Wabi-sabi for Artists, Designers, Poets and Philosophers*, Stone Bridge Press (Berkeley, CA), 1994, p 9.
20 Ibid, p 93.
21 Ibid, p 92.
22 Ibid, p 86.
23 Toshiaka Minemura, *What is Mono-ha?*, Catalogue of Mono-Ha exhibition at Kamakura Gallery, 1986, republished online.
24 Ibid.
25 Ibid.
26 Ibid.
27 Interview with Toyo Ito, in Knabe and Noennig, op cit, p 91.
28 Ibid, p 92.
29 Ibid, p 94.
30 Taro Igarashi, 'Superflat Architecture and Japanese Subculture', in Moriko Kira and Mariko Terada (eds), *Japan: Towards Totalscape*, NAI Publishers (Rotterdam), 2001, p 97.
31 Ibid, p 101.
32 Roland Barthes, *Empire of Signs*, Hill and Wang, The Noonday Press (New York), 1982, p 110.

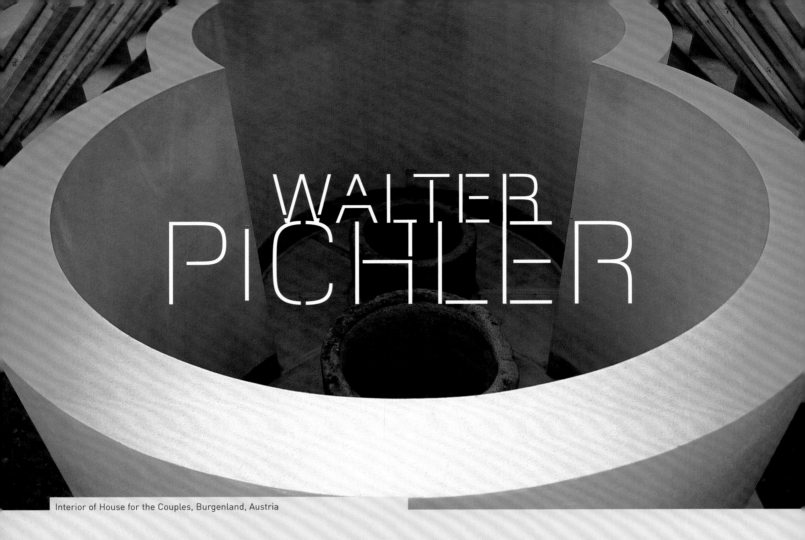

WALTER PICHLER

Interior of House for the Couples, Burgenland, Austria

Throughout his lifetime, the Austrian-born artist, maker and recluse Walter Pichler has defied an easy understanding of his work or its purpose. 'Coming into contact with any product [of Pichler's],' writes critic **David Dunster**, 'elicits for me the sensation of a chilling proximity to the inevitable.' Pichler, the practitioner of personal obsessions, 'created a commentary that is far from private but retains the nature of an archetypal investigation'. In a rare look at his work, Dunster here offers us an eloquent personal insight that stirs a potent array of emotion.

... whoever complains about the inadequate quality of current architecture should ask himself if this architecture actually can be any better. It cannot, in fact, be better because with a few exceptions it is non-functional. It offers man nothing to occupy him; it influences in no manner his great yearning and slight talent for sociability. In a false manner it seeks to take this yearning into account. Our cities are false, and our community centres are false, because no-one can be introduced to communal life merely by the image of community. And this is what we reproach architectural functionalism with: it no longer functions.

What I call for is an architecture which fascinates. This now is commonplace yet there is none better. Whoever finds himself reaching for those attainments which are foreign to us but which tomorrow will be part of us; he will understand what I mean.

— Walter Pichler, 'The Lesson of Pre-Colombian Architecture', *Landscape*, Vol 13, No 3, spring 1964, pp 24–5.

Landscape, the extraordinary magazine edited by JB Jackson, carried the first piece in English that the then young Walter Pichler wrote. In the contributors' list on the contents page (verso and unnumbered), he is introduced thus: WALTER PICHLER studied at the Academy of Applied Arts, Vienna, and is now engaged in writing a book on the Viennese Architect, Otto Wagner.' His piece was in an issue that continued contributions from Michel Dragon and Gaston Bachelard.

Born in 1936, Pichler graduated from the Academy of Fine Art in 1955, and had his first exhibition in the Galerie nächst St Stephan in 1963, alongside Hans Hollein. Five years later he exhibited in New York, in a show called 'Visionary Architecture', with Hollein and Raimund Abraham, and by 1972 he had left Vienna for St Martin an der Raab, Burgenland, where he had already completed his first buildings to house his sculptures. From this point, his work would be exhibited rarely, published in a very controlled fashion, and make of Pichler the most famous artistic recluse in the world. His only pieces that are now purchasable are chairs and a table from the Austrian furniture-makers Svoboda, called Galaxy, designed in 1966 and made from aluminium.

Unlike architects, artists can be obsessed with death. Architects can only project work that makes life better; even those who worked on the design of concentration camps believed that by so doing they would improve life, even if that meant making a master race dominate slaves and obliterate those who could not even be cowed into servitude because their blood was so impure. As such, one of the more cryptic enigmatic suggestions of Adolf Loos about a stone in a forest being architecture because it is a memorial, a tombstone, might be taken to mean that even for him such architecture lacked an interior. That architect appeared to deal with death; Aldo Rossi, in the extension to the cemetery of San Cataldo, Modena, projected a still incomplete project, a necropolis that is itself an idealised city, no longer, *pace* Rowe, fragmentary and collaged, but complete and, therefore, dead. Artists from Goya onwards have made death the subject of their work, and if the horrors of war reappear in our day in the Chapman Brothers' wicked take on our obsession with childish things, then again they, following Goya, make death their subject matter.

Coming into contact with any product of Walter Pichler, the Austrian artist, elicits for me the sensation of a chilling proximity to the inevitable. Pichler does not, of course, make a banner headline out of death, but its presence in his work as a theme makes this work impossible for an architect to have made. Indeed, his almost total withdrawal from the system of purchase and exchange in the international art world means that what we might know of his work depends entirely upon a few publications, infrequent exhibitions, and a visit to the Museum fur Angewande Kunst (MAK) in Vienna. Here, the curator Peter Noever commissioned Pichler to make a door into a courtyard. More than a door, it is a threshold, some steps, and a pair of stub walls executed in concrete, while the door is a magnificent casting ribbed as if part of some prehistoric remnant, not Gormley, and hinged with feral cunning. It is a door so close to being The Door that opening it feels like swinging the Ghiberti portals of the Chiesa, requiring a mighty bodily exertion not required of other doors. The opposite of Pichler's door might be those obedient seeing-eye doors that open automatically as long as there is electricity to power the motor, or the fake heavy doors of new cars that clink to mistakenly reassure the motorist that his or her car is safe at any speed.

Pichler's door needs effort to push it; it does not magically fly open to reveal the bare court beyond as if it were part of Dr No's magical interiors. Perhaps, like most of Pichler's output, the viewer/visitor/reader is forced into a subservient position, made to feel the weakness of this position, and thus made to feel uncomfortable. Only by travelling to Burgenland can anyone see Pichler's work; there is little in public or private collections. The sculptures stand challengingly, and despite the ease with which ordinary things – birds, machines, bodies, clothes and even buildings – may be recognised, we are not placed before them but

have to work to get a place near them. In some ways this reminds me of the intractability of certain architects' work to photographing: think of Borromini or Carlo Scarpa. But, of course, as architects we must travel to see San Carlo alle quattro Fontane in Rome, or the Castelvecchio Museum in Verona. And then can we describe it? As Leo Steinberg showed in his PhD, the precise nature of Borromini's geometry eluded historians until a plan drawing of the church was discovered in the Albertina. If the geometry cannot be described, how can any sense of being inside that miniature miracle be conveyed? Likewise, Scarpa, despite Richard Murphy's excellent work, resists interpretation. However, going to see Scarpa in situ is pure and unalloyed pleasure. Photographs won't do.

With a particular painting, photographs won't do either. Picasso's *Guernica* sits, perhaps not as well hung as it could be, in the converted hospital that is now the Reina Sofia in Madrid, and while one can buy the mug, postcard or tee, the real thing is still the real thing. So Pichler's art, stationed in some out-of-the-way hamlet, is perhaps not so different. Except that it is not for sale. It is his, in at least two ways. His, having been made, drawn, designed and assembled by the human entity we call Walter Pichler. And also on his land, accessible to us only insofar as the legal entity Pichler allows access. Moreover, in extremis, Pichler could destroy all of his work because he owns it, and it is his to do with as he wishes. Thus, as far as an artist can control his work, Pichler has established this control in the most extreme way of any artist. Francis Bacon was known for destroying work, but let enough through to the Waddington Gallery for him to dine as he wished, drink as he saw fit and gamble as much as he wanted to. Jeffrey Bernard tells a story of lunch with Bacon during which, in discussing a painting, Bacon was trying to make a particular point.

Small tower, Burgenland.

Key
1. Living Quarters
2. Workshop
3. Wooden House, House for the Figure With Moveable Parts
4. House for the Steles
5. House for the Wagons
6. House for My Daughter
7. House for the Large Cross
8. Small Tower
9. House for the Torso and the Craniums
10. Cold Storage
11. House for the Ridge and Canyon Project
12. House for the Couples
13. House for the Small Torso, Project
14. House for the Woman and the Woman Made Out Of Metal, Project
15. House for the Staffs, Project
16. House for the Three Planes, Project
17. Three Birds
18. Barn, Project

Plan of Pichler's land in St Martin in Burgenland, including future projects. Reproduced from: *Walter Pichler: Drawings, Sculptures, Buildings*, Stedelijk Museum Amsterdam, 1997.

Many bottles had been emptied, and Bernard slipped a piece of paper towards Bacon, asking him to demonstrate the particular point graphically. Only after picking up the pencil did Bacon push the paper away. Whatever he drew there, Bernard could later sell. Bacon was not playing that game.

To some extent, then, we are denied access to the art of Pichler. Why does this matter? To me his work contains the most beautifully wrought and exquisitely made objects outside contemporary jewellery. I fantasise that the photographs in Pichler's publications were all taken by him on an old Hasselblad in flat sunless light, so that when printed in duotone they give such depth, offer a tactile quality, a nearness and nowness, that you intuit just exactly how even the warm moist touch of a finger would blemish the polished steel of his pieces, provoking clouds of tarnish. Such tactility makes the objects' remoteness even more tantalising. Is this, then, like so much conceptual art, an art that lives in the mind, where a clean description can wring as much interest as the sight of the object itself – those tins of *merde d'artiste* (for example, *Merdes d'artiste*, which '*contenu net gr. 30, conservée au naturel, produite et mise en boîte au mois de mai*

1961', produced by Piero Manzoni, and made in Italy), which were then worth more unopened than opened. Or the *pissoir* of Duchamp into which an artist pissed. (In May 1993, during an exhibition in Nîmes, the artist Pierre Pinoncelli pissed into Duchamp's urinal, the piece known as *Fontaine* (dated 1917 and signed by Duchamp as R Mutt) 'to return the work to its proper use'. At trial he was fined 30,000 French francs: the court was not persuaded of the arguments of his lawyer that 'the provocation of Duchamp is found again in the provocation of Pinoncelli' (*Libération*, 22 November 1999)). No tactility here.

This, then, might be another game that Pichler plays with us, except that because none of his pieces are mass-produced (there is one exception), they cannot be used to assassinate the concept of the institution of art (*pace* Peter Burger) and can only recoil from the machinations of that bad world into the not bad world of Austrian (abandoned) farmland in order to let Pichler himself carry on his own exploration of who he is by making only those things that he is interested in. To say 'obsessed by' pretends to a degree

Detail of the movable figure (steel) clad in red cloak with the shadow figure, made from dark clay, behind.

The movable figure in its house, with a glass roof, 1982. A robot-like figure, it derives from the torso and skulll sculptures made earlier but has movable hands and feet. The statue predates *Star Wars*.

of intimacy that I luckily cannot claim with him, and to call artists obsessed is merely to consign them to some noncapitalist world of functioning loonies. We are all obsessed in one sense or another and, if any great theme unites our obsessiveness, then death bids strongest for first place as the signifying unity *par excellence*.

Why does making have to withdraw in this way from the market? Pichler's work is based in his understanding of our condition. In the 1960s he exhibited, with Hans Hollein, Raimund Abraham and Frederich St Florian at the Galerie nächst St Stephan, with objects, later published as 'Prototypes'. These included a helmet totally enclosing the head with a long protrusion (German name *Fernsehhelm tragbares Wohnzimmer*, 1967). In this was housed a TV, a real predictor of the virtual-reality headpiece of recent sci-fi. He then played with performance art – an illustration shows an arm, presumably Pichler's, having been slashed and now dripping blood on to a white piece of clothing (1971). On to the blood stain, Pichler placed a continent, called *Der Kontinent. Beschreibung einer Reiseroute* (illustrated in Walter Pichler, *Zeichnungen, Skulpturen, Gebäude,* Residenz Verlag, 1993), a rough translation

From left: House for the Wagons, House for the Steles, and House for the Couples, Burgenland.

Walter Pichler, 1997.

Interior of House for the Steles.

By withdrawing from the art world and the consumption of his art by the trade in pieces, Pichler simply asserts that he gained the most valuable commodity — time. Sculpture is the hardest area of work, but by gaining time Pichler felt able to work away at this most unforgiving of artistic labours.

House for the Wagons, House for the Steles and House for the Couples.

House for the Couples.

being 'The Continent, Description of an Itinerary'. Earlier he shows a series of drawings from 1961 that are complex organisms encompassing cuboids and spherical forms, their complexity anatomical. One such drawing is cast and then apparently framed in concrete.

Then there is a move: the family, it seems, left Vienna and began the conversion of a farm at St Martin in Burgenland, where Pichler continued to make and install his objects. In time, specific houses were built for these objects; the houses have nothing to do with the earlier *Kompakt* cities but rationalise the local vernacular. Sketches indicate that in 1970 Pichler embodied human forms within his objects rather than adding the objects to the human form. From this period came the Bed casting of a body that is divided by thick and painful-looking shards of glass. But perhaps the shards are continents. At the same time he drew a chair for suicide in Bergen (Pichler, *Zeichnungen, Skulpturen, Gebäude*, pp 106–7) – a truly painful piece. The chair is again a geometricised mould to hold the human body, which lays out its arms in dishes that channel away the blood from

slashed wrists. Similarly, the stomach and/or penis are also lacerated. The blood returns to the earth. I have written out the most horrific piece because it has always struck a deep chord in me.

As drawings these are terminal in more than one sense. Pichler reached an artistic dead end here with his interest in performance art, one that happily has not been picked up by any other artist. He finally seemed to have found a way of shutting out those parts of everyday life he did not wish to deal with by escaping Vienna for St Martin, where he began to draw in a much more refined and almost relaxed way machines, and the housing for machines (1975, Haus fur den Grossen and den Kleinen Wagen) that were later built. From this point, buildings appeared to always be part of the artistic labour, but buildings that are frames though drawn with an intensity no picture frame has ever enjoyed.

Now to try to answer the question. Pichler's answer is very simple. By withdrawing from the art world and the consumption of his art by the trade in pieces, Pichler simply asserts that he gained the most valuable commodity – time. Sculpture is the hardest area of work, but by gaining time Pichler felt able to work away at this most unforgiving of artistic labours. The subject of his sculpture and architecture is the human body, in parts or totally reduced to machined and machine-like objects highly polished and wrought, a body that is clothed and housed metaphorically and mythically, particularly with reference to religious myths using crucifixes and crosses that in Pichler's hands are both highly crafted and extremely violent. His reductions are nothing if not cruel, and are therefore extremely emotional. By working only to make pieces that gratified him and will never be for sale, Pichler created a commentary that is far from private but retains the nature of an archetypal investigation. He supports this work by the sale of drawings and by his earnings from books, over which he exercises the same degree of control. In the way that he works, I cannot help but be reminded of Béla Bartók, who spent long years notating folk songs in his native Hungary and the surrounding lands, or of Olivier Messiaen, who spent equally large parts of his life notating bird song. Both composers then used this to mould their output. Pichler's material is the world of his past, and what makes him burnish that world is the search for making art. ⌂

91

LEARNING IN NEWBERN:
RURAL STUDIO IN YEAR TEN

Lucy and Anderson Harris House, Mason's Bend, Alabama, 2002
The house was designed and built by Auburn University outreach students Floris
Buisman, Ben Cannard, Philip Crosscup, Kerry Larkin, Marie Richard, James Tate and
Keith Zawistowski. Instructors: Samuel Mockbee and DK Ruth.

Amidst the regulated and increasingly fraught business of architectural practice,
particularly within its homestead of the town of Newbern, Hale County, Alabama,
Rural Studio has entered its second decade as a force to contradict normative
modes of architectural education and practice. In the coming years, we will see
if the wider consequences triggered by this innovative organisation will take root
elsewhere. In the meantime, **John Forney**'s reflective examination of its roots
substantiates the condition that, in times of change, the periphery is a place that
matters greatly.

Auburn University's Rural Studio is an elective, off-campus programme in the undergraduate architecture curriculum, allowing students to design and build dwellings and social facilities for underserved populations in rural Alabama. It has been acclaimed for the projects of its first decade, which are appreciated as the fruits of virtuous methods: pursuing an ethical practice of architecture, providing assistance to disadvantaged communities, and exploring building methods that foster responsible resource use. But the Rural Studio was not born whole, and has followed the crooked path of youth. The messy reality of architecture students building their designs for local communities compromises as many intentions as it resolves. Critics question the wilful quality of student designs, wondering whether these are appropriate to the needs of the 'needy'. The practices of the Rural Studio are not as ecologically sustainable as many wish; the social reforms it has supported fall short of justice, and the craft of its constructions is less than professional. Given its real capacities, the Rural Studio struggles against such standards because learning by doing engages its students and teachers with community members in complex endeavours often beyond their abilities. Does the Rural Studio really work?

This question usually addresses the who, what and why of the Rural Studio, but its location is more telling. It found a place – in US education, in the profession of architecture, and even on earth – that is profoundly peripheral. The choice by Sambo Mockbee and DK Ruth to establish this learning community in Hale County, was motivated by a desire to pursue opportunities unavailable on campus and in centres of architectural practice. The removal of the Rural Studio from both the university and the city affords its students and teachers great freedom – from supervision and regulation, and also from distraction. Its isolation allows an experiment where alternative practices are not only researched, but applied, and where belonging to a

Slippery Elm Field Little League Baseball Park, Newbern, Alabama, 2003
The baseball park was designed and built by Auburn University undergraduate architecture students Julie Hay, Jason Hunsucker, Patrick Nelson and Jermaine Washington. Instructor: Andrew Freear.

Seining net material used in the local catfish farming industry was formed to construct the backstop protecting spectators at Slippery Elm Field Little League Baseball Park.

Lucy and Anderson Harris House, Mason's Bend, Alabama, 2002
The house under construction, using recycled carpet tiles for exterior walls.

Shop and office for the Rural Heritage Foundation, Thomaston, Alabama, 2003
The units were designed and built by Auburn University undergraduate architecture students Kathryn Bryan, John David Caldwell, Emily McGlohn and Walker Renneker. Instructor: Andrew Freear.

community encourages students to reflect on what is central to a life of good practice – for a citizen as well as an architect.

In a way, its location was a defiant choice, identifying opportunity where most see only problems and pathology. The 'Black Belt' is physically beautiful, but by most social science measures it is failing. Hale County lost half its population from 1900 to 1980, while that of Alabama doubled, and that of the nation nearly tripled. In the 19th century growing cotton here made a few rich, but depended upon the exploitation of the land and its workers – first black slaves, but later white tenants as well, yeomen who moved from subsistence farming in the hills to cotton cropping on the prairies as the antebellum plantation system collapsed. The continuing globalisation of textile production forced the abandonment of the cotton economy in west Alabama and the migration of agricultural workers to cities and their factories.

Soil, climate and history marked this place with a difficult legacy, which well serves the studio's educational programme. Students study the vernacular patterns of the Black Belt, finding remnants of local homesteads among the pastures, woodlands and catfish

Perry Lake Park facilities, Perry County, Alabama, 2003
The park facilities were designed and built by Auburn University undergraduate architecture students Sarah Dunn, Matthew Foley, Brannen Park and Melissa Sullivan. Instructor: Andrew Freear.

farms of what is an increasingly industrialised landscape supplying a narrow range of resources for outside demand. Row crops and subsistence farms are rare, demonstrating how economic progress – in the forms of centralisation, the division of labour and distribution of resources – governs not only our work, but where and how we live.

The landscape offers a particularly stark lesson in its legible confrontation between that industrial order and the agrarian one that preceded it. This division has been a source of political and sectional conflict since the founding of the US, contributing directly to the American Civil War. While rural values lie at the foundation of regional identity in the South, national attitudes favouring self-reliant small landowners extend beyond any section. Arguments against centralisation and bigness, and support for social, political and physical patterns based on independent holdings – the family farm – have particular significance for the designed environment of the US. The continuing impact of agrarian thought on our land and building is evident both in Jefferson's ubiquitous national grid and Frank Lloyd Wright's Broadacre City proposal for a continental landscape of small homesteads.

As an architectural programme of the American South, the Rural Studio has been influenced both by traditional critiques of industrialism, and by more recent objections to the implications of market economics like those voiced by the Kentuckian Wendell Berry, who in calling for 'an authentic settlement and inhabitation of our country' argues that the industrial economy is fundamentally colonial, based

'on the assumption that it is permissible to ruin one place or culture for the sake of another'.[2] The Black Belt is filled with the kind of ruined places Berry refers to, and its fallen state provides the Rural Studio with the ground necessary to motivate and test an architecture of reform. Region, landscape, and political and architectural tradition all frame the ethos of the Rural Studio in a broadly agrarian context – less for its rural situation than for its commitment to helping local communities and people be native to their place.

In this commitment, the Rural Studio contradicts assumptions of both the university and the design professions, which reflect the primacy of industrial models in education and commerce today. While the profession of architecture is increasingly driven by contract and documentation structures necessary to manage relationships across the extended hierarchy of the building process, the Rural Studio relies on a flat organisation where designers do their own building. And where the academy is dominated by abstract research in the laboratory, the studio extends land grant university outreach to its limits through a unique service-learning model led by undergraduate fieldwork.

Antioch Baptist Church, Perry County, 2002
The church was designed and built by Auburn University undergraduate architecture students Jared Fulton, Marion McElroy, Gabriel Michaud and William Nauck. Instructor: Andrew Freear.

House for Music Man, Greensboro, Alabama, 2003
The house was designed and built by 32 Auburn University undergraduate architecture students. Instructor: Jay Sanders.

These contrasts with predominant methods suggest an implicit critique of orthodox professional and academic practice. Where the university and profession establish standing and expertise through methods that distinguish and distance their knowledge from the world, the Rural Studio tends to local projects, learning and applying the homely lessons of custom and experience. Students work in communities where skills are shared, expertise is won in doing, and standing achieved by word of mouth. This grounding of Rural Studio method in place not only allows, but demands, an examination of first principles, establishing an exemplary situation in which to begin making architecture. Building is framed as an elemental act, so that student constructions tend to a kind of fundamentalism: big roofs, sheds, basic shelters and simple foundations. Expressive opportunities are discovered and enrich every episode of building, as for once the process and materials of construction are completely familiar to the student. Limited means and skills encourage inventiveness and an opportunistic attitude towards constraint, emphasising the value of specificity and craft.

Simplicity of means, and dependence on local methods, support and goodwill encourage the intimacy with one's work that characterises agrarian life. Instead of encountering sites, clients and buildings as abstractions, students in Newbern grapple with all directly, and are most often humbled in the confrontation. Their situation encourages students to value loyalty and trust over contract; the dignity of working across the whole over the efficiency of dividing labour by task; human contact and community over anonymity and system; and reliance on local things rather than on the products of a factory or the expertise of the city.

The primary lessons taught by the Rural Studio are thus agrarian ones: that place matters, that imagining and making enjoy their fullest power only when intimately linked, that good work depends on the practice of responsibility that exists only when the worker feels a stake in, and affection for, the work.

A dictum ascribed to Thomas Jefferson, that 'design activity and political thought are indivisible', summarises a motivating idea of the Rural Studio. According to Sambo Mockbee: 'What we are trying to create is the citizen architect.' Living in the Black Belt, and in Newbern, makes the potentials and responsibilities of architecture and citizenship more plain – these are places to learn the meaning and value of good work.

In fostering that lesson, however, the Rural Studio only plants a seed. Students return to campus and the design studio, and graduate to pursue careers in cosmopolitan centres. Professional qualification requires three years of internship in established architectural practices, followed by licentiation through examination. These are experiences that enmesh young architects in procedures and habits unfamiliar in Newbern.

The first alumni of the Rural Studio are beginning to establish independent practices, only now walking the new land of their adult lives. Ten years on, their work will make plain whether the lessons of affection and place taught in Newbern are remembered in these practices. Only then will we know if the Rural Studio truly works. ∆

Notes
1 John Crowe Ransom, 'I'll take my stand', in Gail Trechsel and David Moos (eds), *Samuel Mockbee and the Rural Studio: Community Architecture*, Birmingham Museum of Art, 2003.
2 Wendell Berry, 'Sex, economy, freedom and community', in *Sex, Economy, Freedom and Community*, Pantheon Books (New York and San Francisco), 1994.

THE ARCHITECTURE ENSEMBLE

The full intent and scope of design is rarely iterated by information alone. Ultimately, it is a team that ensures the work is executed with skill and care. **Steve Johnson**, project architect for the acclaimed Weald & Downland Gridshell, illustrates how its construction generated an enthusiastic partnership of hands-on expertise that has since led to the establishment of a new visionary organisation.

The artefact store and timber-framing workshop at the Weald & Downland Open Air Museum at Singleton, West Sussex, is one of the world's first permanent timber gridshell buildings. Project consultants included quantity surveyors Boxall Sayer, architects Edward Cullinan Architects, and engineers Buro Happold. However, due to the sophisticated nature of the proposed timber gridshell structure, specialist knowledge of carpentry design was required from the outset, and following a series of competitive interviews the Green Oak Carpentry Company was appointed to work as part of the design team. This was a major breakthrough for the project, as carpenters' inbuilt technical and professional commitment to a project is nowadays rarely found when working with other construction materials and systems such as concrete, masonry and steel.

Lathwork of the Downland Gridshell showing the patented steel node clamps developed jointly by the team. Only timber can achieve the contortions required for the forming of a gridshell.

Left
The carpentry team completing the gridshell-forming process. While the process was monitored and guided using a computer, the bulk of the forming was done by eye, to an accuracy of 50 millimetres over 15 metres.

Middle
English western red cedar and polycarbonate cladding. All cladding had to be cut to size and shaped to follow the double curvature of the gridshell body.

Right
Engineer and carpenter survey the shell. Even at this late stage, adjustments to the position and shape of the gridshell were possible.

As the Downland Gridshell was 75 per cent funded by the Heritage Lottery Fund (HLF), its construction had to be executed through a traditional tender process. We were required to develop the designs to tender stage in order to commission a main contractor. This meant that the winning contractor, EA Chiverton, would be taken on only once almost all of the design and many of the main construction method decisions had been made. Fortunately, the structural engineers had already completed a succession of temporary gridshell projects on the continent, and possessed the wisdom to allow a certain flexibility in their construction method statements – as required by the HLF assessors – which enabled other of the construction professionals involved, including the scaffolding contractors, to add their thoughts and impressions to the potpourri of design information.

The construction of the building was a dynamic process in all respects. The entire gridshell structure was assembled as a flat mat at high level, and then lowered into position through the manipulation and extraction of the special telescoping scaffold system supporting the structure from underneath. The structure was assembled in the air and lowered into its final form through a controlled and monitored step-by-step process, as recommended by the main contractor.

The basis of the project's success was the creation of a system that allowed some of the makers to be drawn into the design team at an early stage. The process required a fluidity of thought, communication and execution that had to be improvised throughout the course of the project, and was very much reflected in the fundamental nature of the building's dominant material – wood. However, it was not all smooth sailing.

In the late 1990s, following decades of neglect and a growing dependence on imported timber to more than 85 per cent, the UK's timber culture had virtually disappeared as far as making use of British timber on UK construction sites was concerned. Forest-management techniques had shifted from long-term to short-term outlooks, with construction taking a back seat. Those few still able to produce construction timber dropped lines of communication.

During design and building stages of the Downland Gridshell, the project team was frustrated in that we were unable to fulfil our original intention to construct the building, as much as possible, from locally grown and processed timber. Although the timber was there, its management was not ideal for producing the extremely long lengths of straight-grained oak required to make and form the gridshell. In short, we discovered a wreck of a timber culture that we had not fully appreciated at the outset of the project. Research and development processes were carried out for both the technical capacities of the timber and for the computer form-finding packages required to design and form the shell. However, the greater unknown was whether the local system was up to providing us with the basic materials and processes. Our findings were that it wasn't at that time.

In the late 1990s, following decades of neglect and a growing dependence on imported timber to more than 85 per cent, the UK's timber culture had virtually disappeared as far as making use of British timber on UK construction sites was concerned. Forest-management techniques had shifted from long-term to short-term outlooks, with construction taking a back seat. Those few still able to produce construction timber dropped lines of communication. This meant that we ended up going to Normandy for our oak. And even the advanced timber-milling machine required for processing the long laths had to be loaned from a German manufacturing firm and temporarily located in Newcastle. The milling contract very nearly went to a firm in Lithuania. Throughout the course of the project, we were aware and observant of a hybrid timber gridshell project at the Woodland Enterprise Centre at Flimwell, East Sussex, where the design and construction team was experiencing parallel problems with procurement, albeit with sweet chestnut rather than oak.

As a result, once the Downland Gridshell was completed we formed a team to try to identify and address some of the challenges we had faced. We concluded that the bulk of our problems lay in a deep-seated lack of confidence and almost nonexistent communications links between timber producers, processors and the construction industry, and in 2003 this inspired us to form the Timberbuild Network, an amalgamation of the Weald & Downland and Flimwell teams, as well as others from woodland and timber-based organisations such as the Forestry Commission, Timber Research & Development Agency (TRADA), several southeast local authorities, and the University of Brighton. Financial support has come from the Southeast England Development Agency (SEEDA) and Wood for Good.

The broad aim of the network is to try to identify improvements and the eventual expansion of the forest culture in the Southeast, which is where most of Britain's woodland stands. The initial point of attack was to re-establish communications channels and get people talking again about the sustainable use of UK timber by the UK construction industry. To do this, the network must create opportunities for foresters and others trying to make a living from timber production. It will provide inspiration through the production of beautiful, innovative and sustainable timber architecture. With inspiration will come increased confidence in the market, and woodlands would flourish and prosper once again.

The first step is to establish an Internet-based network linked to the already successful Weald Woodnet (www.woodnet.org.uk), which was established a number of years ago by East Sussex County Council and based at Flimwell. Woodnet was set up to provide trade forums for foresters, processors and buyers making small-scale use of wood. The main aim was to increase woodland-based commerce within the Southeast. The Timberbuild Network will build on this by re-establishing links between woodland producers and the construction industry. Within our first year, we have produced the basis for an expandable operating system whereby consumers will be able to contact producers directly.

This required a great deal of research into the state of the timber industry and the capacity of the construction industry to take up local timber if offered. It will be crucial to create a demand-pull in order to build confidence within the timber production industry so that if it were to recommence investing in supplying construction timber, there would be a market to receive it. Ultimately, our goal is to develop a network of woodland-based one-stop-shops across the Southeast, where people will be able to visit a local centre to purchase local timber goods, be inspired through exhibitions, research local timber designers, and go for walks and rides through the beautiful woodlands. The centres will be based around state-of-the-art examples of timber architecture that would, in themselves, inspire. In order to achieve this vision, we have decided to start the ball rolling by establishing a first precedent at the Woodland Enterprise Centre at Flimwell.

The completed building set amongst its source material. Even in their standing state, trees clearly demonstrate their potential for forming curved space.

Support scaffolding and the gridmat midway through the forming process, showing the telescoping scaffold system in action.

In 1994, we received funding from the Southeast-based funding body Leader+ for a six-month project called the Timberbuild Workshop. This project has entailed the production of well-detailed design information and physical prototyping for an exemplar workshop building to be constructed as a second phase of development at the Flimwell centre. When complete, it will provide 12 high-specification industrial units intended for start-up businesses making use of wood as a primary resource. The initial design phase of the project has been completed, and the proposals submitted for planning approval. A second part of the project calls for the writing and publication of the *Timberbuild Workshop Workbook*, which will serve as a written template for sustainable industrial shed buildings to be constructed using locally produced timber. If the workshops are approved, the design development and construction will be carried out by a team represented by the original Timberbuild Network steering-group members. As a first model, this is where the real test begins: we are proposing that the group operates as a single design and construction body able to assist clients with the procurement of sustainable timber architecture preferably making use of local timber.

The Timberbuild Network team will be able to provide clients with all of the necessary construction services, from nontraditional services such as development assistance, insurance advice and building control guidance, to academic assessment and monitoring services such as life-cycle analysis and postoccupancy evaluations. Likewise, the network can provide any combination of these services. Members will be autonomous companies and institutions that will have the facility to come together as required to carry out specific projects. We will therefore be able to offer a complete and economic procurement system that will cut out much of the contentiousness of traditional systems and offer much greater cost certainty. All this will be made possible through the coming online of new partnering contracts. We will be able to better certify the true sustainability of a project by tracking all of the materials, systems and components that go into a building. Direct

> The Timberbuild Network scenario demonstrates how it should be possible to close the gap between the design and making processes within the construction industry. We can also demonstrate that, by concentrating on a single construction material, even materials production can be brought directly into the frame of the construction process.

relationships between the various represented construction bodies, including materials producers, will mean that projects are carried out quickly. And importantly, the group's working methods will greatly reduce the risk of potential costly errors.

The Timberbuild Network scenario demonstrates how it should be possible to close the gap between the design and making processes within the construction industry. We can also demonstrate that, by concentrating on a single construction material, even materials production can be brought directly into the frame of the construction process. This will help achieve the verifiable sustainability of a project that is now more frequently required as an integral part of the construction and management process. We hope that through this form of practice we will be able to play a small part in the renaissance of the UK's woodland culture. ∆

FABRICATION RESEARCH

Lloyd's Building expressed sockets in finished beam grid.

The engineer **John Thornton**, formerly of Arup, reflects upon a career that has helped shape the architecture of leading design practices such as the Renzo Piano Building Workshop, Hopkins, and Richard Rogers Partnership. Looking back almost a quarter of a century to a time that preceded digital manufacturing techniques, this frank account of design development for components of the Lloyd's Building reconsiders the notion of fabrication research as an embedded aspect of practice and reminds us of its value as a stimulant for creativity.

A prototype one-piece GRP form for the beam grid of the Lloyd's Building. It was designed to be withdrawn upwards to avoid having the downward tapered beam profile of a conventional waffle floor.

I have always been more interested in research as a tool to develop a particular design than in 'abstract' research, so perhaps a better title would be 'research *through* fabrication'.

Much of what architects and engineers design is straightforward and uses proven components, materials and techniques. Any research involved, whether by a university, institute or company, will have been previously absorbed into products, codes and our design vocabulary. There might be a project mock-up, but this will be as a final check rather than for primary development. Even on those projects where we do explore something new it can be difficult to carry out physical research, as opposed to a desk study, because it takes time and money, even though the cost might be a small part of the project cost and should anyway be set against the reduction in risk and savings that arise from the research. Inevitably, without the reassurance of research, the design must be more cautious. For the relatively few projects where fabrication research can be justified, it is certainly necessary to have a client who is genuinely interested in the design and who supports the research.

The practical benefits of increasing our knowledge, whether from abstract research or as the result of work on some aspect of a particular project, are obvious. I am more interested in the benefits the process of project-based fabrication research brings to both the project and ourselves, if we approach it in the right spirit.

In my view, the best designers know how things work, how they are made, how materials behave and their qualities. They produce buildings of elegance and grace where the concept, the materials and the details are in harmony. They are not necessarily great architecture; they can be simple vernacular buildings built by people who truly understood their materials, the location and how the building would be used. In contrast, there are buildings that appeal mainly to the intellect, while lacking the sensual qualities that an appreciation of material and workmanship can bring, and I believe this means that in time they will just be seen as interesting or spectacular. Of course, there are plenty of buildings with none of these qualities, and even in the best work there are sometimes parts that are not successful or, as we do not always recognise, were extremely difficult to make.

If we work with the surface image without understanding the underlying rationale, the results can look wrong. Sometimes they are only subtly wrong, but this can still leave us with the vague feeling that something is not quite right – even if we cannot say exactly what it is. We are subconsciously aware of how things should be, an awareness acquired over the years.

When I first began to work as an engineer I accepted that architects, with their trained visual sense, knew best how something should look. But after seeing examples of contrived structures, badly sized members, fussy details and inappropriate materials I now think that engineers, who broadly understand how things work, are sometimes better placed to judge. A structural engineer develops the principles of a solution, analyses the forces and stresses, sizes the members and calculates the details. Practice at this develops an intuitive knowledge of how materials are used and which structures work 'easily'. A degree of understanding can be reached by study; a deeper understanding from observation. But real understanding can only be developed through the experience of doing the calculations. Even so, we are often less confident about the details

A prototype folding steel box form for the Lloyd's Building. Turning the screw in the centre of the box drew in the middle of the sides. This reduced the diagonal allowing the box to be withdrawn upwards.

A set of the steel and plywood components used in the elemental formwork system for the Lloyd's floors.

A section of assembled soffit forms showing the reinforcement support cradles for the Lloyd's floors. The raised strips at the intersections are the steel channels which contain the gaskets for the node/beam joints.

of fabrication, although we can learn from the process of developing the shop drawings with the fabricators. This distance from the 'craft', whether of structure or fabrication, is true of other parts of the design, and for architects is accentuated by the roles of the other design consultants.

Few designers actually make things. Perhaps they do not have the opportunity, or lack the skills. Perhaps there is a cultural problem where making things in the broadest sense is not valued, and physically making less so. While preparing a talk recently I found that many of my colleagues had become engineers because they were good at maths or had a relative in the industry, not because they wanted to make things. Similarly, I know architects who became architects because they were good at art.

I do not advocate that we should all start making things. Design covers a wide area and there is room for many skills. I just think that making is very satisfying and improves our use of materials in the sense that one learns what it is to transform 'stuff' into 'things'. I recently built my new ideal workbench out of big sections of rock-hard maple. I knew that the increased size of components and the hardness of the wood, compared with my usual projects, required a different approach and more work. But it was only when I had started that I understood the true extent. If you have experienced the difficulties in working in one material you will appreciate what it is to work in another. You might be unfamiliar with technical detail, but many of the problems are similar and you learn to respect the physical skills involved. If designers had to physically work on site they would appreciate the difficulty of some of the things they expect others to do.

Fabrication research can position us, if we wish, in the making process, free from the contractual constraints and adversarial attitudes that often prevail. Almost invariably we are working with others whose skills we lack or have only to a limited degree. This is a chance to draw on their experience and learn not just technical detail, but the difficulty in achieving what we have drawn and the effect of small changes on how something is made. We sometimes see possibilities that we had not imagined. We joke about solutions looking for problems; however, new ideas often come from making new connections, and the wider our exposure to sources the bigger the data bank to draw upon. What we learn while researching one problem can help us solve another.

We can learn a lot through working with people outside our own field, and can also discover that they approach problems differently from us, just as architects and engineers think differently. But it is also well to be aware of the professional divide that leads people to feel it is not their place to make suggestions.

I recall being told by one foundry that its clients generally specified exactly what they wanted; there was no opportunity for change and suggestions were not welcome. It took them a while to understand that I wanted the design to truly reflect the process and that they should suggest how it could be developed for this to be achieved, and not just in minor details.

Almost every design involves a step, large or small, into the unknown. If this were not the case there would be little need for architects and engineers. However, the word 'innovation' is used too often. It is said that innovation is the art of concealing one's sources, yet in my experience it is often simply that the innovator was unaware that the idea was not new. Innovation is often just a change of context or combination. Nevertheless, whenever you do something new you must be sure it will work before starting construction. Usually this is done on paper, drawing on reference papers, analysis, analogy and experience. If you can test the design before committing it to the contractual process, you can afford to be more ambitious, although you must still be confident since there is rarely enough time for major rework to an idea.

We explore using drawings and models, but models only take you so far, the scale is usually too small, and the materials are docile. When making things yourself, you are free to experiment with the real thing. You might lose some time and waste some materials, but you learn from the 'failures' perhaps more than from the successes because when it goes wrong, you find out why, yet when it goes right, you never really know how close you were to failing. Most importantly, you get a better result.

For some design ideas there is no point in doing more than basic calculations; there might be too many variables, maybe the acceptance criteria would be too hard to define, or perhaps the cost of the time of analysis would not be justified. It would often be easier and more convincing to put the idea to empirical test and use this to refine the design to an otherwise impractical degree. Unfortunately, the usual abstract, compartmentalised design process does not often allow this. However, when we can do fabrication research we get close to the exciting immediate interaction between design and making. The craftspeople, too, enjoy the involvement, in comparison with just making what has been specified

I have been involved in much fabrication research and think my most useful experience was in the development of the floor system for the Lloyd's Building. The floor slab itself is supported by pedestals on a 1.8-metre grid of beams, thus creating a free zone between slab and beams for the distribution of services. It took a lot of development to arrive at this solution. There were two connected strands to the work. The first was the design of a grid system; that is, the arrangement of the beam grid, the depths of the beams, the prestressing zones and so on. But you have to be sure you can build what you have designed, without this being too difficult, and understand how the construction method might influence the design. This was the second strand. It was not immediately obvious how to achieve the required quality of concrete finish, consistently, and at times the engineering and architectural development of the grid was a response to our thinking on the formwork system.

We needed direct experience to test our ideas, and to be sure that the grid could be made to the standard required, before we appointed a contractor. This would have the incidental advantage of reassuring the bidders by showing how it could be done.

We worked on three distinctly different formwork systems and developed them to the point where we built three full-sized areas of the floor to test them. The first results were not good enough, but we learned an enormous amount, particularly about the design of the formwork joints that would give the quality of finish required, and built a second set incorporating refinements. When we went to tender we could demonstrate three ways in which the floor could be built. The bidders had the option of accepting one of these or, if they wished to suggest another way, they had to submit their own mock-up.

This approach was essential to the success of the project because the whole design would have been in jeopardy if the floor bids had been too high. I also learned an enormous amount about the design of high-quality formwork and how this affects the design of the concrete. This was an interesting process, though still constrained by the fact that the formwork systems were made by three different companies, each was procured through a conventional process, and then the modified version procured again.

By contrast, the development of the procedure for making the ferrocement leaves for the Menil Gallery was more immediate and interactive as the specialist contractor had been appointed early in the process. This is perhaps the nearest we, as consultants, can get to the ideal situation, where you can design and test as an ongoing process.

I have written about the lack of connection between design and the experience of making; however, there is also the lack of connection in time. In principle, we complete a design package then, often a lot later, shop drawings are produced and construction follows. The key decisions will have been made long before the construction begins. But design is often not a clearly defined problem; there are many variables and we may have to go through a number of ideas before we hit on the 'best' solution. We are probably not aware of all the inputs, or their importance, at the beginning; rather they come to light as we work and so we spiral down through the detail and then go back and feed what we have learned into the earlier work. We bring this to a conclusion to meet deadlines, though sometimes fail to notice the critical detail that becomes disproportionately difficult or expensive to resolve late in the process. It is what happens when you do something new – and until you have been through the whole process, there is always something to be learned.

Fabrication research can force us down to the fine detail at a time before the design is frozen and, most critically, when the team is still concentrating on this area and has not dispersed on to other tasks. It is a sort of by-product of the research itself.

This point was brought home to me when we made the Lloyd's floor prototype. The steel in reinforced concrete must be maintained at the correct distance from the surface, which is usually done using plastic or concrete spacers. The plastic spacers are often clearly visible on the surface, and even concrete spacers using the same mix as the structural concrete can be seen. Reinforcement spacers are low down the hierarchy of detail, and I suspect that many architects are unaware of the problem unless they have worked with high-quality concrete, while for the engineer it is simply a specification item with a technical function. The options are limited if you do not deal with this issue at the design stage.

As we prepared for the prototype, we turned our attention to this problem and developed a plastic cradle that incorporated a screw-in socket so that it could be bolted to the soffit form and support the reinforcement cage. This was very successful: the cradle was installed before the reinforcement was placed and could not be overlooked, it guaranteed precise location of the steel, could not be dislodged, the bolt socket was revealed as an expressed detail in precise locations, and the socket could be used later as a partition head locator. The technical performance of the cradles was excellent; they simplified construction, had a secondary function in the later use of the building, and added visual interest to the soffit. So, although the prime purpose of the prototype was to develop the formwork, the process helped convert a problem into an advantage.

A characteristic feature of Lloyd's is the visual dominance of the details of the engineering. These were developed in accordance with the architectural 'rules', but are also entirely logical, technically. However, there is a contradiction between the appearance and the fact that Lloyd's was handcrafted. It is a pre-CAD/CAM building. Computers were used in the engineering analysis, but only key floor layouts were produced with CAD. The fabricators, as far as I am aware, did not use computers.

Advances in analysis, visualisation and manufacturing techniques, and the electronic links between them, now allow us to construct forms, details and variations that would have been impossibly expensive a few years ago. Understanding how things are made is transposed into understanding the capabilities of computing systems and manufacturing processes. The danger is that computer power triumphs over design and takes away the need to simplify, rationalise and understand the material. Structural engineers have been concerned for some time that reliance on computers by young engineers can impede the development of their understanding of some aspects of structural behaviour. Since Lloyd's, there have been huge changes in how we design, but we must still know how structures and materials behave and are formed.

As engineers and architects we are lucky to be able to work on a range of problems in different areas. But I envy those who are able to have an idea and then test it themselves. Fabrication research brings us close to this, and gives us a chance to get involved in making. It both improves the design and develops our skills. ∆

CONCEPT PLANNING
PROCESS REALISATION

THE METHODOLOGIES OF ARCHITECTURE AND FILM

Video animation and motion graphics are challenging architectural ideas and practices in relation to people, objects, movement and time. **Nic Clear** reveals how it's done.

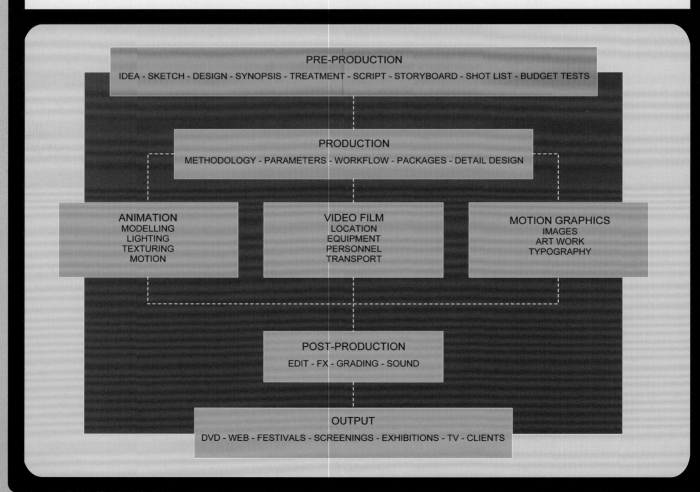

PRE-PRODUCTION
IDEA - SKETCH - DESIGN - SYNOPSIS - TREATMENT - SCRIPT - STORYBOARD - SHOT LIST - BUDGET TESTS

PRODUCTION
METHODOLOGY - PARAMETERS - WORKFLOW - PACKAGES - DETAIL DESIGN

ANIMATION
MODELLING
LIGHTING
TEXTURING
MOTION

VIDEO FILM
LOCATION
EQUIPMENT
PERSONNEL
TRANSPORT

MOTION GRAPHICS
IMAGES
ART WORK
TYPOGRAPHY

POST-PRODUCTION
EDIT - FX - GRADING - SOUND

OUTPUT
DVD - WEB - FESTIVALS - SCREENINGS - EXHIBITIONS - TV - CLIENTS

OUTLINE

The purpose of this piece is to set out at a very basic level the steps by which film and video can be integrated into the design process. I should make it clear that my main interest is in discussing these techniques within the context of academic and speculative work rather than as part of a commercial project. The reasons for this are simple. Firstly, it is the context within which I am trying to develop these ideas as part of a postgraduate unit at the Bartlett School of Architecture and within my own practice as an architect who makes films. Secondly, I am somewhat sceptical about the use of such conceptual methodologies within commercial architecture as they are more often than not merely employed as a smokescreen for more basic and economically driven motivations. Since I stopped working as a commercial architect in 2002, I have little interest in the machinations and perpetuation of the Corporate Architectural Complex, and care not whether any of these ideas are of use to commercial practices; although, judging by the success of many of my students who have left college and have taken these skills into those commercial areas, they obviously are.

METHODOLOGY

The decision to use film as part of the design process should be based upon two factors: i) because it is something that the designer is genuinely interested in, and ii) because it is seen to be appropriate. It is not my intention to be evangelical about using film in the design process – it's not going to change everything, well not yet anyway, and for a lot of designers it will make no sense at all, but for others it will prove an extremely productive and useful tool.

My own interest in film and video came out of an ongoing critique of standard forms of architectural production coupled with a love of film itself. The rise of digital technologies that allow access to a medium that would previously have been extremely expensive and difficult to utilise has obviously played a significant role in turning a fantasy into a reality.

My own problem with traditional forms of architectural representation, particularly orthographic projections, is what they leave out – namely architecture as something that is experiential, performed and immersive. Ideas of duration and movement can never be adequately expressed in a conventional architectural design process nor represented in the traditional forms of architectural notation. By using time-based media these ideas can be addressed, although the experience of using film and animation is still a long way from emulating actual architectural space even in its most advanced filmic and virtual forms.

I wish to make it clear that my interest in film as part of architectural production is not confined to its use as a tool of representation, but extends to the use of the techniques of film and video production as part of the process of inception, generation, development and illustration of architectural ideas – and that doesn't just mean the design of buildings but also of spatial events and spatial practices. The function of film considered solely in terms of the ubiquitous fly-through animation,

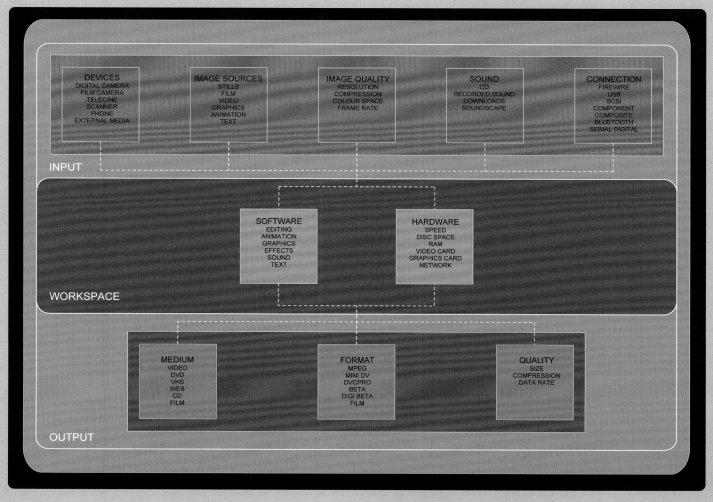

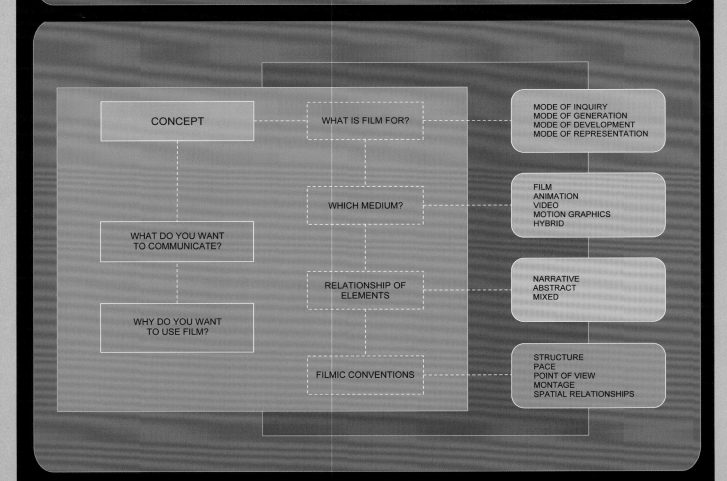

PLANNING

PARAMETERS
WHAT IS AVAILABLE?

AUDIT
WHAT DO YOU HAVE?
WHAT DO YOU NEED?

TECHNOLOGY — SOFTWARE / HARDWARE

SKILLS — SKILLS YOU HAVE / SKILLS TO BE ACQUIRED / SKILLS TO BE BOUGHT IN

TIME — INTERNAL DEADLINES / EXTERNAL DEADLINES / TIME OF OTHERS

SPACE — WORK / STUDIO / LOCATIONS

EQUIPMENT — LIGHTING / CAMERA / AUDIO / ART DEPARTMENT

PERSONNEL — ACTORS / CREW / PRODUCTION STAFF

BUDGET — COST OF EQUIPMENT / COST OF TIME / COST OF PERSONNEL / RUNNING COSTS

CONCEPT

WHAT DO YOU WANT
TO COMMUNICATE?

WHY DO YOU WANT
TO USE FILM?

WHAT IS FILM FOR? — MODE OF INQUIRY / MODE OF GENERATION / MODE OF DEVELOPMENT / MODE OF REPRESENTATION

WHICH MEDIUM? — FILM / ANIMATION / VIDEO / MOTION GRAPHICS / HYBRID

RELATIONSHIP OF ELEMENTS — NARRATIVE / ABSTRACT / MIXED

FILMIC CONVENTIONS — STRUCTURE / PACE / POINT OF VIEW / MONTAGE / SPATIAL RELATIONSHIPS

THEMES
STRATEGIES
ANALYSES

INQUIRY

GENERATION

MODES

DEVELOPMENT

COMMUNICATION

FORMAL
NARRATIVE
RANDOM

REFINE
TEST
COMBINE

IDEA
PROCESS
CONTENT

TIME SPACE MOVEMENT TECHNOLOGY SITE PROGRAMME
PRECEDENT BRIEF COLLAGE PRACTICE OCCUPATION
GENERATIVE ALGORITHM RANDOM SCRIPTING GENDER
VISION MATERIAL COMPOSITION POLITICAL SEXUAL PLAN
STRUCTURAL BUILDING RHIZOME OBJECT TEXTURE LIGHT
UNCANNY PLACE DESIRE PERSPECTIVE EXPERIENTIAL
VIRTUAL NANO CONVERSATION CONSUMPTION ECONOMIC
POWER KNOWLEDGE MONTAGE AUTHENTICITY SECTION
AESTHETIC PHENOMENOLOGICAL ACTUAL HEURISTIC
SOUND GEOMETRY ZOOM TRANSLATION SEX DETAIL
SURFACE POINT SOLID MODEL METHOD DISTANCE CITY
BOUNDARY SHAPE ELEMENT CHANCE EDUCATION DREAM
AVATAR PORN MORPH TRANSGRESSION SIMULACRA HOPE
SEMANTICS TECHNIQUE BIFURCATION ALIENATION
MAPPING SYNTAX METHODOLOGY IMMERSION
RHYTHMANALYSES IMMANENCE EPISTEMOLOGY
VOYEURISM TRANSPARENCY TECTONICS HEURISTIC
REFLEXIVE ACCOMMODATION SURVEY SCHEDULE
PROJECTION TERRITORY FICTION TRANSLATION QUANTUM
SCOPIC PROJECTION AURAL DURATION DECONSTRUCTION
LIMINAL URBAN ENVIRONMENTAL ECOLOGICAL SEMANTIC
DIACHRONIC EXISTENTIAL LIQUID UNITARY IDEOLOGY
COMPOSITION ZOOM FOLD FINITE ARCHITECTURAL

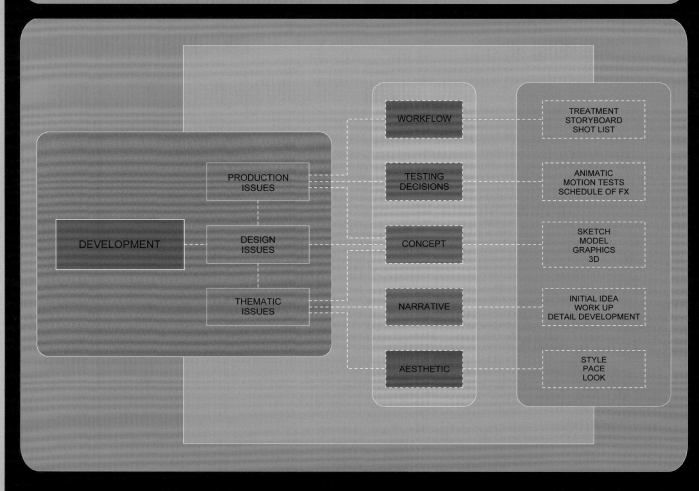

as it often is, is both lazy and reductive. I also wish to make it clear that the techniques I discuss use quite conventional, albeit contemporary ideas of a time line within the context of film and video rather than addressing more interactive technologies. For me the idea of film is to construct something specific that communicates particular values and concepts, and while I find many of the ideas and techniques of interactive media interesting I do not generally choose to use them in my own work.

PEDAGOGY

As part of a teaching regime, the use of film and video to put a project together is a good way for many students to test and develop the ideas of integration needed to deal with the complex processes of architectural production. Making film should involve a great deal of forward planning and complex thinking with regard to how a number of different elements have to be sequenced together. It links writing, designing, scheduling and producing often within a collective environment to create a project. In many ways working with film and video is far more analogous to the wider area of architectural work than simply producing drawings and models because of the high levels of integration of different skills and different types of information it demands.

In most cases the use of film and video doesn't represent an entirely new methodology; what it does for many students is focus and develop their existing skills. Through working with film, students learn how to develop a project by synthesising a number of different components into a single piece that articulates complex spatial ideas – and that seems incredibly beneficial. The use of film and video does, however, require the development of a very particular skillset, and most of the students I teach will have to engage with everything from operating a camera, 3-D modelling and animation, editing and motion graphics to special effects, sound design and authoring DVDs. In addition to this students still have to develop and refine their own particular architectural design skills and strategic interests.

Students who start working with animation and, more particularly, editing programs – and this doesn't just mean throwing a few clips on a time line and putting some cross-dissolves in between them – learn to look at their work in a completely new way. The subtleties and complexities of fine-tuning an edit, an animation or an effects sequence develop levels of visual acuity, attentiveness and consideration of detail that are beneficial in more traditional areas of design. My experience has suggested that students who work with time-based media also develop high levels of confidence when it comes to making decisions as the necessity to continually rework their film with respect to visual, temporal and often audio considerations demands it. Students will often be making changes that are barely perceptible – adjusting a clip by a few frames, for example – yet somehow significant. While this may not have any direct relevance to how to plan a building, the development of abstract methods of thinking and skills in composition and organisation does have directly beneficial consequences no matter what kind of designer the student goes on to become.

PRACTICE

As part of General Lighting and Power and also under my own name I have been involved in a whole range of different film and video projects, from pop promos to corporate video and from TV graphics to short films, and I have always realised that many of

The subtleties and complexities of fine-tuning an edit, an animation or an effects sequence develop levels of visual acuity, attentiveness and consideration of detail that are beneficial in more traditional areas of design. My experience has suggested that students who work with time-based media also develop high levels of confidence when it comes to making decisions as the necessity to continually rework their film with respect to visual, temporal and of ten audio considerations demands it.

the skills I learnt as an architect were wholly applicable to film projects. Indeed the methodology of running an architectural project transferred almost seamlessly with only basic adjustments needed.

My current focus on film and writing projects rather than architecture is testament to the fact that not only do I feel that commercial architecture has increasingly become more bureaucratic and less creative, but also the immediacy that I enjoy in small film projects and the ability to create more narrative and emotive pieces are considerably more satisfying. However, within the role of teaching I think that combining both activities allows a forum where I can be critical of conventional architectural practices while at the same time looking at the greater ability of film to inform architecture.

The function of the diagrams shown here is to emphasise the relationship between the methodologies of architectural and filmic production. Largely based on a model of workflow taken from the *Architect's Job Book*, the diagrams are in no way meant to be exhaustive but hopefully are instructive. △D

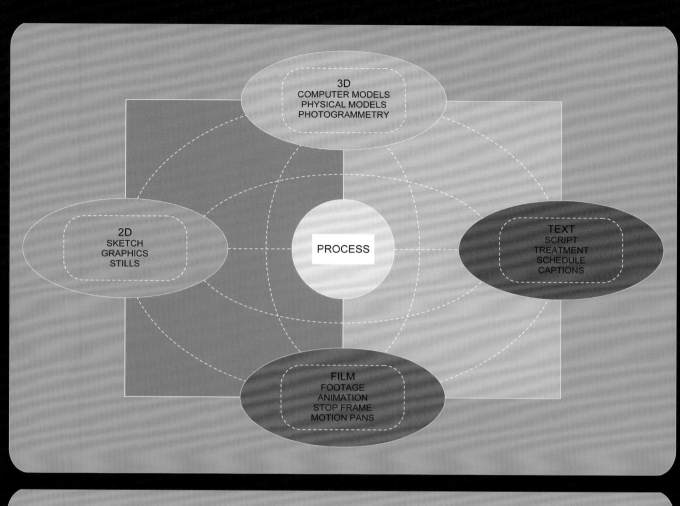

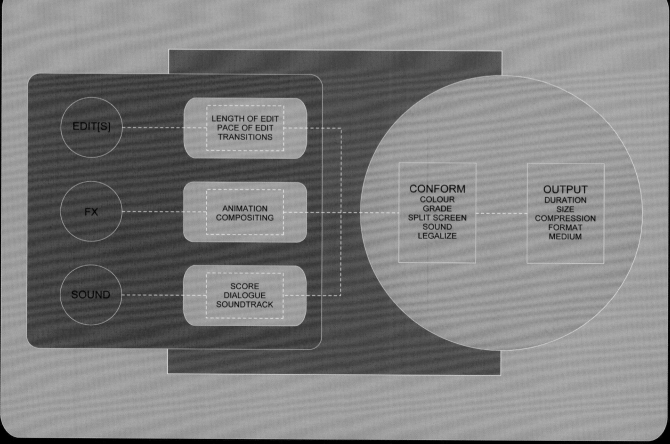

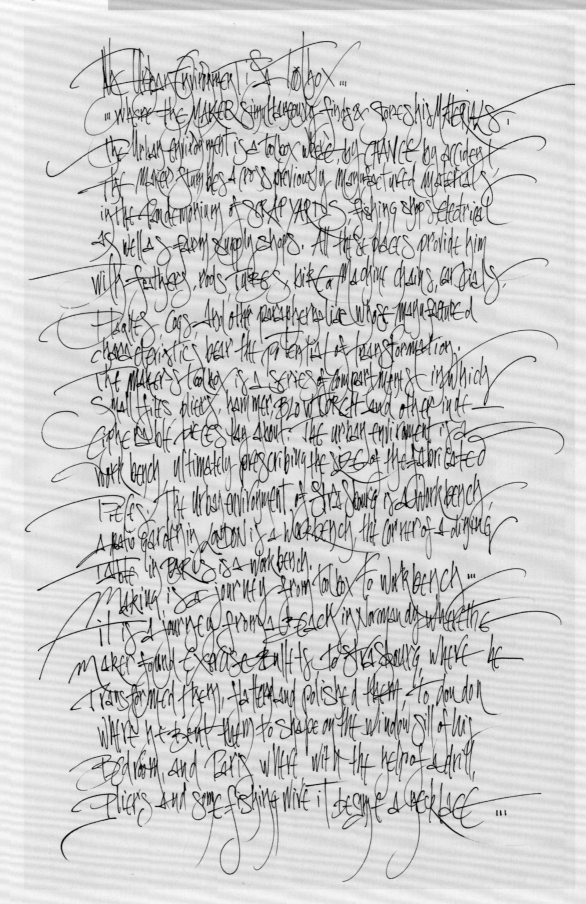

The Urban Environment is a Toolbox...

..."Where the MAKER simultaneously finds & stores his Materials."

The urban environment is a toolbox where, by CHANCE by accident the maker stumbles across previously manufactured materials in the pandemonium of SCRAP YARDS, fishing shops electrical as well as army supply shops. All these places provide him with feathers, rods, tubes, bike & machine chains, car dials, plates, cogs, and other paraphernalia whose manufactured characteristics bear the potential of transformation. The MAKER's toolbox is a series of compartments in which small files, pliers, hammer, BLOWTORCH and other indecipherable off-pieces lay about. The urban environment is a workbench, ultimately prescribing the size of the fabricated pieces. The urban environment of Strasbourg is a workbench, a patio garden in London is a workbench, the corner of a dining table in PARIS is a workbench.

Making is a journey from toolbox to workbench...

...it is a journey from a beach in Normandy where the maker found exercise balls to Strasbourg where he transformed them, flattened and polished them, to London where he beat them to shape on the window sill of his bedroom, and Paris where with the help of a drill, pliers and some fishing wire it became a necklace...

Right
A text on making – words
by Caroline Rabourdin,
calligraphy by Louis Lafargue.

PHIL AYRES

Phil Ayres is a member of sixteen*(makers) and a lecturer at the Bartlett School of Architecture where he tutors Unit 14 with Professor Stephen Gage and Usman Haque. He is also the school's director of computing and runs the CADCAM laboratory. His roles bridge the realms of representation, fabrication and interaction, and feed into his interest in developing exploratory design techniques that are often computer mediated, but always lead to physical output.

PHILIP BEESLEY

Philip Beesley is a practising architect and sculptor at the University of Waterloo where he codirects the Integrated Centre for Visualization, Design and Manufacturing (ICVDM), a high-performance computing and rapid-prototyping centre. He is a specialist in digital fabrication and hybrid architectural envelopes. His work has been recognised by the Prix de Rome for Architecture (Canada), the Governor-General's Award for Architecture, and the Daniel Langlois Foundation for Art and Technology. His practice includes public buildings and interdisciplinary design research. Built projects include the Niagara Credit Union (OAA Award of Excellence 2004), the Gallery of Korean Art for the Royal Ontario Museum, and numerous gallery and stage installations.

MARK BURRY

Mark Burry is professor of innovation (spatial information architecture) at RMIT, and directs the transdisciplinary design studio SIAL. He has published internationally on two main themes: the life and work of the architect Antonio Gaudí in Barcelona, and putting theory into practice with regard to challenging architecture. He has also published widely on broader issues of design, construction and the use of computers in design theory and practice. As consultant architect to the Sagrada Família Church, Mark Burry has been a key member within the small team untangling the mysteries of Gaudí's compositional strategies since 1979. In 2004 he was given the title 'Il.lustrissim Senyor' by the Catalan Royal Academy of the Arts in recognition of his contribution to Catalan architecture and scholarship

NICK CALLICOTT

A former lecturer in architecture at the Bartlett, and author of Computer aided Manufacturing in Architecture – The Pursuit of Novelty, Nick Callicott has taken his extensive experience as a designer and maker to begin a new career within industrial production. Born in Devon, he is now working and living in Wienerode, Germany, where he and his partner Kris Ehlert are fitting out an established firm with new premises and methodologies. By repositioning themselves as designers located within the realm of production, their work is focused at the scale of building production and innovative engineering solutions.

SARAH CHAPLIN

Sarah Chaplin is a qualified architect registered in the UK, where she is head of the School of Architecture and Landscape at Kingston University, London. She is also a director of the design consultancy evolver. She is co-author of Visual Culture: An Introduction (MUP, 1997) which has been translated into Spanish, Japanese and Korean. She also co-edited Consuming Architecture (Wiley-Academy, 1998), and has published chapters and articles in a number of international journals and edited anthologies on digital architecture, cyberfeminism, Japanese spatiality and contemporary urban environments. She has lectured regularly across the UK and overseas, and is chair of the judging panel for the RIBA President's Medals, awarded each year to the best student dissertation. She is a panel member for Architecture and the Built Environment for RAE2008, and is an external examiner at Oxford Brookes University and at the Bartlett.

NAT CHARD

Nat Chard is a professor of architecture at the Royal Danish Academy of Fine Art School of Architecture in Copenhagen, and leader of its research institute for design and visual communication. Since running highly successful units at London's Bartlett and at Metropolitan University in the 1990s, his work has explored the ways in which architecture might take its meaning as much from the present moment as from prescription. He studies this by proposing new architectures and also by taking possession of the existing city. He is currently working on a research project by design entitled 'Drawing indeterminate architecture, indeterminate drawings of architecture', for which he makes bespoke speculative machines.

NIC CLEAR

Nic Clear is a registered architect and teaches at the Bartlett School of Architecture where he runs Unit 15, a postgraduate design unit that specialises in the use of video, animation and motion graphics in development and representation of spatial and architectural ideas and practices. A founding director of the now defunct General Lighting and Power, whose work covered everything from pop promos to architecture and from advertising campaigns to art installations, he now divides his time between writing fiction and making drawings and films.

DAVID DUNSTER

David Dunster is Roscoe professor of architecture at Liverpool University. Amongst an extensive body of international works on architectural criticism, history and theory, are his publications Key Buildings of the 20th Century (Vols 1 and 2, 1985 and 1990) and Architecture and the Sites of History (1995), co-edited with Iain Borden (both for the Architectectural Press). He continues to research the history of 19th- and 20th-century urban planning in Europe and America, with particular reference to Chicago. His article on Pichler marks a return to another passion, that of architecture's fascination with death.

JOHN FORNEY

John Forney is a native of Birmingham, Alabama, where he is an architect. He is a graduate of Dartmouth College, and received his MArch from Princeton University. He practised with Venturi, Scott Brown and Associates in Philadelphia before teaching in the School of Architecture of the University of Arkansas. He was the Paul Rudolph visiting professor at Auburn University's School of Architecture, later joining its Rural Studio outreach programme faculty from 2002 to 2004.

JONATHAN HILL

An architect and architectural historian, Professor Jonathan Hill is director of the MPhil/PhD by architectural design at the Bartlett School of Architecture, University College London. He is the author of The Illegal Architect (1998), Actions of Architecture: Architects and Creative Users (2003) and Immaterial Architecture: Hunting the Shadow (2005). Jonathan is the editor of Occupying Architecture (1998), Architecture – the Subject is Matter (2001) and the 'Opposites Attract: Research by Design' issue of The Journal of Architecture (2003). Galleries where he has had solo exhibitions include the Haus der Architektur in Graz, and Architektur-Galerie am Weissenhof in Stuttgart.

STEVE JOHNSON

Steve Johnson was born in Minneapolis, Minnesota, and trained in architecture at Kansas State University where a small battle was being waged between professors of 'high design' from the East Coast and behaviouralists/environmentalists from the West Coast. This brought about a typical Midwestern storm where two system fronts often collide. A permanent move to London in 1985 resulted in a two-year postdiploma course at the Architectural Association and employment within a succession of London firms including Paskin, Kyriakides, and Sands, Gus Alexander Architects, Lifschutz Davidson, and Edward Cullinan Architects where he served as project architect on the Downland Gridshell. In 2002, he established his own firm, the Architecture Ensemble, which focuses on the advanced use of sustainably produced timber in architecture.

CHRIS LEUNG

Chris Leung's research interests lie in the design, analysis and making of responsive systems in architecture. He has followed these interests in tandem with a professional career in architectural practice. Of particular emphasis in his work are the use of computers, the embedding of intelligence in the construction fabric of buildings and their subsequent monitoring. Chris divides his time between working for YRM Ltd and the Kielder residency programme with sixteen*(makers).

RON PACKMAN

Engineer Ron Packman was born in Deptford, London. On graduating from Imperial College, he started a development company specialising in interesting refurbishment projects. After two years he joined MMP as a consultant on a number of UN and FAO projects in developing countries. He then established the consultancy Bryan Packman Marcel, and later Packman Lucas, which now specialises in interesting and diverse areas of building structures. He taught at the RCA from 1994 to 2000 where he met Thomas Heatherwick, with whom he has continued to work on such projects as Harvey Nicholls, the Buddhist temple for Kagoshima, Japan, Rolling Bridge at Paddington and the B of the Bang. Their close collaboration led to the formation of a branch of his consultancy within Thomas' studio.

MARK PRIZEMAN

Mark Prizeman was born and raised in central London in a family of architects. He now teaches Diploma Unit 8 at the Architectural Association, which advocates studying the 'means of production' as the basis of design. He formerly ran the Tent project in the first year, a programme that by coincidence used the fields around Hooke Park as test sites. A strong believer in 'designing by making' and 'learning by intuition', he ran a workshop for 10 years after the demise of NATO making architectural artefacts and repairing redundant machines. He is now in solo architectural practice concentrating on the domestic and shops.

BOB SHEIL

Made in Dublin, Bob Sheil is an architect and senior lecturer at the Bartlett School of Architecture, UCL. He has worked as a designer and maker in architectural practice, furniture and exhibition design, light engineering fabrication, information management and education. Following 10 years in practice, his teaching career began in the Bartlett workshop in 1995, where his key interest and curiosity in the relationship between architecture and making evolved from practice to research. Since 1994, when he co-founded the workshop-based practice sixteen*(makers) with Nick Callicott, his work has been shown and published internationally. In 2004 he was appointed coordinator of the Bartlett's diploma programme.

MICHAEL STACEY

Consultant and professor Michael Stacey is an architect and architectural technologist practising and teaching in London. He is the author of Component Design (Architectural Press, 2000), a textbook providing detailed analysis of current fabrication technologies and detailing strategies for architecture. His research draws upon his expertise both in automated fabrication and in a range of handcraft and guild-based artisanal trades. He has been designing component-based architecture for 20 years. He is currently codirector of the Digital Fabrication Research Group at the Metropolitan University of London.

JOHN THORNTON

John Thornton is a structural engineer with a particular interest in problems that call for unconventional solutions. While working at Arup he was responsible for a wide variety of significant projects including Lloyd's (architects: Richard Rogers Partnership), the Mound Stand at Lord's and Glyndebourne Opera House (architects: Hopkins), the Grand Stand at Lord's (architects: Nicholas Grimshaw & Partners) and the Menil and Nasher galleries (architects: Renzo Piano Building Workshop). Many of these projects, of the so-called hi-tech era, were carried out in a time preceding digital fabrication where quality assurance of bespoke components required considerable manual input on the part of consultants and prototype fabricators.

Where can you find the best architectural thinking?

Launched in 1930, *Architectural Design* is regarded worldwide as the most influential and prestigious architectural journal. It has an unrivalled reputation for being at the forefront of cultural thought and design. Provocative and informative, AD has throughout its history inspired key theoretical and creative advances - from the modernist to the digital. It successfully combines the currency and topicality of a newstand journal with the editorial rigour and design qualities of a book. This allows it to provide space for topical architectural issues in a way that is no longer possible in other publications.

To mark the 75th anniversary of its first publication, *Architectural Design* is now available online through Wiley InterScience.

Ask your institution to visit http://www.interscience.wiley.com/journal/ad for more information.

Only £18 / $30 more per year than a Print Only subscription!
Institutional Rate
Print only or Online only: £175/$290
Combined Print and Online: £193/$320

Now you know.

wiley.com

Just Build

New Yorkers are doing it for themselves: Craig Kellogg looks at the new American DIY architects.

Below
For Manhattan's Fluff bakery, a 2004 retail design by architects Lewis.Tsurumaki.Lewis, the design partners composed a wall-and-ceiling surface of stained plywood and coloured felt strips, tackling the installation themselves.

Below
In Lewis.Tsurumaki.Lewis's sketch, the new glass facade for the
Fluff bakery highlights cantilevering benches in the window bays.

Some of us suffer unending trials and tribulations. Others find the creative process no more complicated than cracking open a can of Coke and putting pencil to paper. Any two architects you ask are likely to describe personal methods that differ at least a little. Rem Koolhaas told a writer from the *New Yorker* magazine that he carves foam blocks to seek inspiration – whereas one of his competitors instead retreats into the woodshop.

It remains difficult to imagine Robert AM Stern, the dean of Yale University's architecture programme, in the shop with sawdust on his loafers and a framing hammer in his hands. But a surprising number of promising recent graduates in architecture seem as comfortable banging away with manly tools as their predigital counterparts were with electric erasers. Just think of the young architectural firms toiling each spring in the museum courtyard at PS1, in Queens, to install temporary summer-shade structures of their own design. Underfunded and dependent on donations and volunteer workers, the young PS1 architects have pushed up their sleeves and pitched in. What they lacked in resources was more than counterbalanced by an overwhelming desire to build.

The late educator John Hedjuk, of New York's Cooper Union, helped focus Manhattan's attention on architectural methods. His emphasis on the design-and-build process turned architecture into a sort of hands-on performance art. Naturally, the output from young 'process-oriented' firms was, shall we say, a bit experimental at first. The projects were easy to recognise, as the term 'process' became synonymous with structures assembled from latticed wood modules slotted together, or lots of fiddly pieces cut, perhaps, with a computer-controlled milling machine. Sometimes, a slapdash element was noted. The downtown firm Lot-ek adapted old newspaper-dispensing boxes into bay windows and colourful plastic laundry-detergent bottles into collectible little lamps. But never mind. The installations were spirited, harmless. They were nonstructural interiors created within pre-existing shells. So any lapses in craftsmanship simply served to remind that the architects themselves were the ones working the table saws and tin snips.

Though still in their teens, architecturally speaking, the creators attracted attention by stretching the traditional boundaries of architecture. When projects by Sharples Holden Pasquarelli (SHoP) were published, 'process' started to seem less like a back-to-basics buzzword and more like a movement deeply rooted in technique. Then all at once – definitely at a point in the last several years – some of the larger process firms reverted back to plain old architecture. SHoP's new commissions began demanding teamwork with professional builders, and SHoP was not alone. Having mounted an elegant minimalist installation in which curving bamboo whips overarched the PS1 courtyard last summer, nArchitects began a small apartment tower on Manhattan's Lower East Side.

Today, nArchitects still shares a modest shopfront with nine other small firms, on a slightly gentrified block of Manhattan's Lower East Side. (A woodshop and metals studio occupies the basement.) One cotenant is Lewis.Tsurumaki.Lewis (LTL), which, after the three principals joined forces, in 1993, built out of necessity the interiors they designed. From the look of things, they still do. All three supplement their incomes by working as academics. David J Lewis directs the masters programme in architecture at Parsons School of Design. Paul Lewis directs graduate

architectural studies at Princeton University, and Marc Tsurumaki teaches architecture at Columbia University and Parsons.

The firm's work remains suitably experimental. Two new restaurants opened last winter, not long after the debut of Fluff bakery, a tiny coffee shop by LTL near 50th Street and Ninth Avenue in New York. Photographs lend Fluff the appearance of a high-end digital rendering, though the design displays more grit to visitors. Over the entry is a bespoke branched chandelier of brushed stainless-steel tubes and dimmable linear incandescent lamps. The walls and ceiling surface are 18,500 linear feet of white and battleship-grey felt strips combined with three-quarter-inch stained-plywood strips. Each was aligned and glued independently. The darker effect at bench height lightens as the frequency of white stripes increases near the ceiling, in an 'excessive' effect the architects have termed 'horizontal vertigo' – it helps attract passers-by peering in from the street.

Of course, LTL not only designed the bakery but built it, too. No shock there, perhaps. But it is at least a bit surprising in an era when architects have been sucked almost completely into their computers. Young designers are bound to ask: Why bother building at all when rendering imaginary spaces is so much easier than working in the real world? The new digital models of space can be so lifelike. Advanced visualisation software such as Realtime, a modelling program from Arup Research & Development, is based on gaming technology. Fun! Why would anyone even want to design for life in the real world? In the light of swiftly advancing digital technology, projects by DIY firms such as LTL have come to represent the most compelling alternative for young designers who would otherwise be obliged to an architectural life lived almost exclusively onscreen. ⌂+

Varying the proportion of dark to light strips produced
a graduated effect on the walls from bottom to top.

Grand Central Bar, Shoreditch, London, 2001
Streaming lights as reference to the informational
exchanges and high mobility of the modern city.

BLOCKARC
HITECTURE

Curation or selection offers up probably the greatest challenge for the contemporary architect. With the onslaught of information, the emphasis is now on what an architect chooses to respond to rather than what is available to him or her in terms of sources. Iain Borden discusses how Block Architecture's responsive position enables the firm to react with immediacy to its urban surroundings, while also resulting in highly attuned 'architectures of suggestion and momentary thinking'.

In the 15th century, Renaissance intellectuals and artists such as Alberti or Leonardo da Vinci could, conceivably, know all that was knowable in their worlds – all books, all arts, all sciences, all languages could just about be absorbed by a single mind, if only that person could get hold of the materials. The challenge, therefore, was not so much to understand as to uncover, locate, unearth. Five centuries or so later, the exact reverse is the case: our problem is no longer how to locate new materials or forms of knowledge, but how to deal with the incredible onslaught of information – arts, cultures, data, events – that sweeps over us every day. Our problem, unlike that during the Renaissance, is one of filtering, ordering and selecting.

For architects who seek to relate their designs to the world outside of architecture, the challenge is even greater. Not only do they have to process the world around them, they also have to find a way to translate that processed information into spaces and symbols, into an architecture that is visual and spatial. This, of course, was part of the context for the move into Postmodernism, most notably Robert Venturi's *Complexity and Contradiction in Architecture* (1966) and, with Denise Scott Brown and Stephen Izenour, *Learning from Las Vegas* (1972), which sought to find a way of using popular symbols – from elements of domestic architecture to neon signs – to respond to the complexity of the contemporary world. A number of successors to Venturi have tried to continue with this game, creating a collage of materials and signs that expresses aspects of everyday life, often wrapped up in a narrative that provides both popular accessibility and, frequently, an evident strain of humour.

Which is partly what Block Architecture do, and partly what they don't. On the one hand, it is clear that London-based Block – formed by partners Zoe Smith and Graeme Williamson – are immersed in an intense negotiation with the (post)modern world. As they explain in their practice lecture (a constant and evolving reference point for the two partners): 'Our approach is derived from an innate need to continually reassess and validate responses to the city, or environment, we live in.' Unsurprisingly, then, many of their earlier projects are particularly explicit in the way they disclose what Block calls the 'Found City' – scavenging the city for spaces, materials and sites that are ripe for appropriation and intervention. For example, a bar project for the ICA in London explores the relationship between the borrowed and the made through the use of materials deployed out of their expected contexts, including cellbond (lightweight aluminium honeycomb core with GRP lining, normally used in aircraft) for a backlit billboard, and white fire-clay urinal slabs for the front and sides of the bar itself.

In a similar vein, a later London bar, Grand Central, draws its inspiration from another aspect of urban life: the transitional spaces, informational exchanges, control systems and high mobility of the 'living city'. The fluid language of traffic lights and city movement is invoked in a series of 'lightstream' walls manufactured from strips of live-edge, coloured Perspex and plywood, and backlit to create the impression of car head- and tail-lights. Overhead, a lighting rig – constructed from galvanised-steel conduiting and junction boxes, nodal downlights, red LEDs and mirrors – weaves its way through the space like a Metro map.

On the other hand, this is far from being an architecture that relies solely on Postmodern symbolism, shape or iconography for its effect. In Block's architecture, the city is also seen as 'a myriad of individual stories, intertwining or overlapping, frictionally weaving in and out of contact'. As a result, the materials and imagery invoked are not so much applied on to an architecture as used within architecture, or as Smith and Williamson put it: 'We're not interested in developing a style, but rather in

Top left
Museum of Modern Art, Oxford, 2002
Enigmatic space: the entrance area.

Bottom left
Treehouse apartment, Hoxton Square, London, 2000
A contrasting landscape of inside and outside: enclosed and floating bed deck.

Below
Text Map
'Text Map' used to translate conceptual ideas into design interventions for the Hussein Chalayan store, Tokyo (2004).

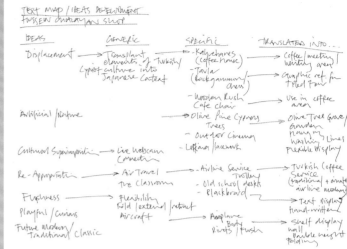

producing responses to the immediacy of what surrounds us, both in visual and experiential senses.'

Other Block designs thus also operate in ways different to Postmodern symbolism, exploring qualities of space and intimacy and other of the more subtle arts of architecture. This is the 'dreaming city' of their Treehouse apartment in London or Museum of Modern Art project in Oxford, refitted spaces that rely on atmosphere, charm and a sense of the enigmatic as much as they do on specific materials or visual codes. Indeed, it is the very degree to which these works cannot be defined, classified or codified that provides much of their quality – these are social spaces in which human beings meet, discuss and become close, and so their success relies not so much on the ability of the architecture to communicate as on its operation as a space of cultural depths and resonances. It is as if these designs are not so much reflections of the world as spaces in which to reconsider and ponder the city – architectures of suggestion and momentary thinking.

So in this sense, Block Architecture is very far away indeed from the accessible, populist, yet ultimately caricatured and decidedly unsuggestive nature of some of the crudest of Venturi-esque po-mo architecture. This is readily discernible in the firm's most recent architectures. For example, the Tokyo shop for Hussein Chalayan, which in many ways uses the same material and narrative strategies as the ICA Bar, now brings in a considerable degree of maturity to present interwoven narratives and hybrid cultural resonances within a complex and subtle game of materiality and graphics. Despite this being a high-fashion retail environment, there is also an evident concern 'to produce an antidote to what we see as our increasingly packaged environment'. Thus the delicate use of olive trees, backgammon and aeroplane detailing, an understated playing of references that tells not a single story but instead invokes multiple traces and histories.

Magasin 3, Stockholm

Magasin 3 is a large contemporary art gallery in the docklands of Stockholm, with an annex gallery, studio and café in the Djurgårdsbrunn – a park near the city centre. This annex building is a postwar single-storey pavilion constructed in a traditional Swedish style.

Block was approached at the beginning of 2004 and asked to produce ideas for an external installation in front of the building. This was not as easy as it might have seemed, as stringent planning regulations dictated a nonintrusive intervention. In addition, Magasin 3 plan to relocate within a few years' time, so a language of transitoriness was also thought appropriate.

The solution is simple in construction, yet highly complex in effect. In material terms, a four-metre-high timber and aluminium fence lines the exterior, with one split to allow for entrance to the gallery. Metal louvres are hinged, allowing them to rotate 270 degrees.

At once subtle and precise, the foil front reflects the park landscape and sky while the spacing between each post still allows the form of the building line to remain. The existing building consequently partially disappears into the landscape of the park, fading from public collective memory.

Thus also the environmental concerns evident in the 6000 Miles project for the Isle of Skye. This project marks a significant change of scale for Block, moving outside of their more normal interior-oriented projects to a larger, landscape-sited intervention. In 6000 Miles there are also different politics at play, and here the socioeconomic conditions of the villagers of Kyleakin are counterposed against a protected maritime ecology, all brought to play within a quiet yet subtly atmospheric machinic architecture.

Different again are the Dan Graham-like reflections of the Magasin 3 annex in Stockholm, where public perceptions of the building are treated visually, allowing it to disappear in both space and time. Here the concerns are less overtly political, but just as sensitive in the way that the practice skilfully negotiates the needs of the client, audience reception and their own architectural artistic playfulness. 6000 Miles and the Magasin 3 project together show how Block is always keen to experiment, and never to be pigeonholed or stereotyped by its most famous and successful works. Mind you, this is not likely to happen, certainly when the practice shows as much concern with process as with the final product, a concern that allows such things as their teaching (with Bob Sheil) a Diploma Unit at the Bartlett School of Architecture, and the text maps used in their collaboration with Hussein Chalayan.

All of these are works of suggestion, of possibility, of opening; Block's architecture is, then, not about knowing the world in any absolute manner. Instead, their designs create spaces which are intrinsically involved with their physical and social contexts – accessible and relevant to society and culture, yes, but also, as Block say, 'inviting enquiry from and engagement with the people that interact with it'. This is an intelligent and knowing position, allowing architecture to offer something to those who use it. These are architectures not of certain or closed knowledge, but of integrated and potential urban action.

Hussein Chalayan Store, Tokyo

Block Architecture's first retail project is a shop in Tokyo for the Turkish-Cypriot, British-based fashion designer Hussein Chalayan. The underlying concept, materiality and detail of the project were all developed through close collaboration with Chalayan himself – an unusual yet entirely appropriate approach given that Chalayan is well known for deploying a strongly conceptual narrative behind each of his projects, while Block's designs similarly draw on cultural references and commonly held experiences.

In order to progress this collaboration, a series of 'text maps' were used to outline thematic relationships such as cultural displacement (in particular, the superimposition of Turkish-Cypriot references into a Japanese cultural context), air travel and associated airplane detailing, the juxtaposition of the modern and classic, and a sense of timelessness and charm within the retail space.

For example, Womenswear, situated on the ground floor, is visualised as an olive-tree garden mapped out on a grid of points. Some of these points locate actual olive trees, which grow out of the floor; other points situate 'washing posts', forming a flexible hanging system with a washing line tied between the posts. By contrast, two storage walls resemble the fuselage of an airplane with flaps – some of which open to form shelves. And different once again, to the rear of the store a backlit wall contains display boxes which hold

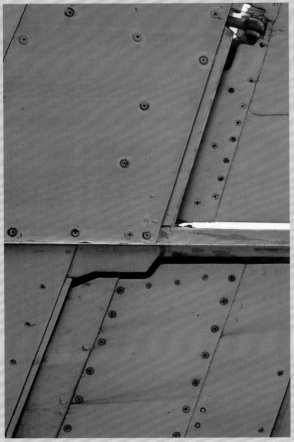

Chalayan's Airmail T-Shirt range, where each box is labelled like a filing system and so invokes post office pigeonholes.

This montage of cultural superimposition is also explored through materials. At the entrance, triangular ceramic tiles are laid out like a backgammon board, and then reappear upstairs in Menswear to define a film-screening area – populated by traditional Cypriot chairs and set out like an open-air cinema/courtyard. Here the air travel aesthetic is further augmented, this time by hanging rails on seat-belt material and creating mobile display units to look like airline service trolleys.

Text and graphics are another device used by Block, most dramatically as full-height blackboards where handwritten text (English and Japanese) describes Chalayan's approach to each fashion season. The airmail wall and service desk are subtly engraved with packaging and folding instructions.

6000 Miles, Kyleakin, Isle of Skye

The Isle of Skye had been separated from the Scottish Highlands since the Ice Age – until 1995 when a new bridge replaced the old ferry service between the mainland over the Kyle of Lochalsh and the Skye village of Kyleakin. While the bridge connected the island and the mainland for motor traffic, it also bypassed Kyleakin, thus severing the mutual dependence that had previously existed between the two territories – today, Kyleakin seems like a place without purpose.

Hope, however, is on the horizon. In 2005 the water between the mainland and Kyleakin – which includes shellfish and reef beds as well as seal, dolphin, whale and shark – is to become a marine Special Area of Conservation. Block see this as a new opportunity to reinvigorate both the social community of Kyleakin and its relationship with the coast, creating a coastal machine which will relate to the rhythms and cycles of tides, currents, seasons, erosions, landfalls and other processes of the environment.

This intervention is an artificial archipelago of platforms, extending from the slipway at Kyleakin out towards the mainland, thus reinstating a trace of the old ferry route.

Each platform functions as a seacroft growing scallops and mussels in cage and rope structures. In addition, temporary cabin accommodation above water acts as an environmental buffer, providing shelter from rain and high winds. These cabins accommodate changing uses throughout the year, responding to seasonal change and the weather. They are at once floating caravan park, providing midge-free residences, and science facility with in-situ laboratories monitoring marine life.

The ferry slipway will also be developed as a marine-life study centre, gathering the existing privately run boat trips into a single organisation, and supporting an auditorium structure which dips into the sea at high tide. An array of reef markers extends between Kyleakin and the mainland, outlining areas of specific conservation. *Δ+*

Iain Borden is director of the Bartlett School of Architecture, UCL, where he is professor of architecture and urban culture. He is the author and co-editor of 12 publications, including, with Sandy McCreery, *The New Babylonians* issue of *Δ* (Vol 71, No 3, June 2001).

BLOCKARC
HITECTURE

RESUMÉ

Block Architecture was established in 1998 by Scottish architects Graeme Williamson and Zoe Smith. Over the last six years they have received critical acclaim for their innovative and experimental approach to architecture through a broad range of commercial, residential, retail and arts projects, predominantly in London but also in New York, Tokyo and Stockholm. In 2005 Block won the Blueprint Sessions Interior Designer of the Year award.

MAJOR WORKS (selected)

1997	Tomato Building (studios and exhibition space), Soho, London
1998	The Klinik (hair salon), Clerkenwell, London
2000	ICA Bar, The Mall, London
	Treehouse apartment, Hoxton Square, London
2001	Grand Central Bar, Great Eastern Street, Shoreditch, London
	Market Place Bar, Oxford Circus, London
2002	Loft apartment, Soho, New York, US
	Museum of Modern Art, Oxford
2004	Hussein Chalayan store, Tokyo, Japan
	The Building Centre exhibition space, London
2005	Residential live/work development, Brighton
2005	Office refurbishment for Glue London, Shoreditch, London

AWARDS (not including nominations)

2001	FX Interior Design Awards – best leisure product
2002	FX Interior Design Awards – best bar
	FX Interior Design Awards – best residence
2004	Time Out Design Awards – best local bar
	FX Interior Design Awards – best retail interior
	FX Interior Design Awards – best installation for public space

Bottom left
AHMM has turned the patterns made possible by the prefabricated module into a powerful composition that speaks functionally and symbolically of the role of housing.

Bottom right
At six storeys in a predominantly low-rise neighbourhood, Raines Court establishes a civic presence and gives its residences views towards the City of London.

RAINES
COURT

Much of what has been written about the Raines Court housing project in Hackney, East London, has focused on the logistical challenges of prefabrication. Here, Jeremy Melvin also acknowledges the contribution that Allford Hall Monaghan Morris (AHMM) has made at Raines Court with a high-density scheme that makes a conscious effort to address the public realm, but also uses modular units to advance internal planning.

Top
Raines Court caters for a diverse population.

Bottom
Each of the live/work units on the ground floor has its own entrance,
creating an engagement between the building and the public realm.

Anyone who wants a quick rundown on why social housing in Britain failed and what might be done about it, could do far worse than visit Allford Hall Monaghan Morris's Raines Court in Hackney. From charitable almshouses to Edwardian tenements, from 1950s 'peoples' detailing' to that stripped form of Neo-rationalism that was the swan song of local authorities before Margaret Thatcher put an end to them, the area could be an encyclopaedia of a century of attempts to solve the housing 'problem'. Whatever the mode of expression or manner of financing, all share one characteristic: low density. Most of the projects are only two or three storeys, but even where they rise rather higher, they are still surrounded by that *cordon sanitaire* with which planners isolated the poor, not just from traffic, but also from any normal contact with the urban realm.

AHMM's design is different in almost every respect. At six storeys it achieves about three times the density specified in the local unitary development plan. It also makes a conscious effort to address the public realm, pulling back from the street line to widen the pavement around a bus stop and its own entrance, and each of the live/work units on the ground floor has its own entrance from the street. With a long cantilevered porch and a volumetrically generous foyer, the main entrance also has a civic rather than an apologetic character. The presence of such mixed-use accommodation may have been a sop to the planners who wanted to retain some 'employment' on the site – it had previously been a dairy depot – but that in itself is a radical break from the notion that living and working should happen in separate zones. The architectural logic might have suggested shops, but not the commercial logic. There are plenty of empty or low-cost units in the area and, as Simon Allford points out, in an AHMM scheme down the road in Dalston, for flats above retail premises, the shops took a long time to let. Yet even so, Raines Court stands as vitiation of previous housing paradigms.

But its relationship to the history of housing is more complex than a simple counterproposal to earlier mistakes. The client is the Peabody Trust, whose origins go back to the 1860s when the childless American banker George Peabody gave £500,000 to house London's teeming poor, and ever since has been a major player in housing provision. Recently, under its dynamic and far-sighted director of development Dickon Robinson, that relationship has taken a twist as the trust has steadily challenged the conventions of social housing that emerged from the wreck of the postwar programme. It pioneered live/work units as a prelude to mixed use, varied forms of tenure from rental through shared ownership to more or less market price.

As a shared-ownership scheme, Raines Court is not really for the lumpenproletariat. It caters for key workers – often professionally qualified but in low-paid employment such as teaching and nursing, who take a mortgage for the maximum a lender will advance on their salaries, while the housing association charges rent on the rest. In theory, as salaries increase and more can be borrowed, the proportion of ownership changes until the apartments are entirely in the

Top left
The access galleries facing the courtyard are supported on a minimal structure, but still establish a frame. The larch boards are common: residents are free to colour their recessed kitchen walls as they please, allowing for variance of infill.

Bottom
The workers have 'never had it so good'.

Top right
Balconies on the inner block with three-bedroom apartments balance privacy with the communal aspects of high-density living.

possession of the occupants, the freehold remaining with the association. It is a neat kind of 'third way' in housing tenure, though at present low interest rates cause the anomalous position that rents cost more than loans. But it recognises a maturing of the social-housing industry, starting with a realisation that housing alone is not enough to break the cycle of deprivation. Public services, and those who operate them, also need provision, and this in turn suggests a more diverse community and the potential for deeper integration into its social and physical context.

At this point in a review of traditional social housing, one used to be able to say, 'Enough economics, what about the architecture?' At Raines Court one can't because of the most piquant intersection between it and the history of social housing – its prefabricated construction. This technique was revived more or less single-handedly in the 1990s by Peabody, which, though deeply aware of its flawed history, sullied reputation and complexities, firmly believed the imbalances in the housing market to be so great that only radical new thinking could solve them.

Top
Plan of standard two-bedroom unit. Making the flats from two 3.6-metre-wide modules avoids the tunnel effects of narrow units such as London terraced houses. Slipping them past each other gives privacy to the entrance and bedroom, as well as creating an entrance court and usable balcony.

Bottom
The three-bedroom units are customised from the two-bedroom layout, with two adjacent ones sharing an extra module for the third bedroom. The wider balconies provide alternative means of escape for the third bedroom, avoiding the living room; third bedrooms in those with square balconies escape to the access gallery.

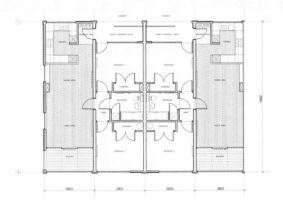

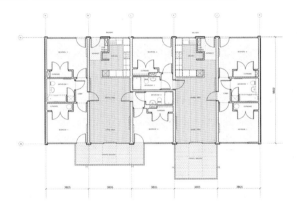

Signing up to prefabrication is a little like joining Opus Dei or a hard-line communist party: it affects almost every decision the designer makes, even where it does not absolutely dictate the outcome. Diversion from the discipline leads to excommunication and the gulag of professional opprobrium, while the rewards have yet to be seen in this world.

At Raines Court, even 50 per cent prefabrication determined the unit and overall volumes. It has a great bearing on the finishes, the composition of the facades and the planning layout. And it governs the construction process and its contractual arrangements. What is remarkable about AHMM's design is the way it accepts these strictures and even intensifies them, weaving from them a powerful image that arises logically from function and construction. They are, says Peter Cook, with whom the partners taught and occasionally sparred at the Bartlett, representatives of the 'polite modern' school of London architecture, but their politesse has a force to it.

Designing for prefabrication calls for a different sensibility, where the designer can conceive both of the prefabricated unit, and the way it fits together. AHMM decided on units 3.6 metres wide internally, the maximum width that can be transported by road without a special escort, and sufficiently generous for more or less any domestic use. Faced with such a discipline, the old GLC architects obsessed about how narrow a minimum dwelling could be (3.15 metres was generally accepted), but AHMM cast off such inhibitions in favour of making apartments from two units, the standard layout having two bedrooms in one, and the living and kitchen spaces in the other. Having these modules to play with, they slid them along each other so that they project at opposite ends. This move creates little entrance recesses at one end, and usable covered balconies at the other. The effect is not only to lend some sublimated expression of construction to the exterior, but also to echo another aspect of social housing history: John Habraken's old distinction of frame and infill. The front building line with its expressed dimensions of the individual units stands for the frame, while the recesses, with their potential for individual customisation, are clearly infill.

Most of the 61 apartments are two-bedroom above the ground-floor living/kitchen units, though at the rear is a small wing of three-bedroom apartments. This cannibalises the standard layout by taking half of a third module for the third bedroom and a second shower, but here too the exterior expression reveals something of the interior arrangement. Third bedrooms have their secondary means of escape on to the access deck or a balcony that runs the width of the living room into another bedroom in alternate flats. This determines a balcony pattern depending on whether or not it provides a means of escape.

Raines Court experienced many of the problems that might be expected in a revival of prefabrication. Simon Allford rues that only 50 per cent of construction was actually off site. Though not unexpected, the additional cost of about 20 per cent above conventional construction evinced negative publicity. But AHMM and Peabody are trying to capitalise on this extra investment in a project called MoMo (Mobile Module),

Signing up to prefabrication is a little like joining Opus Dei or a hard-line communist party: it affects almost every decision the designer makes, even where it does not absolutely dictate the outcome. Diversion from the discipline leads to excommunication and the gulag of professional opprobrium, while the rewards have yet to be seen in this world.

Top
The live/work units are essentially tight one-bedroom
flats with studios of more than 7 metres by 5 metres.

Bottom left
Ground-floor plan, showing the live/work units to the front.

Bottom right
Typical (second-) floor plan. Note the balcony configuration
on the rear (three-bedroom) block.

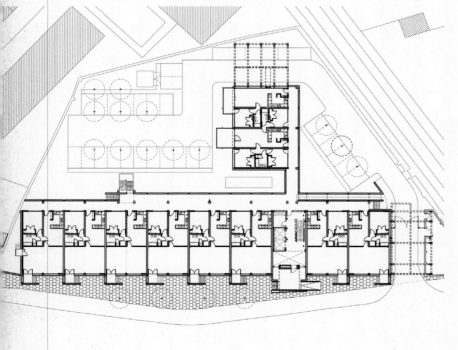

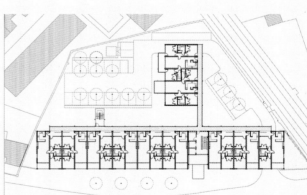

based on the proven technology of self-supporting
shipping containers. Designed to be mobile, it has
no site in mind, and with a simplified plan and
construction, as well as piggy-backing on an already
sophisticated production system, it should offer savings.

But that is for the future. For now, Raines Court
stands as a testament to the potential of prefabricated
construction to provide architectural expression,
maximise use of a particular site and, above all,
provide decent, affordable homes. Δ+

The design of the Brunswick Centre leaves no room for indecision: people either love it or hate it – there seems to be no middle ground.

THE BRUNSWICK CENTRE

MARCHMONT STREET LONDON WC1

Some 30 years after completion, one of London's most iconic postwar schemes is being refurbished by Levitt Bernstein, with its original architect, Patrick Hodgkinson, on board as a consultant. Bruce Stewart describes the plans and asks what the impact of the renewal of the building might be on residents and on the immediate local area.

Top
The building has not weathered well, with large areas of the render now missing, exposing the structural brickwork and the steel reinforcing mesh.

Bottom
The entrance into the piazza from Brunswick Square shows the monumental scale of this Modernist masterpiece.

Situated in the centre of London's Bloomsbury is one of the city's and, indeed, the UK's most iconographic postwar housing schemes. With Trellick Tower by Ernö Goldfinger in west London, and Alexandra Road by Neave Brown in north London, the Brunswick Centre – or Foundling Court – by Patrick Hodgkinson is now one of a growing number of Modernist buildings that have been awarded listed-building status. This is recognition that many buildings, of all types, constructed in the years following the Second World War are of significant architectural importance and need to be protected as part of our ongoing cultural history. Opinion on all of these buildings is quite firmly divided – people either love or hate them.

Conceived in 1959, the Brunswick Centre was finally completed in 1972 after many changes to both the design and the personnel involved. The aim of the original scheme was to test the possibilities of high-density, low-rise urban housing combined with a commercial centre. Initially working with Sir Leslie Martin, Hodgkinson sought to provide the 20th-century successor to John Nash's Regent's Park terraces of the early 19th century. The residential accommodation was to take the form of high-quality speculative apartments, of several plan types, positioned above retail units and basement garaging. However, a change in the freeholder of the site, with Camden Council becoming leaseholder for the housing, dictated a greatly simplified arrangement of studio, one- and two-bedroom flats for low-income residents.

Consisting of two large, stepped wings flanking an open central piazza-esque space, the building was constructed by the McAlpine Design Group and is a reinforced-concrete frame 'with a surprising amount of structural brickwork'.[1] The flats themselves are all single aspect with reasonable-sized balconies, their most distinctive feature being the large area of glazing to the living space, known as the 'winter gardens'.[2] Though the apartments were eventually finished in rendered blockwork, the grey concrete 'superblock'[3] was originally to be substantially longer and finished with a buttery cream paint to echo the Nash terraces Hodgkinson so admired.

This incomplete scheme is now undergoing refurbishment by the current freeholders, Allied Land. Using the architectural practice of Levitt Bernstein, with Patrick Hodgkinson as a consultant, plans have been agreed to radically remodel the commercial areas of the ground floor and to upgrade the residential accommodation. (Interestingly, both David Levitt and David Bernstein worked with Hodgkinson on the original project and are therefore very familiar with the evolution of the development.)

Granted grade II listed status in 2000, the building now looks tired and frayed at the edges. Nearly all of

Top
View of the west flank. The bridge and much of the balustrade to the podium open space have had to be removed for safety reasons. Unfortunately, the bridges are not being reinstated as part of the refurbishment.

Bottom
The shop units, which are currently mostly empty, are set back behind the colonnade created by the edge of the podium. The newly refurbished units will be brought forward to the line of columns, thus removing the covered walkway.

the units on the retail level are empty, and the remaining ones are, for the most part, budget shops and cheap cafés, plus a Morrison's/Safeway supermarket. Possibly the most successful commercial venture on the site has been the Renoir Cinema that nestles beneath the heroic columns on the entrance from Brunswick Square. Above the shopping arcade is the 'podium' level, which houses a large open area and a few office units, as well as the first of the housing units. The building's north–south flanks were originally connected to each other by three bridges at this level, but these are no longer present, having been removed for safety reasons. Walking around the

building it is easy to see quite large areas where the render has come away, revealing both the structural brickwork and the steel reinforcing mesh. In addition, many of the residents have painted the exterior of their homes, which has led to a patchwork of various shades of white and cream covering the building.

In the new plans, both the residential and retail areas of this large building will be upgraded, though the main focus will be on the retail zone. A new supermarket unit will close off the northern end of the site, and the shop units will be upgraded. Currently accessed from within the colonnades that define the edge of the upper podium level, the shopfronts will be brought forward, thus removing the covered walkways provided by the colonnades. The piazza will be upgraded and a new series of water features are being designed in conjunction with the artist Susannah Heron. The residential units will be upgraded to provide independent heating (at present there is only a hot-air, centralised system). And the drainage of water from the balconies is to be revamped, doing away with the narrow internal downpipes and providing more substantial external drainage.

However, the main cause for concern has always been the extensive amount of glazing provided by the 'winter gardens', as during the summer this results in excessive heat gain, and in the winter heat loss and condensation problems. It is cost-prohibitive to replace the original structure of the glazing, and thus the

133 +

Top and bottom
Before and after. The apartments are spacious and have
plenty of light coming in from the 'water garden' glazing.

maintenance, gardens. But it is the plans for the ground floor that are most likely to change the spirit of the building. The removal of the colonnades is a big gesture and could reduce the impact of the retail area to little more than an outdoor mall or even to the blandness of airport shopping. The closing off of the northern end of the piazza with an upmarket supermarket will reduce its visual impact and stop the natural flow of the area. In addition, the building exterior will finally be painted a pale cream. Although this was always Patrick Hodgkinson's intention, most people think of the Brunswick Centre as a concrete mammoth; it will be interesting to see how the colour change will affect not only the building, but its impact on the surrounding area.

This refurbishment is, of course, not only timely, but necessary now that the building is listed. But what will be the effects of its renewal on the residents and the local area? Many residents have lived at Foundling Court since it was completed, and enjoy living there. As is the case with most public housing, there are an increasing number of privately owned apartments, yet happily no conflict between the two types of neighbours. There is very much a village atmosphere, with people looking out for each other, and the non-threatening architecture gives the feeling that this is a very safe place to live. In fact, as one explores the building, it is almost amazing to find that instances of graffiti or vandalism are virtually nonexistent.

But despite all of this, the majority of the residents fall within the very low income brackets, and the proposed refurbishment of the retail area is therefore of great concern. As the building exists now, the tenants can afford to shop locally, in the downstairs Safeway, and the little cafés and snack bars are used by many as community spaces to meet friends and neighbours, somewhere they can buy a cup of tea and sit for hours. It is the loss of this focus of the community that is worrying to those who live in the Brunswick Centre. If the large open space on the first floor were to be dealt with in a sensitive manner, perhaps there could still be a heart for this community. ⌂+

conservatories will remain single glazed with replacement double-glazed units to the ceiling, but an integral gutter to help with water run-off is to be removed in order to reduce the effect of the cold bridge in winter.

There are criticisms that can be made of the new architecture of the Brunswick Centre. The plans for the upgrading of the flats could be described as a swings-and-roundabouts situation: for example, the removal of the hot-air heating system could free up the flexibility of the plan, yet the introduction of radiators restricts the available wall space; unfortunately, there are no plans to upgrade the residents' public space at the podium level; and the bridges are not going to be reinstated. Recently, some of the residents have tried to show how significant this space could become by holding a series of workshops that created four, temporary, low-

Notes
1 Stuart Tappin, 'Building of the Month', May 2003,
The Twentieth Century Society: www.c20society.demon.co.uk.
2 In conversation with Peter Sanders of Levitt Bernstein.
3 Ibid.

Bruce Stewart is currently researching and writing *The Architects'
Navigation Guide to New Housing,* to be published in early 2006
by Wiley-Academy. He trained as an architect and is currently a
college teacher at the Bartlett School of Architecture, UCL London.

McLean's Nuggets

End of the Sign Age?

A whole set of forces are conspiring against the 'information age'. Visual information in both text and image in the form of flyers, fly-posting and proliferating road and street furniture are all currently challenged. Firstly, mean-spirited Transport For London (TFL) has produced 'cancelled' overstickers to discourage fly-posting of events on its property. Camden Council has served antisocial behaviour orders (ASBOs) on the record companies who pay for the illegal bill-posting of bands and events, and in south Buckinghamshire, councillor Richard Pushman has written to the Cabinet member for roads to complain about what he sees as the pointless litany of signs that have appeared on the county's roadsides. As reported in the *Bucks Free Press*, Mr Pushman was particularly incensed by the recent erection of a large sign advertising a local radio station's travel information on a habitually traffic-congested section of road. His protestations have received support from the National Trust and local conservation groups. Meanwhile, plans for London's Exhibition Road propose to do away with street signs, road markings, safety

barriers and traffic lights, but not traffic. Research from the town of Drachten in the Netherlands suggests that the removal of barriers between pedestrians and vehicles has not resulted in any more accidents, and that their removal actually helps to limit traffic speed.

In this visual cull, few other than former pop Svengali Malcolm McLaren have defended the practice of fly-posting, which seems a reasonably informal method of (passive) communication or 'ambient media'. Jon Goodbun of Weisser and Goodbun (WaG) Architecture has, though, proposed a challenge to what fellow architect Simon Allford describes as the 'permanent ephemera' of street paraphernalia. The Democratic Billboard was part of a proposal for the relandscaping of Old Street in east London. A community-based electronic notice board, a negotiable mix of advertising (70 per cent), public information (10 per cent), public entertainment (10 per cent) and art (10 per cent) would provide news, entertainment and income to the local community.

Jack Boat

A solution to house building on the flood plains of the Thames Gateway has recently been spotted in the area, albeit temporarily. The giant 14,850-tonne jack-up barge, *The Resolution,* has just completed piling in the Thames estuary for 30 offshore wind turbines, which will sit 70 metres above sea level. As reported in the *New Civil Engineer,* this purpose-built Chinese-fabricated vessel can be 'jacked-up' during pile installation, lifting the hull several metres above the water line, and creating a stable work environment. How about some of the estimated 128,000 new houses along the Thames estuary on legs? A typical three-bedroom house of brick (minus foundations) weighs a mere 150 tonnes. Other possible solutions to the issues of flood-plain building have been tested in the Netherlands, where construction firm Dura Vermeer has developed a timber-framed house built on a hollow concrete pontoon that will float in flood conditions and is equipped with the necessary flexible service inlets/outlets. Also, currently moored in Middelburg in the southwest Netherlands, is Herman Hertzberger's stylish Watervilla prototype. These three-storey dwellings are built upon a floating hexagonal pontoon fabricated from 2-metre-diameter steel tubes. Creating enough buoyancy to support 135 tonnes, the tubes also double up as storage space. Robert Webb of energy consultants XCO2 explains that building on flood plains is problematic unless flood protection is seriously considered, and that this protection is 'upgradable to protect against future risk'.

Systems Failure

If architecture is not a serious problem-solver because, as Cedric Price would say, 'it is too slow in the gestation period', then how good are architects at anticipatory design? As a field, anticipatory design seems to have really been explored and articulated only by Price and his friend Buckminster Fuller; this is odd. In a recent issue of the *European Journal of Information Systems* there was an analysis of 'decision support systems' and their level of user participation. Systems were classified as High, Medium and Low impact and included: AVOMAN – 'providing management tools and information to improve Avocado orchard productivity'; RAINMAN – 'aims to raise understanding of El Niño ... to achieve better management of climate risk'; and WEEDMASTER – 'providing farmers with herbicide options to deal with weed infestations'. Where is ARCHIPERSON, a nongender-specific tool to determine the usefulness of architecture, or architects for that matter? To what extent does anticipatory design need to define or describe its consumers? In the *Journal of Food Marketing*, Martine de Boer, Mary McCarthy and Cathal Cowan analyse the classifications in the 'food-related lifestyle (FRL) instrument' developed by MAPP (market orientated production and product development in the food sector) Denmark, where food consumers are classified as the following 'food-related lifestyle (FRL) segments':

Hedonistic	28%
Conservative	21%
Extremely Uninvolved	16%
Enthusiastic	14%
Moderate	13%
Adventurous	8%

Where are these categories within architecture, and what might a hedonistic or extremely uninvolved consumer of architecture be like? 𝝙+

McLean's Nuggets is an ongoing technical series inspired by Will McLean and Samantha Hardingham's enthusiasm for back issues of AD, as explicitly explored in Hardingham's 𝝙 issue *The 1970s Is Here and Now* (March/April 2005).

Will McLean is joint coordinator (with Pete Silver) of technical studies in the Department of Architecture at the University of Westminster, and is currently working on a low-cost factory-produced house with architect Adam Kalkin.

HAPTICITY & VISION

The Eyes of the Skin has become an architectural classic. Here, on the publication of a new edition, its author Juhani Pallasmaa reflects on why a sensory understanding of the world has grown in an increasingly digital age.

During the 10 years since my little book *The Eyes of the Skin: Architecture and the Senses* (Academy Editions, 1996) was published, interest in the significance of the senses has grown considerably, both philosophically and in terms of experiencing, designing and teaching architecture. My assumptions of the role of the body as the locus of perception, thought and consciousness, as well as the significance of the senses in articulating sensory responses, have been confirmed. Recent philosophical studies have even established the central role of the body for human memory and thought.

The title of the book referred to the significance of the tactile sense for our understanding of the world, but it also intended to create a conceptual short circuit between the dominant sense of vision and the culturally suppressed sense of touch. It has been found, however, that our skin is capable of distinguishing a number of colours; we actually do see by our skin.

The primacy of the tactile sense for complete and satisfying architectural experiences has become increasingly evident. Hapticity is the sensory mode that integrates our perceptions of the world and ourselves. Even visual perceptions are fused and integrated into the haptic continuum of the self; my body remembers who I am and where I am located. My body is truly the navel of my world, not in the sense of the viewing point of a central perspective, but as the very site of reference, memory, imagination and integration.

All the senses, including vision, are extensions of the tactile sense; the sense organs are specialisations of skin tissue, and all sensory experiences are modes of touching, both literally and metaphorically, and thus related to tactility. Our contact with the world takes place at the boundary line of the experiential self through specialised parts of our enveloping membrane.

Artists who are deeply engaged in experiential qualities of light, for example James Carpenter and James Turrell, speak about the tactility of light itself. 'There is a tactility to something which is immaterial ... With light you are dealing

Juhani Pallasmaa

THE EYES OF THE SKIN

Architecture and the Senses

Preface by Steven Holl

with a purely electromagnetic wavelength coming in through the retina, yet it is tactile ... Your eye tends to interpret light and bring to it some sort of substance which, in reality, is not there,' writes James Carpenter.[1] In emotionally charged experiences of light, the immaterial phenomenon of light tends to be

Top
Vision is suppressed in heightened emotional states and deep thinking.
René Magritte, *The Lovers*, 1928, detail. Private Collection, Brussels.

Bottom
Vision and the tactile sense are fused in actual lived experience.
Herbert Bayer, *The Lonely Metropolitan*, 1932.

experienced as some sort of liquid or substance;
touching light turns it into a substance.

Today's high levels of illumination may impoverish
our visual perception. 'Normally, in daylight, our eyes
are almost entirely closed, that is, the pupil is a tiny
dot. Obviously we are not made for that light, we are
made for twilight. Now what that means is that it is not
until very low levels of light that our pupil dilates.
When it does dilate we actually begin to feel light,
almost like touch,' writes James Turrell.[2]

A remarkable factor in the experience of enveloping
spatiality, interiority and hapticity is the deliberate
suppression of sharp-focused vision. Photographed
architectural images are centralised images of focused
Gestalt. Yet, the quality of an architectural reality
seems to depend fundamentally on the nature of
peripheral vision, which enfolds the subject in the space.

One of the reasons why the architectural and urban
settings of our time tend to leave us as outsiders, in
comparison with the forceful emotional engagement
of natural and historical settings, could reside in the
poverty of their field of peripheral vision.

The significance of peripheral and unfocused vision
in our lived world, as well as in the experience of
interiority, is also beginning to awaken interest. The
very essence of the lived experience is moulded by the
fusion of haptic and peripheral visual stimuli. Focused
vision confronts us with the world, whereas peripheral
vision envelops us in the 'flesh of the world', to use
Maurice Merleau-Ponty's evocative expression.[3]
Alongside the critique of the hegemony of vision in our
culture, we need to reconsider the very nature of sight
itself, as well as its unconscious contents and fusion
with other sensory modes. ᴆ+

Notes
1 Lawrence Mason, Scott Poole, Pia Sarpaneva and James Carpenter
(eds), *James Carpenter* (interview), Architecture Edition (Blacksburg,
Virginia), 2005, p 5.
2 James Turrell, 'The thingness of light', in Scott Poole (ed), *James
Turrell*, Architecture Edition (Blacksburg, Virginia), 2000, p 2.
3 Maurice Merleau-Ponty, 'The Intertwining – The Chiasm', in Claude
Lefort (ed), *The Visible and the Invisible*, Northwestern University Press
(Evanston), 1969.

Juhani Pallasmaa runs his architectural office in Helsinki and
teaches, lectures and publishes extensively internationally.
He is author of *Encounters: Architectural Essays* (2005),
Juhani Pallasmaa: Sensuous Minimalism (2002) and *The
Architecture of Image: Existential Space in Cinema* (1998).

Juhani Pallasmaa, *The Eyes of the Skin: Architecture and the
Senses*, 2nd edn, Wiley-Academy, 2005, is available in paperback
at £14.99 (ISBN: 0-470-01578-0) and in hardback at £45
(ISBN: 0-470-01579-9). It can be purchased direct from John Wiley
& Sons online at www.wiley.com, or by email at cs-books@wiley.com.

MALEDICTION
D'AGAMEMNON

JARDIN DE LA GUERRE
LA GUERRE DU JARDIN

Charles Jencks describes how the theme of chaos at the Chaumont Garden Festival in France in 2004 inspired an interactive garden of attack.

Art and politics don't mix, and when they do the result is usually one-sided propaganda. But, if films such as *Fahrenheit 9/11* can resist the Bush Junta, then why not a garden – after all, as Ian Hamilton Finlay famously put it, 'a garden is not just a retreat, but an attack'. This idea led to an interactive landscape in the Loire valley at Chaumont, one where the people of many nations could shoot water at each other and at the plants, thereby inadvertently creating beauty, growth and laughter. This interactive landscape also produced a form of chaos and death (dead plants), as war does.

In 2004 the Chaumont Garden Festival, which focuses on a single theme, chose the idea of disorder or, as the organisers put the growing variety, Vive le Chaos. Chaos is the popular word for the science of nonlinear dynamics, and a hopeless misnomer. Its real subject is the opposite of disorder; that is, the way organisation grows out of apparently random activity. It grows, in the phrase that became famous, on the edge between order and chaos, that edge where nature self-organises, and a garden flourishes. Thus the subject is fitting for garden art, even if the label is a mistaken cliché. Since so much of my design has been involved with complexity theory, I was asked to do a keynote water garden, and as the US and British governments at the time were misleading their publics to war, with the spectre of a 45-minute holocaust on the horizon, I thought of a water-war garden.

Charles Darwin saw the war of nature as a fundamental truth that drives natural selection, the decimation of nine in ten so that the tenth might prosper, and statesmen from Hobbes to Churchill have seen human war as an eternal condition. Both nature and culture are perpetually struggling, competing, killing each other off. Whatever the larger truth of this proposition, it is apparent that war causes chaos, particularly today among civilian populations. The phrase 'total war' is now used by historians to signal that, in the last 100 years, war against civilians has become the norm, our particular contribution to the history of strife. The curse of Agamemnon, the tit-for-tat response that locks in species to perpetual warfare, also blights generations of people who must avenge a deed or ritually attack an adversary. The most obvious example is the Middle East or, in the West, Ireland.

In the Chaumont water garden, the visitor enters on wooden decking that curves across the shallow water and sees to the right a high point. This is the symbolic source of wealth and dispute, a V-shaped cistern with exit spouts to either side. The one to the left spills on to a waterwheel. The spinning wheel is set a-centrically, so that it moves in chaotic motion, fast then slow, and it also creates pulsating optical illusions. These explode at the viewer in white flashes – blades of light. Water, the source of life and power, is seen to cause sudden bursts and flares, explosive visual reactions that portend the role of water in war, and in this garden.

To the right, the spout of the V-cistern falls into a sequence of six galvanised-metal spouts which, pivoting chaotically as water passes over them, give off an a-periodic drumbeat. These drums of war fill up with water, tip over and then fall back on top of reverberant metal cylinders of different shapes and sounds. Since the water flows through this sequence in a regular yet somewhat random manner, the musical beat is like syncopated machine-gun fire: ratta-tat-tat.

Proceeding on this large curved segment, one sees two of the five gunnera flares. The life cycle of this water plant is shown in various stages of life and death, flaring out from a growing specimen. The dead and rotting elements are set on top of curved metal mesh that undulates in self-similar shapes. This formal pattern relates to the three large chaotic attractors, or strange attractors, that create the grammar of the garden. The gunnera flares vary from more ordered to more chaotic in the way they are stacked and in their stage of decomposition. Living at the base, recently dead in the middle, and very dead, and brown, at the top.

contenders are stencilled on top of the red planking, in light orange lettering: La France and Allemagne to the left, Grande Bretagne and Espagne to the right, and USA in the centre. They aim at three boats, small floating vessels with water shields on two sides. These protect the growing species and plastic flowers laid out like white corpses on a black bier. The force of the water hose guides the boats as if the wind (water) were pushing against sails (the shields). The game of superpower control is to aim a stream at these boats. Two superpower hoses work in conjunction, or strategic alliance, forcing the satellites to get back in their place. Their pigeonhole is two harbours of similar species, colour and shape. While this ordering of chaotic boats is possible, once they are pushed inside their harbour and left alone they tend to drift towards freedom.

Threaded through the wooden decking are two other strange, or chaotic, attractors. The larger one, coming from the gunnera under the V-cistern, is made from metal channels with different low-growing water weed floating on the top: duck weed, algae, cape pond-weed and water lily. Their flares follow the self-similar curves that sometimes reveal water between the channels. The third chaotic attractor, made from coloured metal channels placed deeper in the water, visually connects elements and ends in a small curved dish.

Orange lettering on the walkway identifies the superpowers, the tit-for-tat and various themes, such as *La Vie – Le Grand Ordonateur, La Mort – Le Grand Désordre*, and those Presidential Kings (*Les Bushs – Voodoo Bush Pere, et bush tres petit*, a dangerous, prickly bush). Harmonious and self-similar curves are woven through each other, the destructive creation that can result in regeneration and beauty, partial consolation for the curse of war. *Δ+*

The rust-red wooden decking, and major route, is the first chaotic attractor that leads to different interactive war games. In the middle of the decking are two waterpults. These are two catapults throwing water at each other, incidentally hitting the porous moss-covered rocks at the base and helping them to grow. The way the waterpults fill with water and suddenly release is determined by the constant input (a forceful rush of water through a hosepipe) and made random by the initial conditions and the unpredictable interactions. Thus tit-for-tat, 'deterministic chaos', the curse of Israel and Palestine today.

At the head of the strange attractor, visitors can take part in the Superpower Settlement. Here, shoot five hoses. In case viewers have trouble with the symbolism, words naming the

Known for his books questioning Modern architecture and defining its successors, Charles Jencks divides his time between lecturing, writing and garden design projects in Europe and the US. He studied under the Modern architectural historians Sigfried Giedion and Reyner Banham, and now designs landscape and sculpture and writes on cosmogenic art.

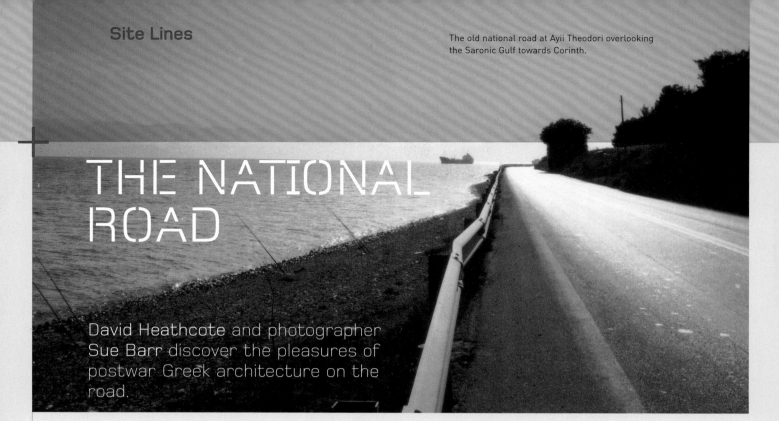

The old national road at Ayii Theodori overlooking
the Saronic Gulf towards Corinth.

THE NATIONAL ROAD

David Heathcote and photographer
Sue Barr discover the pleasures of
postwar Greek architecture on the
road.

At the dentist recently I read an Italian essay by a follower of
Eco on the littoral city, which proposed that Naples lay on the
cultural border between Europe and the Levant. As anyone who
has been to Pireaus will know, that port and Athens stand more
clearly on the border of East and West than anywhere in Italy.
I mention the Italian essay because it stands for the unspoken
cultural prejudice of many in the original EC nations that holds
that places like Greece are not really European. In our
architectural culture there is an equally unthinking assumption
of cultural superiority: the idea that countries like Greece, being
poorer nations, are somehow less European, less able and less
responsible nations – a kind of smugness that one finds in
adherents of Frampton's critical regionalism. Thus, while
Greece may have a history of architecture, it has no present.

It is true that Greece is different to its neighbours; its
geography and history have given it different challenges and
freedoms. Greece is a diasporic nation whose citizens have
always formed large parts of the populations of the major
cultural centres of the world. This diasporic tradition
contributes a culturally promiscuous and materially pragmatic
creative character. In fact, Greek Modern architecture is in
many ways far more heterodox than the architecture of other
European nations because of this tradition, and far freer from
the dead hand of history because of the ravages of the recent
past: the ethnic cleansing of the 1920s, invasion by Italy and
Germany in the Second World War, civil war immediately
afterwards, and a dictatorship that ended in 1974.

The post-civil-war generation of Greek architects had the
perverse benefit of reaching maturity at a time when the
country was finally able to modernise, and when there was
already a mature body of postwar architectural innovation
from which to take inspiration and no real local architectural
orthodoxy. These local conditions combined with an openness
to architectural ideas from both sides of the Atlantic, because
of the Greek diaspora, and created a modern architecture in
Greece that has the quality of eclecticism and dynamism
that for many cultural analysts is the essence of Modernism.

You can actually see the forces of Modernism on the
national road from Athens to Patras as it takes you
through the trashy chaotic poetry of roadside industries
seen through choking particulate fumes, past the
Saronic armada of dead and alive ships bringing
goodness knows what to vast fungal troops of tanks,
pumping stuff into a kerbside chemical cracker painted
and supergrafficked. This is archireal not archigram.
The national road itself is in some places two choked
lanes of trucks; in others three separate roads, each
laying aside the other in an ever bigger unlaned chaos
of dead dogs and crystalline light.

As you leave the grip of Athens and travel the older
national road you can feel history catch up with you; the
stillness of the mountains, the sea and light pull at the
wheels, ships slide towards the canyon of the Corinth
canal and disappear into the land. Beyond Patras the
road has the feel of Steinbeck's California – of sheds and
groves – but even here the future can suddenly intervene
in the form of a derelict flying saucer parked by the road.

Near the inappropriately named Kineta and between
the 50 metres that separate the Aegean from the road
and the Peloponnisos railway beside it, are, in
unconscious emulation of the Pacific highway south
of Los Angeles, the weekend houses of the Athenian
industrious middle-class. Our reason for travelling the
old national road was to find the Svolos summer house
by Alexandros Tombazis (built around 1970) that we
had seen in an old *Architectural Review*.

Tombazis heads a large and successful international
architectural practice in Athens, specialising in
environmentally friendly, bioclimatic and passive solar
design, built up since the mid-1960s. He is renowned
for his honesty and integrity and has said of his practice:
'It is essential not to forget, first, that architecture,
when built, is something more than just theory, it is a
solution, a statement; and second, if one is too cautious,

Clockwise, from top left.
Alexandros Tombazis, Helios 1 family house, Trapeza Aigialeias, Patras, 1977
View from the verandah across the patio and garden.

View of upper storey of the Heliosd 1 children's room with the solar panels mounted on the pitched side.

Vacuum-moulded plastic windows of the upper levels of a child's room at Helios 1.

Alexandros Tombazis, Svolos summer house, Ayii Theodori, 1970
Detail of kitchen and spiral stair to garden.
Detail of living-room fireplace at Svolos.

View of national road facade and entrance ramp of Svolos summer house.

Abandoned GRP 'clampshell' of uncertain date on the national road south of Patras towards Kyparissia.

if one mixes all the colours together in an equal amount, the result is grey, and neutral grey is not always what one desires.' Of his approach to work with others he remarks with candour: 'I have no patience with personal egotism such as who thought of an idea first. The real challenge is to have a dialogue of quality, and to do that the more participants of quality you have the better the end result, as long as someone leads the way.'

A shock amongst the respectable, almost Californian homes of Kineta's beach suburbs, Tombazis' Svolos villa is a very individualistic essay in space-age castellar Brutalism whose board-marked modularity hovers above fruit trees and peppers spanned by a vast overgrown drawbridge. The house enjoys uninterrupted access to the sea, and beside the baroque and futuristic use of concrete, the house is designed around the problem of climate control. At the villa's centre is an open atrium that picks up coolness sucked in from the sea by the heat of the land. Dense shutters keep the direct sun out as it transits the house, and the elevation of the main structure several metres from the ground pulls fresh sea air under the floor. Inside is a large wooden fire for chilly evenings, and a spiral stair down from the kitchen allows outside living in the space below the house, further shaded by the entrance ramp. The whole effect is a combination that looks both forward and back – a futuristic belvedere planned with Palladian regard for climate in a garden of simple Plinian virtue.

Much further along the same road at Trapeza Aigialeias, near Patras, is Tombazis' own weekend retreat (Helios 1,1977), where the virtuous crudeness of the Svolos home is replaced with an equally appropriate attention to detail. The spirit of the house is its view across the Gulf of Corinth to the high mountains, and when we saw it, it was spanned by a storm underlined by a rainbow over a true wine-dark sea. It only has this view because for the most part Helios 1 is buried in the ground, being Tombazis' first essay in positive climate control.

Planned as an L-shape, much of the house beyond its retaining wall is a Mediterranean essay in Scandinavian timber and light – sliding picture windows (using the same system as the apartments at the Barbican in London) blur the division between the outside room of the courtyard and the interior of bedrooms and split-level living and cooking areas. This littoral is blurred further by the fireplaces inside and out at the foot of the periscope chimney. The other vertical feature of the house is the tower facing to the rear with its solar panels, and to the front with vacuum-moulded Perspex bubble windows for the children's rooms. These are a reminder of a more liberated

child-centred architecture, with their parent-lethal entrance ladders leading to secluded chambers, and a bed for a friend up another vertiginous tiny ladder. From this eyrie the children share the Turneresque view that all the rooms have to offer. The villa has the same sculptural quality found at the Svolos house, but here created by the combination of striking verticals, the beautiful contrast of materials, and weathered lead sheets that protect the wooden structure from the peninsular climate.

Tombazis' work is full of the freedom of Greek architects to do as they please. Unfettered by expectation, Tombazi sculpts his work according to pragmatic needs and personal desire – free to be in or out of fashion. Where price is an issue, detail gives way to massing elsewhere, where form is self-expression exquisite details prevail. Evident throughout is a sense of responsibility – in his consistent interest in energy efficiency and also those children's rooms so empathically formed.

What you don't get is duff architecture made to sparkle by rhetoric. ⏃+

David Heathcote is the author of *The 70s House* and *Barbican: Penthouse Over the City*, by Wiley-Academy with photography by Sue Barr. *The 70s House* is being published in Winter 2005. For further details see www.wiley.com or email cs-books @wiley.co.uk.

Subscribe Now

As an influential and prestigious architectural publication, *Architectural Design* has an almost unrivalled reputation worldwide. Published bimonthly, it successfully combines the currency and topicality of a newsstand journal with the editorial rigour and design qualities of a book. Consistently at the forefront of cultural thought and design since the 1960s, it has time and again proved provocative and inspirational – inspiring theoretical, creative and technological advances. Prominent in the 1980s for the part it played in Postmodernism and then in Deconstruction, △ has recently taken a pioneering role in the technological revolution of the 1990s. With groundbreaking titles dealing with cyberspace and hypersurface architecture, it has pursued the conceptual and critical implications of high-end computer software and virtual realities. △

△ Architectural Design

SUBSCRIPTION RATES 2005
Institutional Rate (Print only or Online only): UK£175/US$290
Institutional Rate (Combined Print and Online): UK£193/US$320
Personal Rate (Print only): UK£99/US$155
Discount Student* Rate (Print only): UK£70/US$110

*Proof of studentship will be required when placing an order. Prices reflect rates for a 2005 subscription and are subject to change without notice.

TO SUBSCRIBE
Phone your credit card order:
+44 (0)1243 843 828

Fax your credit card order to:
+44 (0)1243 770 432

Email your credit card order to:
cs-journals@wiley.co.uk

Post your credit card or cheque order to:
John Wiley & Sons Ltd.
Journals Administration Department
1 Oldlands Way
Bognor Regis
West Sussex PO22 9SA
UK

Please include your postal delivery address with your order..

All △ volumes are available individually. To place an order please write to:
John Wiley & Sons Ltd
Customer Services
1 Oldlands Way
Bognor Regis
West Sussex PO22 9SA

Please quote the ISBN number of the issue(s) you are ordering.

△ is available to purchase on both a subscription basis and as individual volumes

○ I wish to subscribe to △ *Architectural Design* at the **Institutional rate** of (Print only or Online only *(delete as applicable)* £175/US$290.

○ I wish to subscribe to △ *Architectural Design* at the **Institutional rate** of (Combined Print and Online) £193/US$320.

○ I wish to subscribe to △ *Architectural Design* at the **Personal rate** of £99/US$155.

○ I wish to subscribe to △ *Architectural Design* at the **Student rate** of £70/US$110.

○ △ *Architectural Design* is available to individuals on either a calendar year or rolling annual basis; Institutional subscriptions are only available on a calendar year basis. Tick this box if you would like your Personal or Student subscription on a rolling annual basis.

Payment enclosed by Cheque/Money order/Drafts.

Value/Currency £/US$ _____

○ Please charge £/US$ _____ to my credit card.
Account number:

Expiry date:

Card: Visa/Amex/Mastercard/Eurocard *(delete as applicable)*

Cardholder's signature _____

Cardholder's name _____

Address _____

_____

_____ Post/Zip Code _____

Recipient's name _____

Address _____

_____ Post/Zip Code _____

I would like to buy the following issues at £22.50 each:

○ △ 176 *Design Through Making*, Bob Sheil
○ △ 175 *Food + The City*, Karen A Franck
○ △ 174 *The 1970s Is Here and Now*, Samantha Hardingham
○ △ 173 *4dspace: Interactive Architecture*, Lucy Bullivant
○ △ 172 *Islam + Architecture*, Sabiha Foster
○ △ 171 *Back To School*, Michael Chadwick
○ △ 170 *The Challenge of Suburbia*, Ilka + Andreas Ruby
○ △ 169 *Emergence*, Michael Hensel, Achim Menges + Michael Weinstock
○ △ 168 *Extreme Sites*, Deborah Gans + Claire Weisz
○ △ 167 *Property Development*, David Sokol
○ △ 166 *Club Culture*, Eleanor Curtis
○ △ 165 *Urban Flashes Asia*, Nicholas Boyarsky + Peter Lang
○ △ 164 *Home Front: New Developments in Housing*, Lucy Bullivant
○ △ 163 *Art + Architecture*, Ivan Margolius
○ △ 162 *Surface Consciousness*, Mark Taylor
○ △ 161 *Off the Radar*, Brian Carter + Annette LeCuyer
○ △ 160 *Food + Architecture*, Karen A Franck
○ △ 159 *Versioning in Architecture*, SHoP
○ △ 158 *Furniture + Architecture*, Edwin Heathcote
○ △ 157 *Reflexive Architecture*, Neil Spiller
○ △ 156 *Poetics in Architecture*, Leon van Schaik
○ △ 155 *Contemporary Techniques in Architecture*, Ali Rahim
○ △ 154 *Fame and Architecture*, J. Chance and T. Schmiedeknecht
○ △ 153 *Looking Back in Envy*, Jan Kaplicky
○ △ 152 *Green Architecture*, Brian Edwards
○ △ 151 *New Babylonians*, Iain Borden + Sandy McCreery